New Immigrants
and the Radicalization
of American Labor,
1914–1924

New Immigrants and the Radicalization of American Labor, 1914–1924

Thomas Mackaman

McFarland & Company, Inc., Publishers
Jefferson, North Carolina

LIBRARY OF CONGRESS CATALOGUING-IN-PUBLICATION DATA

Names: Mackaman, Thomas, 1975– author.
Title: New immigrants and the radicalization of American labor, 1914–1924 / Thomas Mackaman.
Description: Jefferson, North Carolina : McFarland & Company, Inc., Publishers, 2017. | Includes bibliographical references and index.
Identifiers: LCCN 2016024886 | ISBN 9781476662497 (softcover : alkaline paper) ∞
Subjects: LCSH: Foreign workers—United States—History—20th century. | Immigrants—United States—History—20th century. | Working class—United States—History—20th century. | Labor movement—United States—History—20th century. | Radicalism—United States—History—20th century. | Industries—United States—History—20th century. | Social change—United States—History—20th century. | United States—Economic policy—To 1933. | United States—Ethnic relations—History—20th century. | United States—Emigration and immigration—History—20th century.
Classification: LCC HD8081.A5 M33 2017 | DDC 331.6/2097309041—dc23
LC record available at https://lccn.loc.gov/2016024886

BRITISH LIBRARY CATALOGUING DATA ARE AVAILABLE

ISBN (print) 978-1-4766-6249-7
ISBN (ebook) 978-1-4766-2468-6

© 2017 Thomas Mackaman. All rights reserved

No part of this book may be reproduced or transmitted in any form or by any means, electronic or mechanical, including photocopying or recording, or by any information storage and retrieval system, without permission in writing from the publisher.

On the cover artwork entitled *Steelworkers*, Gerrit Beneker, 1920 (© 2017 PicturesNow)

Printed in the United States of America

McFarland & Company, Inc., Publishers
  Box 611, Jefferson, North Carolina 28640
    www.mcfarlandpub.com

Table of Contents

Preface   1
Abbreviations   3
Introduction: "Got a match?"   5

1. "Our lives, our thoughts and our allegiance":
   New Immigrants in 1914   23
2. "A war of coal and iron": 1914–1917   59
3. Securing "the industrial forts of America": 1917–1918   87
4. "The Revolt of the Rank and File": 1919   115
5. Reaction in New Country and Old: 1920–1924   142

*Epilogue: The Nation-State, Immigration Restriction
    and Fordism*   169
Chapter Notes   175
Bibliography   199
Index   209

Preface

New Immigrants and the Radicalization of American Labor, 1914–1924, analyzes how new immigrant workers changed American industrial society through a comparative study of iron mining in Minnesota, steel milling in the Calumet district of the south Chicago area, and coal mining in central Illinois.

By 1914, new immigrants from Eastern and Southern Europe had come to dominate industry's dirtiest and most dangerous jobs. Such was the case in the iron, coal, and the steel industries of the western Great Lakes—the heart of industrial growth prior to World War I. The decade that followed was bookended by interruptions to mass immigration, first brought on by the eruption of war in Europe, and then in 1924 by the virtual banning of new immigration through the Johnson-Reed Act. The intervening years were characterized by acute economic and demographic change on the one hand, and on the other by the saturation of new immigrant populations with ideology generated both in the U.S. and Europe, including the competing claims to loyalty of nationalism and various currents of radicalism. These changes coupled with the new immigrants' position at the bottom rungs of industrial hierarchy to advance a tendency toward interethnic labor militancy and to augment the audience for radicalism.

In the 1920s government and industry, as well as American nationalist organizations, reacted against this immigrant militancy and radicalism of the preceding years. New immigrants then found themselves caught in dual reactions, in their new land and old.

This book advances on previous studies by synthesizing various elements of the labor, immigration, and political history of the period and comparatively analyzing different industries and immigrant groups in a transatlantic context, while recognizing new immigrants as actors in the period's crucial changes.

Abbreviations

A.A.L.D. — American Alliance for Labor and Democracy
A.F.L. — American Federation of Labor
The Amalgamated — Amalgamated Association of Iron and Steel Workers
A.P.L. — American Protective League
C.C.F. — Central Competitive Field
C.C.S.P. — Cook County Socialist Party (Chicago)
C.F.L. — Chicago Federation of Labor
C.I.O. — Committee for Industrial Organization, formed in 1935; from 1938, Congress of Industrial Organizations
C.I.R. — Committee on Industrial Relations
C.N.D. — Council of National Defense
C.P.I. — Committee on Public Information
C.P.S. — Minnesota Commission of Public Safety
C.S.M.U. — Chicago Steamshovel Men's Union
Dillingham Commission — United States Immigration Commission
F.B.I. — Federal Bureau of Investigation
F.M.R.S. — Federal Mediation and Reconciliation Service
F.S.F. — Finnish Socialist Federation
F.S.I. — *Federazione Socialista Italiana* (Italian Socialist Federation)
F.T.C. — Federal Trade Commission
I.E.B. — International Executive Board of the United Mine Workers of America
I.W.W. — Industrial Workers of the World or "Wobblies"
The Klan — Ku Klux Klan
N.A.M. — National Association of Manufacturers
National Committee — National Committee to Organize Steel Workers
N.M.R.S. — National Mediation and Reconciliation Service
N.M.T.A. — National Manufacturing and Trade Association
Oliver — Oliver Iron Mining Company (U.S. Steel subsidiary)

Peabody Commission — Committee on Coal Production
P.S.F. — Polish Socialist Federation
S.L.P. — Socialists Labor Party
S.P. — Socialist Party (USA)
S.S.S.F. — South Slavic Socialist Federation
S.W.O.C. — Steel Workers Organizing Committee
U.M.W. — United Mine Workers of America
U.R.W. — Union of Russian Workers
W.F.M. — Western Federation of Miners
W.P.A. — Workers Party of America

Introduction: "Got a match?"

The cartoon appeared in the *Duluth News Tribune* in October of 1919, in the midst of the largest strike wave in U.S. history. With one hand, a swarthy figure labeled "foreign element" whispers to a figure representing "American labor," and with the other holds a fuse labeled "industrial revolution and communism" that leads to a stockpile of "gun powder" and "dynamite." The explosives lie beneath depictions of American mines and mills, the "Foundation of American Wages and Prosperity." High on a hill above the industrial scenes we see a wooded town, the cartoonist's illustration of an imperiled society.

Commentators employed terms like "foreign element" to suggest that "industrial revolution and communism" were alien imports. The cartoon depicts a number of the major problems from a troubled period of U.S. history. Present is the fear of the new immigrant—racialized with dark, protruding features, and standing in stark contrast to the fair and upright characterization of the idealized American worker. We also see the fear of workers' revolt conjured up by the Russian Revolution. Yet the cartoon's unmistakable implication, given its date and nod to "industrial unrest," was that the foreign origin applied to more than revolution: class conflict itself was an import and a grave danger to "American wages and prosperity" and the society built up on industry.

A deeper reading, however, shows that the cartoonist must have had doubts about the foreign nature of class conflict. We note, for example, that the "foreign element" is not depicted as an intellectual or a soap-boxing rabble rouser; rather, he is clad in the garb of a worker. Strikingly, the figure representing "American labor" shows no hostility to the "foreign element." On the contrary, his eyes are trained on the

"Got a Match?" Source: The cartoon originally appeared in the *Des Moines Register* on October 10, 1919, and can be found in Drake University Library's Cowles Collection.

latter with a look of curious study. Brow furrowed and hand-to-chin, he is clearly contemplating the appeal of "industrial revolution and communism." And by the immense stockpile of explosives underlying industry, the cartoonist perhaps unwittingly suggested that the basis of labor struggles in the period literally arose out of the mines and mills themselves. The "foreign element" needs only a match to set the whole works ablaze.¹

This is a study of "new immigrant" industrial workers from Southern and Eastern Europe during a critical period of U.S. history, from 1914 to 1924. Through comparative case studies of coal mining in Illinois, steel milling in the Calumet area around Chicago, and iron mining on Minnesota's Iron Range, I argue that new immigrant workers played a critical role as both actors in, and objects of, important changes to the working class, organized labor, industry, politics, and culture. These changes were transnational in origin, bound up with transatlantic ideologies, world-historical events like World War I, and the Russian Revolution, and the processes of immigration and return migration.

By 1914 immigrants had come to dominate in whole sectors of industry, such as the iron, coal, and steel industries of the western Great Lakes, a region of rapid industrial growth prior to World War I. The ten years included in this study were bookended by interruptions to immigration, first brought on by the eruption of war in Europe and then in 1924 by the Johnson-Reed Immigration Act. The intervening years were characterized by acute economic and demographic change, on the one hand, and on the other by the saturation of immigrant communities with ideology generated both in the U.S. and Europe, including the competing claims to loyalty of both U.S. and "old country" nationalism, as well as socialism inspired by the Russian Revolution and other currents of radicalism. These changes coupled with the immigrants' position at the bottom of industrial hierarchy to enhance inter-ethnic labor militancy and to augment the audience for radicalism, manifested in the largest strike wave in U.S. history (1916–1922) that gripped these and other industries.

Within this historical context, this study concentrates on the mutual and dynamic interaction between immigrants on the one hand, and industry and the late Progressive Era state on the other. That is the central drama, to borrow a metaphor from the theater. But the scene's setting is crucial. The story unfolds amidst the turbulent development of the industrial economy within the U.S. and a crisis of the entire world order, punctuated by war, revolution, and reaction. The stage is populated with an array of actors—Progressive Era managerial elite and politicians, trade unionists and radical leaders, reactionary and vigilante Americans. Yet here the leading performance belongs to new immigrants, who were protagonists in important changes to unions, radicalism, industry and American citizenship. As is the case with a good theatrical performance, which requires effort for an audience to interpret the actors' motivation, so for the historian the great challenge remains to arrive at an assessment of the consciousness of historical actors.

In considering the question of new immigrant consciousness, I make reference throughout the book to "labor militancy" and "radicalism." By the former, I refer to various forms of labor struggle that arise out of the point of production or the local community, such as union organization, strikes, labor marches, bread riots, and clashes with strikebreakers, private security forces, police, and so on. There has been no shortage of bloody labor militancy in U.S. history—in spite of prevailing assumptions based on the relative absence of strikes and the decline of unions during the last three decades. By "radicalism," I refer to ideological formations—such as the Socialist Party (S.P.), the Industrial Workers of the World (I.W.W.), and the various communist parties—that sought to articulate what they perceived to be the class interests of workers. While it has often been the case that radical groups have tried to anticipate and advance working class struggle through their activity and theory—and though many radicals have themselves been workers—there have been long periods during which radicalism has operated at a distance from the practical and day-to-day struggles of masses of workers.

And then there have been periods where the two streams—labor militancy and radicalism—both appear to be growing in strength and bound for convergence, threatening to lift radical ideas upon the crest of powerful popular social movements. Such was the scenario developing in the period of this study, when a convergence of radicalism and mass labor militancy emerged first among new immigrant workers. The historian's most articulate commentators during such moments are often those whose interests appeared most menaced. Whether or not business leaders and politicians overreacted to the actual danger posed in this period can never be proven. This is the prevailing viewpoint, and has led to an assessment of the first Red Scare as a gross overreaction. Yet whether they were right or paranoid, contemporaries counted the very real development of mass labor struggle and radicalism as a dangerous threat.[2]

The period of political reaction that began in the Wilson administration, and accelerated through the Red Scare and the early 1920s can only be understood in this light. During World War I, the American state attempted to head off the convergence of mass labor militancy and radicalism through a combination of cooption and coercion. The Wilson administration invited labor figures such as Frank Walsh and Samuel Gompers close to the citadels of state power and offered an unstated quid pro quo to much of the labor force that included increasing wages (which nonetheless still fell behind inflation), federal mediation of labor disputes, and a friendlier regime toward A.F.L.–style organized labor. It also invited "Americanization" of immigrants as a prominent part of a nationalist propaganda mobilization. On the other hand, government meted out savage repression against political dissenters. Radicals and immigrant workers suffered unconstitutional and quasi-legal censorship, mass arrests, deportations, beatings, court injunctions and law suits, ransacking and burglaries, and frame-ups. This was conjoined to a darker side of the propaganda campaign that demonized difference and dissent. At the same time the state "deputized," so to speak, hundreds of thousands and then millions of middle-class Americans into organizations such as the American Protective League (A.P.L.) and later the American Legion and Ku Klux Klan. These organizations, some of the largest mass volunteer organizations in U.S. history, armed themselves, carried out vigilante attacks and intimidated radicals, workers, and immigrants. They also acted quite self-consciously as a social counterweight to the largely immigrant industrial working class. The parallels with the more-or-less simultaneous emergence of fascism in Europe are striking.[3]

The fear of the new immigrant was doubled by the fact that many came from lands caught up in the revolutionary fervor of Europe after 1917. By means of repression, government and business leaders sought to decapitate radicalism and thereby prevent it from giving expression to widespread antiwar sentiment and the strike wave. By the early 1920s, the racialized association between new immigrants and radicalism laid the groundwork for the passing of the Johnson-Reed Act of 1924 and its de facto banning of Eastern and Southern European immigration. This was a watershed moment in U.S. history. Not only did Johnson-Reed repudiate the long-standing open immigration policy, which had been progressively eroded after decades of singling out Asians, anarchists, and the infirm, it also initiated a sharp change in the composition of the working class and the advent of a new approach in labor-industrial relations that favored stability and employee loyalty over labor market flexibility. Whereas the growth of industry from the 1890s until World War I had been predicated on an enormous and fluid labor force, during the war for the first time industrial experts began to concern themselves with "turnover" and its problems. The transition was from the sort of labor market favored by the steel industry, contingent upon mass immigration, to that associated with what would come to be known as "Fordism."[4]

In spite of many cultural differences, new immigrants were categorized together by contemporaries and engaged in labor struggles together across national and ethnic boundaries in these years. There are important historical works that present quite a different picture. Lizabeth Cohen, in her treatment of Chicago's industrial workers between the two world wars, *Making a New Deal*, views the massive steel strike of Chicago's new immigrant workers in 1919 as the premature birth of something that could have arrived only much later—successful union and political struggles waged by industrial workers across ethnic lines. For Cohen, it was only the process of cultural Americanization and assimilation—and afterwards labor's alliance with New Deal liberalism—that cleared the way for workers to build up industrial unions' clout within a popular-front style political alliance. Prior to that, she assumes, new immigrants were hopelessly separated. "Working men and women were politicized with their 'local' worlds of race, ethnic group, neighborhood, and job and were not oriented toward broader political alliances or solutions," she writes.[5]

The new immigrants' labor struggles and political radicalization of the period between 1914 and 1924, however, demonstrate that national and ethnic rivalries did not form an insurmountable barrier to solidarity. Indeed, at times nationality, ethnicity, or race, as it was then most often called, became very much conjoined in the consciousness of new immigrants with class grievances arising in the workplace or community. New immigrant workers felt that dirty and dangerous work, poor living conditions, and bigotry resulted from their being categorized as lesser Italian, Slavic, Hungarian, or Finnish workers. But they also learned that these conditions were shared by others in the same mine pit, steel mill, and industrial community. Yet simultaneously World War I, and the prospect of independence for a number of Eastern European states, authored competing nationalisms among new immigrants. New immigrants united in labor struggles both *in spite of and because of* their cultural or "racial" differences, a process that James R. Barrett has called "ethnocultural class formation." John J. Kulczycki, in his study of Polish coal miners in the Ruhr, has found a similar tendency, what he calls "ethno-class consciousness," although he goes so far as to call for the invalidation of the "analytical dichotomy between national and social solidarity," rather than seeing the two identities in motion, at times working in harmony, at times at cross purposes. In the period of political reaction that emerged in the early 1920s, however, the disaggregating elements of identity pushed to the fore, and those elements tending toward class solidarity, which had tended to unify immigrants across many transplanted borders, receded. Cohen is right about the 1920s, but wrong about 1919.[6]

The new immigrants' labor struggles in the period were typified by long, violent, and whole-community fights in which women and children figured prominently. The militancy of the new immigrants interacted with existing trade unions in seemingly unpredictable ways, which can be seen in the relative success in the coal industry, led by the United Mine Workers (U.M.W.), and the ultimate failure to organize the steel industry. In both industries new immigrants tended to be the most militant portion of the workforce, at times running into conflict with conservative trade unionists. Because in both industries the militancy of the new immigrants was a constant factor in the period, understanding the success of the U.M.W. and the failure of the A.F.L. to organize the steel industry demands further explanation.

The question of the rationalization of industry holds the key. Rationalization was a major underlying force of U.S. economic development from the 1890s on. In the steel industry, finance capital took the lead and affected a sweeping reorganization not just of the production process, but of the entire industry. Craft unionism stood in the way, but because its peculiar form was rooted in earlier relations of production, business leaders were able to largely eliminate the craft unions from steel and other industries, in spite of the bitter resistance of skilled workers. However, due to the peculiar nature of the coal industry, which stemmed from the superabundance of coal deposits and the low level of capital needed to extract and transport it, coal interests could not carry out an equivalent form of rationalization. In the absence of capitalist monopoly, the U.M.W. played an important role in leading the efforts to regulate competition in the major fields of the Midwest. In general, it did not stand in the way of technological development, even if technology was far less advanced in coal than in many other industries. Yet this rationalizing role, which hinged on the defense of contractual obligation, brought the national and state U.M.W. bureaucracy into frequent conflict with workers, especially the immigrants.

Radical immigrants launched struggles within the U.M.W. to broaden its political and economic demands. Among other things, they demanded the nationalization of the entire industry. This did not happen. Its basis in the Midwest ultimately pitted the U.M.W. and its allies among the coal operators against the non-union producers of West Virginia and Kentucky. The U.M.W. would reach its high water mark in terms of membership and strength during World War I, yet soon after the war it faced fierce competition from the non-union fields, and entered a period of protracted decline. In coal the problem was overcapacity—"too many mines, too many miners," as John L. Lewis put it. The struggle within the U.M.W., which was particularly ferocious in Illinois, continued to hinge on the question of how the problem of overcapacity would be resolved.

The interaction of industry, trade unionism, and the new immigrants took a different form in the steel industry. The early craft unions in the steel industry did not fall victim to an "immigrant invasion," as their leaders sometimes claimed, but to changes in the nature of the steel industry. Later the attempt to organize steel workers in 1919 along industrial lines under the National Committee to Organize Steel Workers (National Committee) failed after a spectacular strike involving as many as 350,000 workers. The strike exposed major fissures along lines of race/ethnicity and skill, which the National Committee was unable to overcome. But as was the case in the coal towns, the immigrants reached an extraordinary level of militancy in 1919, and evidence from the strike suggests a widespread embrace of radicalism. Indeed, these characteristics—what unionists called "impetuousness"—brought the new immigrants into conflict with the organizational effort. Owing to the nature of the coal industry and its rationalizing role therein, the U.M.W. proved much more capable of overcoming national and racial divisions in the workplace than the craft unions.[7]

The basis of shared identity among new immigrant resulted from the shared experiences of labor migration and hard, dirty work. In steel milling and iron mining, distinctions between the kinds of jobs allocated to "American," "old immigrant," or "skilled" workers—jobs that paid better, and were cleaner and safer—and new immigrants, whose work was dirty, dangerous and lesser paid, both fed off and reinforced the formation of a new immigrant identity. Cultural differences, the focus of much contemporary commentary on immigrants, provided a racial explanation for social inequality.

Unlike the steel industry, coal proved resistant to mechanization, Taylorization, and indeed monopolization. The divide between "American" and "Hunky" work was never so stark. Yet there too, new immigrants increasingly dominated the workforce, a similar sense of grievance emerged, and tendencies toward labor militancy and radicalization came to the fore contemporaneously to similar developments in such a highly concentrated industry as steel. The development of consciousness among new immigrants, therefore, must also be explained by broader factors. I argue that the shared experiences of work and living conditions were shaped and given meaning by a series of world historical developments unfolding during the years of this study that acutely impacted new immigrants—depression, war, inflation, revolution, reaction, and depression again.

The immigrants led transnational lives; their ideologies, cultures, and movements were of necessity transatlantic. Europe and the U.S.—and the rest of the world—grew in dynamic interaction. No process reflects that more than mass immigration. If World War I represented the revolt of the means of production against the nation-state system to which they had been confined, as Trotsky argued, then the phenomenon of mass international immigration was perhaps that revolt's most consciously-experienced element, involving as it did millions upon millions of people. It was in large part a response to the struggles of the new immigrants, imbued with a spirit of internationalism, that the U.S. would move decisively away from its old position that advocated open immigration from Europe, and toward the Fordist model of steady employment, employee loyalty, and Americanization—a system that gained state sanction with the triumph of the Johnson-Reed Act, or Immigration Act of 1924, and which would characterize U.S. capitalism until the new globalization that emerged from the 1970s on.[8]

New Immigration and the Age of Steel

> Deposits of iron, coal, and limestone—the essential raw materials of iron and steel production—are enormous, and they occur in a form that makes them easily and therefore cheaply worked.... The Lake Superior ore region is several hundred miles distant from the coking-coal producing centres in the Pittsburgh and Chicago region ... [but] the Great Lakes, navigable from Duluth, the center of the world's greatest iron ore production region ... form the greatest internal waterway in the world. Further, they constitute the northern boundary of the largest manufacturing belt in the country.[9]

In order to understand the development of the new immigration, its political implications, and the consciousness of new immigrant workers, it is necessary to consider the development of industry to which it was conjoined. The enormous scale, complexity, and interconnectedness of industry contributed to what contemporaries referred to as the "mass mindedness" of the immigrants. Industrial development from the 1890s on linked, moreover, new immigrants into circuits of labor migration both national and transatlantic in their dimensions.[10]

The growth of industry was heavily based on the production of steel. Steel was necessary for the final surge in the growth of the railroad network that reached its pinnacle shortly after World War I. The steel beam and rail allowed for the enormous expansion of the cityscape—both upwards and outwards. The production and distribution of steel, in turn, relied on four essential ingredients—iron, coal (converted into coke), a transportation network capable of bearing heavy loads, and labor. Fortuitously for the growth of American capitalism, the Great Lakes region supplied the first three of these ingredients in abundance. The fourth, labor, would have to be supplied largely through immigration.

Iron ore had been produced in the Great Lakes region for decades prior to 1914, regular shipment of ore having begun in the 1850s from Michigan's Upper Peninsula. By the early 1880s, Minnesota had joined the ranks of the ore producing states through the development of the Vermillion Range. Then in the 1890s, the development of the Mesabi Range touched off a bonanza. Ore deposits were enormous and located conveniently close to the surface in a 120-mile stretch of northern Minnesota timberlands. Collectively, Minnesota's three ranges—the Mesabi, the Vermillion, and the Cuyuna—came to be known as "the Iron Range" and produced nearly 60 percent of the total dollar value of U.S. iron output by 1910, when 50,000 people, mostly immigrants, inhabited the area. To its great advantage, Iron Range ore deposits were easily transportable. Heavily laden trains coasted a gradual descent to Lake Superior's major U.S. harbors situated in and around Duluth, Minnesota, which came in short time to be among the nation's largest port in terms of tonnage. The trains then travelled out above Lake Superior on enormous scaffolding called "ore docks" where they dumped their payload into the open hulls of waiting ore freighters below. In this way 12,000 tons of ore could be loaded per hour. From the Superior ports the trains then ascended empty to the mines of the Range, and the great maritime steamships transported the ores over the length of the Great Lakes to their destinations in Pennsylvania, Ohio, New York, Wisconsin, Michigan and the Calumet district of the south Chicago area. There the ore was unloaded by the recently developed "Hulett electrical unloader," which could unload, remarkably, at nearly the same rate the ore trains dumped. By 1913, the Lake Superior District produced 84.5 percent of all U.S. iron.[11]

Chicago proved to be fortuitously located at the center of the Great Lakes maritime routes and the U.S. rail network. The bulk and weight of both raw materials and finished product made it necessary to place new steel centers within reach of both minerals and markets. Chicago's position and its ability to generate enormous investment capital allowed for the building up of the Calumet steel-milling district which stretched from South Chicago to Michigan City, Indiana, and encompassed the U.S. Steel–designed Gary, Indiana, built in 1906. By World War I, the Calumet district was challenging Pittsburgh as the nation's leading steel

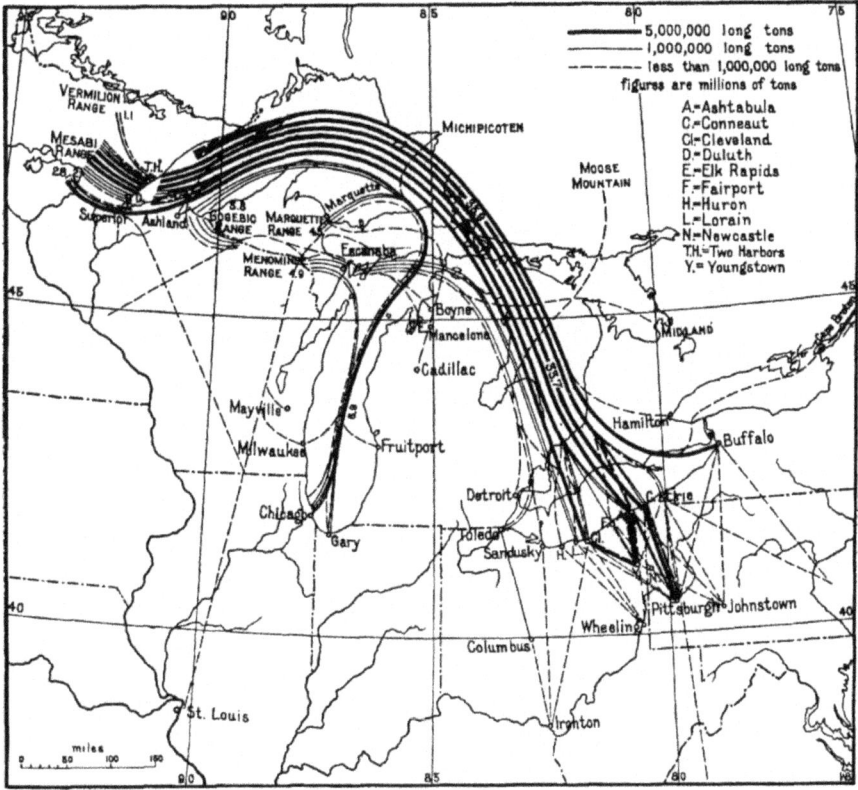

A map from a contemporary geological survey of the Lake Superior ore district, with the destination of ores. Source: George J. Miller, "Some Geographic Influences of the Lake Superior Iron Ores," *Bulletin of the American Geographical Society* 46, no. 12 (1914): 881–916.

center. It had numerous advantages, not the least of which was that it developed later and with the most modern technology. The vast sandy flats on the approaches to Lake Michigan, furthermore, allowed for the expansive horizontal growth of enormous factories, while the lake made possible the transportation of heavy iron ores from the Lake Superior District and limestone from northern Michigan without any rail transport required. The Calumet district indeed produced iron more cheaply than Pittsburgh (as did other Great Lakes milling centers such as Cleveland and Buffalo) but was somewhat restrained in its growth by the "Pittsburgh Plus" system of price-fixing inaugurated by U.S. Steel in 1901, by which steel prices nationally were fixed based on the costs of production in the Pittsburgh District (including Southeast Ohio) plus the cost of transport to market.[12]

The growth of U.S. industrial output was dependent upon the expansion of the U.S. coal industry, which by 1910 had come to represent nearly 40 percent of world output. A significant share of this growth took place in Illinois. Though Illinois had been a significant coal producer for decades, its production expanded rapidly beginning in the 1890s. By 1910 it was the nation's second leading coal-producing state after Pennsylvania. Coal production increased from 2,624,163 tons in 1870 to 51,317,146 tons in 1907, and the workforce grew from 6,301 in 1870 to 65,581 in 1907. Steel plants consumed 6.4 percent of all bituminous coal production. Prior to the nineteen-teens, Calumet's steel mills supplied their need for coke—which is created through the processing of bituminous coal—largely from eastern Kentucky and West Virginia. However, the development of the by-product coke oven allowed for the conversion of lower-grade Illinois and Indiana bituminous to coke, thus further uniting the regional economy of the Western Great Lakes. The new coke ovens converted coal to coke directly at the modern steel plants, and managed to utilize every by-product of the conversion— ammonia, tar, and benzol—which had formerly been discarded.[13]

Chicago came to be the center of the coal trade as well; one observer calling it "the coal trade cockpit of the country." It was the battleground for Illinois and West Virginia coal production, even if "rate differentials long ago drove eastern industrial coal of out of the market." This struggle played out in Minnesota as well, where "at St. Paul the all-rail coals from Illinois and Indiana clash with the eastern dock coals from Duluth and Superior."[14] An enormous industrial region, in short, had developed around the Great Lakes, and much of the growth since 1890 had hinged on the development in the western Great Lakes region, dependent upon

A magazine cover promoting the Calumet steel milling region (Chicago Historical Society).

the iron ore of Minnesota and the coal reserves of Illinois. The Calumet region was the lynchpin—the transportation and processing center—of this development.

U.S. Steel, together with a few other much smaller rivals (later dubbed "Little Steel"), accounted for virtually all steel production and iron mining. "The Steel Trust," as it was commonly known, was among the first corporations organized for the benefit of bank investment, or finance capital, as opposed to the industrial empires of individuals or small groups, which Andrew Carnegie's empire had epitomized. The triumph of finance capital in the steel industry, which was mirrored in many other sectors of the U.S. economy, marked a shift from the ruthless and chaotic competition of the period lasting from the 1870s through the 1890s, which had encompassed years of sharp deflationary pressures and two major depressions, toward a more "rational" form of capitalism designed to ensure the profit margins of large investors, run by bankers and financial experts.[15]

But finance capital did not prevail in every sector of the economy. The coal industry proved resistant to the triumph of the financiers that had changed so many other industries in the U.S. and internationally during the period. As had been the norm during the Gilded Age, ruthless competition, overcapacity, and overproduction—and thus deflation—characterized the coal industry, much to the chagrin of its leaders, who wished for nothing more than to follow the monopolist trend ubiquitous elsewhere in the economy, and who lobbied unsuccessfully for a relaxation of anti-trust legislation to allow for greater industrial "cooperation" in setting prices and practices. Several factors explain this critical difference. Numerous regions—Appalachia, the Midwest, and the Rocky Mountain West—had abundant reserves. Much of this coal was fairly easily extracted and lay close to major transportation arteries, both river and railroad. Railroad companies often opened their own "captive" mines to supply their own demand, as did U.S. Steel for its Pennsylvania mills. Iron deposits, on the other hand, were concentrated in the Lake Superior region, making them more easily controlled by a handful of interests. Furthermore, iron ore required intense capital investment to extract, either through deep shaft mining or highly-mechanized strip-mining. Large capital expenditure was also necessary for steamship transport on the Great Lakes. By the end of the 1890s all the small time iron mine owners had been chased out by the likes of Carnegie, John D. Rockefeller, and the railroad magnate James J. Hill. Carnegie later bought out Rockefeller, and eventually sold out to J.P. Morgan and U.S. Steel, through which iron production was linked up with an industrial empire the likes of which the world had not seen.[16]

The deflationary pressures on coal, however, were quite useful for other sectors of industry: not only the steel industry, but the railroads, the steamships, and almost all factories were powered by bituminous coal. In 1914, bituminous coal supplied about 70 percent of all U.S. energy requirements.[17] Cheap coal was good for everyone, in other words, except those in and around the massive coal industry itself. Paradoxically, that both operators and workers in the coal industry suffered due to the chaos of competition opened up the possibility for a degree of cooperation absent in other sectors of the economy. Lacking the ability to rationalize their own affairs, operators tacitly invited labor to assist. This the U.M.W. did through its exclusive Trade Agreements with the coal operators of the Central Competitive Field (C.C.F.) which consisted of western Pennsylvania, Ohio, Indiana, and Illinois. The U.M.W. collaborated with the owners to regulate prices, wages, and, most importantly, competition.

This contributed to a limited rationalization of the C.C.F. and helped the U.M.W. emerge as a formidable union. However, even as the U.M.W. solidified its cooperation with Midwestern coal operators in order to reduce the havoc created by the free market, new competitive pressures emerged with the opening of new coal fields in Appalachia, from West Virginia to Alabama. The Appalachian fields held numerous competitive advantages. Like the C.C.F., they had coal in super-abundance, but they tended to produce a higher grade coal than the C.C.F. Government regulation was more advanced in the C.C.F., which added to the cost pressures faced by operators. And while the U.M.W. served as a useful tool for rationalizing the chaos *within* the C.C.F., once installed it tended to impose a significantly higher wage structure on the C.C.F. operators, over and above the higher wages that typified the North as opposed to the cheaper-labor South.[18]

Shared by the steel and coal industries was a seemingly insatiable demand for labor. This would be met primarily by the massive influx of new immigrants from Eastern and Southern Europe. On Minnesota's Iron Range, Finns, Slovenians, Italians, Croats, Serbs, and Montenegrins joined more established groups of Cornish and Swedish miners. In Illinois coal mining, Italians, Lithuanians, Russians, Poles, Slovaks, and Hungarians joined older groups of German, Scottish, and Belgian miners to meet the growing production demands. In Calumet, all of these groups and many others manned the steel industry. The dynamic interaction of these newcomers with industrial development, punctuated by world-historical events, propelled the period's momentous changes that this book's chapters address.

Chapter 1, "'Our lives, our thoughts and our allegiance': New Immigrants in 1914," addresses the forms of social distance separating and marginalizing new immigrants from society and trade unionism. The chapter examines the relationship of skill to that of race/ethnicity in the three industries. The chapter establishes that the new immigration was a labor migration and that new immigrants were overwhelmingly congregated in what were called "unskilled" or "semi-skilled" forms of labor. These menial jobs had become practically a preserve of the new immigrants. Social advancement to skilled work was largely, with certain variations, the preserve of "American" or old immigrant workers from northern and western Europe. New immigrants and other observers were aware of this social reality, the chapter shows, contributing to a shared identity. I also consider various forms of testimony from social reformers and new immigrants to paint a portrait of living conditions among new immigrants, which in spite of the differences among the industries studied, bore striking resemblance in their isolation and insularity from larger U.S. society. These characteristics, I argue, contributed to the formation of a new immigrant consciousness and to the coming period of labor militancy. Finally, I consider the position of the trade union movement toward the new immigrants, comparing the success of the U.M.W. in its organization of the new immigrants with the failure of the craft unions in steel.

Chapter 2, "'A war of coal and iron': 1914–1917," treats the changes that were precipitated by the eruption of war in Europe, which combined with the social position of the new immigrants to propel a wave of labor militancy that erupted in numerous short and local strikes in coal mining and steel milling, and the bitter and I.W.W.–led Mesabi Range strike of 1916. After a brief depression caused by war-related economic dislocations, industry began to boom in 1916 as U.S. commerce sought to meet the demands of the European belligerents. The war virtually ended new immigration and laid the groundwork for the Great Black, southern white, Mexican, and Caribbean migrations that would take its place, and which would begin to change the steel industry labor force in particular. The chapter also addresses the beginning of the politicization of the new immigrants, as they followed closely events in Europe, and various ideologies engaged in heightened competition for their loyalty.

Chapter 3, "Securing 'the industrial forts of America': 1917–1918," analyzes the two years in which the competing claims for new immigrant loyalty reached their most fevered pitch, a situation greatly exasperated by the Russian Revolution, U.S. entry into World War I, and the growing likelihood that a number of new states might emerge from the wreckage of the German, Austro-Hungarian, Russian, and Ottoman empires. Government and the corporate elite pursued a carrot-and-stick strategy with new immigrants. On the one hand, there was an unprecedented demand for "Americanization," by which new immigrants seemed to be offered a path toward social acceptance. On the other was a shrill and oppressive nationalism that could brook no opposition or disloyalty, real or imagined, and that was increasingly directed against the new immigrant communities. At the same time, U.S. industrialists and the government wanted to keep new immigrant workers in production behind the war effort and off the picket line. But in spite of all efforts, and the loyalty of the A.F.L., new immigrants struck in enormous numbers in 1917 and 1918, including a general strike led by new immigrant coal miners in Springfield, Illinois.

Chapter 4, "'The Revolt of the Rank and File': 1919," considers the year when new immigrant radicalism and militancy came to a head. The largest strike year in U.S. history to that point, massive strikes gripped the steel and coal industries. In the former, divisions between new immigrants, "Americans," and African Americans played a prominent role in the strike's defeat. In both the steel and coal strikes, new immigrant radicalism appeared to be dangerously close to escaping the bounds of traditional trade union struggles. Radicalism held perhaps its greatest appeal among new immigrants, but the year was also ground zero for the American and new immigrant left after the twin shocks of the Russian Revolution and intense government repression, which continued during the first Red Scare. A number of new states were born in Eastern Europe, and return migration—a possibility for the first time in a number of years—attracted hundreds of thousands of new immigrants.

After 1919 a number of reactionary currents which had emerged already during World War I consolidated and exacted an enormous impact on the new immigrant communities, a process I examine in Chapter 5, "Reaction in New Country and Old: 1920–1924." The economic situation changed markedly, as wartime production levels receded and depression emerged in 1920–1922, leading to higher levels of unemployment. Significant right-wing vigilante movements, such as the American Legion and the Ku Klux Klan, emerged in coal and iron mining communities to intimidate immigrants. American industry, chastened by the powerful militancy of new immigrants in the preceding years, slowly altered its labor policies, pushing back on workers' wartime gains. Industry became more interested in developing a stable and loyal workforce, hallmarks of what came to be known as "Fordism." Gradually U.S. industry came to favor, for the first time, a closing of mass European immigration. This joined with a changing political mood to allow for the passing of the National Origins acts of 1922 and 1924. The developing national reaction in the U.S. coincided, moreover, with a period of transatlantic reaction, particularly in the homelands of the new immigrants. By 1923 fascism had triumphed in Italy, and nearly all of the Eastern and Southern European states had installed right-wing militarist and royalist dictatorships. In the Soviet Union, the ebb tide of revolution corresponded with bureaucratization and the gradual consolidation of power by Joseph Stalin. It was in this national and international context of reaction that new immigrant radicalism and militancy waned, and nationalist sentiment and rivalries among the new immigrants reappeared with great force.

Chapter 1

"Our lives, our thoughts and our allegiance": New Immigrants in 1914

New immigrant life in the factory, mill, and mining towns of the industrial U.S. has struck observers, past and present, for its enormous distance and isolation from the presumptions of normal middle class American life. This distance can be appraised in numerous ways. In the first place, we may speak of a spatial distance. The expanse separating the overwhelmingly new immigrant Iron Range from what was thought of as "civilization," was measured in the hundreds of miles and in days, rather than hours, of travel. Long travel by train through cut-over timberlands added to the effect. The milling neighborhoods of Calumet seemed a world apart from the middle class and business districts of Chicago. This physical distance could be easily spotted once again in Illinois' downstate mining towns, where small middle classes huddled together; a few large houses set off against dozens or hundreds of miners' shacks and crowded boarding houses.[1]

Spatial distance was but one evident aspect of a gulf that appeared to separate the immigrants from their new country. Other forms of distance may have been less tangible, but if anything they have absorbed the attention of observers even more. Perhaps foremost among these was the gulf that separated the new immigrants socioeconomically from middle class standards of living. Poverty, poor living and working conditions—these seemed to be the natural state of affairs for the immigrants. Opponents of immigration simplistically associated these problems of social inequality with supposed cultural and "racial" barriers that appeared to separate the new immigrants from the traditions of Anglo-Saxon America. New immigrants were overwhelmingly Roman Catholic,

Jewish, and Eastern Orthodox in a predominantly Protestant land; they spoke strange Italian dialects, Yiddish, and an array of Slavic, Baltic, and Finno-Ugric languages, in addition to Romanian, Albanian, Greek, Turkish, and Arabic. Hundreds of local and national customs were conflated in the contemporary public eye under the somewhat pejorative moniker "foreign." An observer of Russian immigrants could thus conclude that "the majority of Russians ... are almost as completely isolated from the American people as if they would live in the heart of giant Russia."[2]

This distance—spatial, social, and cultural—was of primary concern for numerous agents who attempted to bridge the gap. Progressive reformers feared that the isolation would lead to social unrest. How could the new immigrants in their insular industrial communities be reached and the barriers of separation pierced? Could the new immigrants be influenced, settled, Americanized? What sort of citizens could be made of individuals seemingly locked away in isolated communities? A whole wing of progressivism, of which Jane Addams is the best known representative, was focused both politically and in its practical work on precisely this question. This dilemma—at heart a question of authority—was also quite a serious and important matter for the state, at all levels of government, as the propaganda and repression of World War I would soon make clear. From the perspective of indigenous American radicalism, practical and ideological questions prevailed. What *were* new immigrant workers in relationship to the "American" working class? How could new immigrant radicalism, evidently growing in strength, be tied to American radicalism? What role would the new immigrant radicals play in the volatile divisions within the ranks of the left? The labor movement faced a similar dilemma: Could the new immigrants be reached? Could they be organized? Would it not be better to just keep them out of industry, and failing that, the country?[3]

New immigrants felt this social distance keenly. Though the new immigrant industrial communities were insular, paradoxically they housed within their oftentimes invisible boundaries cosmopolitan and politicized populations. More importantly, while enormous barriers did indeed separate the new immigrants from the "host" society, new immigrant industrial communities proved to be acutely sensitive and responsive to the global changes that would become manifest with the onset of World War I.[4]

At its basis, the problem of social distance was a manifestation of what contemporaries called "the labor problem." It was so at two levels. First, immigration was itself a worldwide mass labor movement over and beyond the borders of numerous nation-states, a migration generated by dramatic changes to economic production on a world scale. The U.S. economy played a catalytic and interactive role in these changes. Its rapid growth accelerated market integration in Europe's predominantly agricultural regions. The growing reach of the market, in turn, tended to push people out of agricultural and handicraft production and into a worldwide labor market, of which the U.S. was itself the most important beneficiary, culling millions of new workers for the same industrial growth that was propelling the market advance in the first place. Thus, even prior to arrival in the U.S., broad economic tendencies had generated certain similarities in the migratory experience for people coming from Eastern and Southern European lands to the U.S.

Second—and turning to the topic of this chapter—industrial work gave rise to shared experiences in the coal mining, iron mining, and steel milling communities, and by extension in U.S. industry more generally. Among these similarities were low-paid, dangerous, and dirty work, the living conditions which resulted from this work, and a perception that advancement out of these positions was virtually blocked. Secondarily, changes to the division of labor related to skill, mechanization, managerial practice, and capitalization, interacted with the "racial" (or "national" or "ethnic")[5] composition of the rapidlychanging workforce. In this atmosphere, industrial labor and race came to be mutually constitutive. Certain forms of labor became "hunky" work. Other forms of labor associated with skill and the operation of expensive machinery were very often the preserve of old immigrant groups from northern and western Europe, workers increasingly thought of as "American" in the period. The forms of social distance confronting new immigrant coal miners were the same. These similarities structured many aspects of life for diverse new immigrant groups in the U.S, and contributed to the coming years of militancy and radicalism, as well as to the forms that new immigrant struggles would take.[6]

The New Immigration as Labor Migration

The new immigration was the corollary to profound changes to industry: its monopolization into financial empires; its "Taylorization" of labor by which the manager sought to put his brain "under the workingman's cap"; its drive for technological innovation that increasingly reduced industrial labor to an extension of the machine; its enormous growth of infrastructure, much of it still built by "pick and shovel men"; and of course, its unrelenting drive for profit, by which it sought to extract more and more at the point of production. As Bruno Ramirez has put it, U.S. immigration policy amounted, if not in so many words, to a "labor-market policy." A vast supply of cheap labor was the prerequisite for the reorganization of the workplace. Indeed, the characteristic of the immigrant communities that caused more suspicion among contemporaries than any other—mobility—was in fact the characteristic U.S. industry found most attractive.[7]

A narrow layer among new immigrant communities made their living as clergy, professionals and small businessmen; one scholar has found that among Yugoslav immigrants "up to the First World War it was not possible at all to talk about a Yugoslav middle class in the U.S.A."— only some "who attempted to attain a better material position" such as "merchants, innkeepers, saloon owners, bankers, *sifkartasi* (ticket agents for shipping companies), and later translators, writers, priests, and an occasional doctor or lawyer."[8] What was true of Yugoslav groups was more or less true of the whole new immigration. Even this minority owed their livelihoods to the communities of immigrant workers that they served as bankers, lawyers, food wholesalers, and so on. These middling strata—*i prominenti* as the Italian immigrants called them—oftentimes represented themselves as the leadership of new immigrant communities to the outside world. Yet their position was more akin to that of a mediator operating between new immigrant workers on one side, and a number of power structures on the other: both old and new world governments, religious hierarchy, and U.S. industry. The small numbers of the immigrant elite, coupled with their social and cultural proximity to the much larger numbers of working class immigrants, ensured this ambiguous position. Before 1920, only in the rarest occasions were new immigrants and their children found at the head of major companies that did significant business outside of the new immigrant community.

Just a small portion succeeded in finding work as independent land-owning farmers, in stark contrast to the "old immigration" of Scandinavians and Germans—but not the Irish—whose arrival at a time when vast agricultural tracts in the Upper Midwest and Great Plains were available for purchase on the cheap made possible a more variegated occupational picture. Among Hungarians, even though a majority had been engaged in agriculture in the old country, and though 35 percent lived in "rural non-farm areas," less than one percent found work in agriculture. Some new immigrant groups gained a slightly larger foothold in farming; for example the Czechs, whose large scale migration began earlier, in the 1870s, and the Finns, a significant minority of whom scratched subsistence farms out of the rocks and stumps of the cutover logging areas of northeastern Minnesota and Michigan's Upper Peninsula.[9]

In the U.S., new immigrants congregated overwhelmingly in unskilled and semiskilled occupations. Michael La Sorte has estimated that 80 percent of Italian migrants from 1871 to 1910 wound up in positions of common or agricultural labor. Similarly, by one author's estimate, fully 80 percent of Polish immigrants lived in industrial cities and worked as laborers prior to World War I. According to a 1922 study the vast majority of Russian immigrants found employment in just two industries: steel and coal. In 1910 40 percent of Hungarians labored in steel mills and the same proportion worked in coal mines. Another historian has concluded that already by 1900 nearly three quarters of all Italian, Slavic, and Hungarian immigrants lived in the six most highly industrialized northern states that together accounted for over 60 percent of all manufacturing and mining production. A major 1910 survey of immigrants in industry found that two thirds of all miners in both the iron and copper industry were foreign born; in coal mining the figure was one half. Another study, published in 1917 and based on the 1910 census, found that for 15 leading industries the foreign-born comprised a large majority of the workforce; for industrial workers in all "leading" industries, the average was 58 percent.[10]

These trends found abundant expression in the three industries studied here, although in different ways and to varying degrees. Of 12,018 workers employed by the Oliver Iron Mining Company (Oliver) in 1907, U.S. Steel's Iron Range subsidiary, 84.4 percent were foreign born, and half of those had lived in the country for less than two years. Surveying 1,708 Iron Range miners in 1909, the Dillingham Commission (or the United States Immigration Commission, formed in 1907 to investigate immigration and propose legislation) found that only 3.5 percent were native-born of native-born white fathers. The European origin of the Iron Range miners was so overwhelming that the category "American" had, by 1910, come to subsume the old immigrant groups. Thus, on the Iron Range, the so-called "American element" included both the native-born of fathers from "old" immigrant groups and even the foreign-born of the old immigrant groups, among whom Cornish, Scandinavian, and German workers predominated. Even so, only 18 percent of the mine work force on the Iron Range would have been called, by the parlance of the time, "American."[11]

In 1910, fully 55.4 percent of the Mesabi Range towns' populations were foreign born. Of 2,328 day laborers in the Eveleth, Minnesota, labor force, only 118 were described as "American-born"—a figure which thus included the second generation of new immigrant workers entering the work force. In Virginia, Hibbing, Chisholm, Eveleth, and Ely—the Iron Range's five largest towns—respectively only 35, 17, 10, 8, and 18 percent of inhabitants were the children of a native-born parents. The census breakdown for Virginia (the only Range city for which observations based upon nationality were made) indicates that the overwhelming majority of the town's foreign born and children of foreign born were new immigrants from Finland, "Austria," "Russia," Italy, and "Hungary."[12] For the five leading Iron Range towns, there lived only 17 "Negroes," according to the census, and 50 Chinese, Japanese, "Indian"—i.e., Native American—"and all others."[13]

America's steel mills were also heavily new immigrant, with as many as two thirds being foreign born.[14] The Dillingham Commission did not study the Calumet steel district individually, but instead produced a representative study based on 12,053 workers for steel milling in the "Middle West," a geographical category which included Illinois, Indiana, Wisconsin, Michigan, and part of Ohio. Certain things stand out from the study. First, like the Iron Range, the share of white native-born of native-born fathers was very small—just over 15 percent of the total. Unlike the Iron Range, steel mills did employ some black workers, but they represented a small share of the workforce—only .5 percent of the total in 1909. "Old Immigrant" groups formed a considerable share, about 30 percent, of the workforce, counting both those born of immigrant fathers and those who themselves immigrated. Yet new immigrants had come to dominate the industry, representing over 50 percent of the workforce and coming from a wide range of Eastern and Southern European backgrounds. In one "representative" Midwestern steel milling community, the Dillingham Commission found that fully 99 percent of the foreign-born workforce had been in the country for less than ten years. Polish immigrants comprised a large share—nearly a quarter of the workforce—compared to Italians, who comprised just over one percent.[15]

Statistics for South Chicago support the larger demographic view for the Midwest as a whole. The Dillingham Commission estimated that there were 90,000 inhabitants, of which approximately 30,000 appear to have been old immigrants, 15,000 were "American (White and Negro)," and 45,000 were new immigrants. The report noted that "Scandinavians" had begun to leave the steel mills in the 1890s and that "by the year 1900 practically all of the Scandinavian workmen had disappeared." Among the new immigrants themselves the trend for employment seemed to be continuing an eastward and southward arc across the map of Europe, with Poland and the Czech lands supplying the first large numbers of new immigrants, and numerous Balkan nationalities coming in large number only after 1904. This view is supported by an earlier sociological study, published in 1901, which also noted the decline in South Chicago's old immigrant groups and a corresponding increase in the new immigrant population, with Poles then predominating. Not surprisingly, the new immigration was even more marked in Gary, the U.S. Steel company town founded in 1906. Of a total estimated population of 15,000, only 4,200 were counted as "American, German, Irish, English, and Swedish" (it is telling that these nationalities were conflated into one group). The Poles were still among the largest single groups, but they were outnumbered barely by Hungarians, and fourfold by Croatians. In addition to Croatians, various groups of South Slavs were well-represented, as were Slovaks.[16]

Census data confirms that in the Calumet region's recently built up industrial areas, new immigrants dominated. In Chicago's 33rd Ward, which contained South Chicago and U.S. Steel's South Works, out of a population of nearly 71,000, only 12,123 were the native-born children of native-born parents. New immigrants appear to have comprised about one-third of the population, with Russians, "Austrians," Italians, and Hungarians all well represented. Thus notwithstanding employment patterns in the mills, the old immigrant groups still comprised the majority of the population, with Swedes, Dutch, and Germans represented in very large numbers, followed distantly by the Irish and English. In the newer districts of the Calumet region, the new immigrant proportion of the population was more marked. In Chicago Heights, of 14,525 inhabitants, about 44 percent would have been classified as "new immigrants." But here the Italian proportion of the population was the largest by far, constituting well over half of the total. In East Chicago, Indiana, out of a population of 19,098 in 1910, only 3,013 could be described as "American." Over half of the population was foreign born, with "Austrians" and Hungarians predominating. In Gary, out of 16,802 inhabitants, half were foreign born, with large numbers of "Austrians," Hungarians and Russians. For Lake County, Indiana, as a whole—the county containing Gary, East Chicago, Whiting, and Hammond—the population of 82,864 was over half foreign born. Meanwhile, the African American population of the Calumet region in 1910 was, relatively-speaking, as small as it was on Minnesota's Iron Range, which suggests that even the very small portion of blacks actually working in the steel mills was forced to commute from the Black Belt. In Lake County, Indiana, the African American population was just under .06 percent of the total; in Chicago's 33rd ward, it was just over .01 percent.[17]

Coal mining presents a somewhat different picture. Though new immigrants and their children formed a large share of the total workforce, "old immigrants," native white Americans and native African Americans comprised a significant share. Coal mining communities could be "mosaic[s] of nationalities and religions." At the most general level as one moved from north to south across the United States the native element became larger, so that it appears coal mines in Pennsylvania, Ohio, Indiana and the northern portion of Illinois were mostly worked by new immigrants, while in Kentucky, West Virginia, and southern Illinois native whites and African Americans formed a relatively larger share of the population. This difference is likely owed to the fact that the southernmost coal mining regions lay in close proximity to abundant cheap labor from America's own agricultural periphery in the U.S. South. Yet in a number of southern Illinois coal towns new immigrants constituted a large majority.[18]

The nature of work in the coal mine also tended to allow for a more mixed workforce, with certain positions—especially those related directly to extraction—requiring greater levels of skill and experience. A number of new immigrants, especially those from northern Italy, had gained experience prior to immigration, so that in instances where skilled immigrant workers labored in mines with large new immigrant workforces, such as in Spring Valley, Illinois, by World War I a certain degree of occupational mobility among the immigrants had taken place. This tended to favor the possibility for cross-ethnic organization and the sort of cooperation between old and new immigrants that was developed under the auspices of the U.M.W.[19]

Synthesizing statistics for various new immigrant groups compiled by Lauck and Sydenstricker, it appears that new immigrants comprised just over half of the total workforce in the bituminous coal industry nationally. Detailed local statistics are more difficult to come by. For the Springfield area, U.M.W. sub-district president John Clark estimated that in 1914 fully 80 percent of the local mine workforce was comprised of new immigrants. Caroline Merithew found that in four northern Illinois coal towns, the combined first- and second-generation population was 85–90 percent. For its part, the Dillingham Commission compiled data on the Midwestern coalfields that included reports from "all sections" of Illinois, Indiana, and Ohio. The resulting report was based on nearly 19,000 workers out of a total estimated workforce of over 130,000. Among these 19,000, just over half of the total was foreign-born. Native-born of foreign-born fathers accounted for 14.5 percent of the total, but these were nearly all sons of old immigrant groups. The new immigrant share of the total labor force for the three states, then, appears to have been just above 35 percent, slightly larger than the native-born of native fathers, which was 32 percent. Blacks accounted for 3.1 percent of the workforce, and old immigrants approximately 30 percent, among whom British and German miners figured prominently. In other words, in 1910 the Midwestern bituminous coal mining workforce was split almost evenly in thirds among new immigrants, old immigrants, and Americans, while blacks accounted for a not insignificant share.[20]

Yet in general, the Commission noted a marked shift toward employment of new immigrants among the foreign born that began after 1890, a tendency that has been substantiated by historians of coal mining. Prior to that mining had been dominated by British and German miners. Analyzing one representative coal mining town, the Commission described the demographic picture in the following way:

> The population is made up exclusively of white races and embraces Native-born Americans, and native and foreign-born English, Irish, Scotch, Welsh, Germans, and foreign-born Italians, Ruthenians, Poles, Slovaks, Lithuanians, and a small number of Hebrews. These races form three more or less clearly defined groups. The natives, together with the British and German races, make up the first group and constitute about one-half of the population. The Italians stand about midway between the other two groups in point of Americanization, and are said to furnish nearly 30 per cent of the population. The Lithuanian and the Slavic races form the third group, comprising approximately one-fifth of the combined population of the three towns.

The "midway" position assigned to Italians here is noteworthy and unusual, but Merithew's research on Italians in the Spring Valley area suggests that this position may be owed to the fact that numbers of North Italians arrived with some experience in coal mining.[21]

In the steel industry a workforce divided in two along lines of both race/nationality and skill had emerged. New immigrant workers, predominately unskilled or semi-skilled, stood on one side of this divide.

On the other were the old immigrants, as the Immigration Commission and other contemporaries referred to workers of northwest European background. The former could also be referred to as "foreigners" or by epithets such as "Hunky," while the latter were increasingly referred to as "American." This division was not so marked in coal mining, due to the organizing of the U.M.W., although the influx of new immigrants had created an increasingly international workforce. Prior to 1916, new immigrants encountered African Americans only in small numbers in the steel mills. In coal mining, they contributed a sizeable proportion to the workforce and were also organized by the U.M.W., but this was especially true in downstate Illinois, and mine operators typically employed either African Americans or new immigrants, but not both together. Native Americans, despite inhabiting northern Minnesota in the Ojibwe nation, were evidently not hired in significant numbers by U.S. Steel, although it is probable that some workers referred to as "French Canadian" may have in fact been of Native American ancestry.

Mechanization, Skill and the New Immigrants

In the space of fifteen years, beginning about 1900, the steel industry was reorganized by machine technology in most aspects of production. Likewise, the development of the Mesabi Range, with its vast ore deposits close to the surface, allowed for the extensive introduction of machinery in iron ore mining. Even in coal mining, notably resistant to technological innovation, machine mining was making considerable headway, so that already by 1904 more than one third of all Midwest coal was machine-extracted. The new immigration was certainly linked to these developments, as well as with mechanization and efficiency more generally, although demonstrating a relationship between cause and effect proves to be a more difficult pursuit.[22]

In many industries divisions in the labor process relating to skill tended to play out along ethnic or "racial" lines, so that "American" and old immigrants tended to dominate skilled and supervisory roles in production, while new immigrants tended to be confined to the un- and semi-skilled positions.[23] This was very much the case on Minnesota's Iron Range. In the iron mines, only in the skilled jobs—steam shovel operators, railway employees, engineers and mine management—did the native-born outnumber the new immigrants. The Immigration Commission thus described the occupational structure on the Iron Range:

> On the Mesabi Range [...] the Finns, Italians and Austro-Hungarian races were first in the lower occupations where they are still found. The Montenegrins and Servians are doing the most common or unskilled labor such as track laying and tram work. The Scandinavians, Irish, English, and Americans are in the skilled occupations in all mines on the range. Slovenians and Finns are found in the unskilled occupations, chiefly in the underground mines, where great physical strength is required. The reason for this lies in the fact that none of the other races in the unskilled class can stand the work.

One mine superintendent who oversaw numerous mines was categorical in his description of the division of labor: "Slovenians and Finns do the common heavy work, while the English, Irish, and Scandinavians carry on the skilled work."[24]

The division true of iron mining was equally true of the steel industry as a whole. As was the case with iron mining, the new immigration did not displace native or old immigrant workers. Rather it corresponded to the enormous growth of the steel industry, notwithstanding a decline of skilled trades associated with mechanization. The overall effect was that forms of unskilled labor came to be viewed as "hunky" work.[25]

The division of labor that was so marked in iron mining and steel milling tended to be more porous in coal mining. The majority of new immigrants began as loaders or in other unskilled positions, but not always, and there was considerable movement upwards toward all except supervisory positions. Yet at its heart, like the new immigration to the iron mines of northern Minnesota, the massive new immigration to the Central Competitive Field was both effect and prerequisite for the reorganization and enormous expansion of coal mining, which grew enormously in the thirty years preceding this study.[26]

Contributing to the rise in new immigrant employment in the coal fields was what the Dillingham Commission called "machine mining," most advanced in Illinois, which "reduc[ed] the miner's occupation to that of an unskilled laborer, loading and cleaning up the coal after the machine." As elsewhere in American industry, the installation of machine methods carried with it advantages from the perspective of the employer: "There can be no doubt that machine mining decreases the number of strikes, as each man is working for his own interest. There are no standing shots to delay the miner; skilled labor is necessary only in a few places; and with the machine the mine necessarily developed more systematically and a steadier output can be relied upon." In short, machinery made possible the use of a large amount of unskilled labor.[27]

Yet if it were true that mechanization was the *cause* of the new immigration, then we would expect that immigrants would be most numerous in coal locations where highly-mechanized open-pit mining prevailed, and least numerous in shaft mining areas where a considerable premium was based on a miner's skill and experience. In the case of coal mining in Illinois, the cause-effect relationship between mechanization and immigration was likely overstated by the Dillingham Commission. Indeed, as Amy Gottlieb has noted, in Illinois machine mining was least advanced in the most northerly sub-districts, where shaft mining prevailed. Yet those were exactly the mines where the new immigrants comprised the largest share of the workforce.[28] Furthermore, if we make a comparison to iron mining on Minnesota's Iron Range, we find that different groups of new immigrants dominated *both* shaft mining and open pit mining. There the Dillingham Commission investigators acknowledged that while shaft mining required more skill, those sorts of dangerous "skilled" positions were also reserved for new immigrants, while skilled Cornish miners were very often promoted to supervisory roles.

Examples from other industries also cast doubt on the direct link between high numbers of new immigrants and mechanization. Scholarship has demonstrated the new immigrant domination of lowly-mechanized industries such as garment making, textiles, cigar making, construction, and even meatpacking with its minutely sub-divided hand work, while common labor absorbed a significant share of the workforce even in the highly mechanized steel industry.[29] One noted observer of coal mining, Carter Goodrich, lamented how little machinery had actually been introduced in the coal mines, and where it had how little it had done to actually lessen worker control over production. While "the arrival of the newer stream of immigration has of course changed the whole color of life in the mining communities," wrote Goodrich in 1923, "the striking thing is not the far-reaching effect of the change but rather the surprising continuity of the miner's tradition in spite of it ... [the new immigrants] seem to have taken over quite thoroughly from the older miners the attitudes that were customary in the rooms and on the gobiles; and the union that was so largely founded by British miners has passed on its traditions and polices with very little change in spite of its membership."[30] The composition of the work had changed, but the methods—and militancy—of the miners had not.

These observations suggest two tentative conclusions. First, it appears that where capital-intensive innovations in machinery were applied to the production process, they paved the way for the mass entry of new immigrants into employment elsewhere in the mine, mill, or factory, while also allowing an avenue of advancement—or else displacement—for skilled old immigrant or "American" workers. These processes were most visible and noted in steel plants, as Brody, Bodnar, Fitch and others have shown. In other words, the new immigration was not solely the *result* of mechanization, Taylorization or other shop-floor innovations, but was either the prerequisite for, or the corollary to, those innovations. As Montgomery has written, for immigrants "the skill and knowledge required by manufacturing occupations in which they were engaged were embodied not in their training but in the technical organization of the factory itself." Therefore, and second, the causes of new immigration—the famous "push" and "pull" factors—can best be understood at a sociological level that takes into account much broader factors of settlement patterns, industrial development, political economy, and even international events.[31]

In the steel industry, managerial reform focused primarily on corporate welfare. Though pioneering, it was also experimental. The most important development in terms of the management of the workforce, instead, was carried out through mechanization and the reorganization of the production process, creating a "homogenization" of labor, registered most clearly in the decline of skilled and the growth of semi-skilled labor.[32] Meanwhile, in the coal industry there is little evidence that labor management reform gained any significant traction.

Whatever the extent of reform, from the perspective of the new immigrant workers, American industry could scarcely have been called "rational." For beyond the stopwatch and the newfangled machines, turbulent labor markets and brutal working conditions prevailed. The frequency of periods of unemployment no doubt added to the mobility of the workforce, and must be considered a salient feature of new immigrant life. In fact, high fluidity in the labor market was both the unstated policy and cornerstone of U.S. industrial practice prior to World War I. Concerns about the costs, both economic and social, of high labor turnover only began to be broached during the war years.[33] In each of the three industries, the majority of new immigrant workers went through periods of seasonal unemployment or underemployment during periods of "slack" production. In iron mining, slack periods typically came in the winter, when Lake Superior, the only transportation artery for Minnesota iron ore, became impassable, and when frigid temperatures hindered work in the Mesabi's open pit mines. The opposite was true in coal mining, when the fall and winter months sharply increased demand for coal for heating, and periodic gluts of overproduction in the coal market suspended operations. Weinberg has found that coal miners rarely worked more than two-thirds of a possible 300 working days in a year. In 1913, Sangamon County mines were only open an average of 181 days. In one representative steel town, the Dillingham Commission found that fewer than half of workers from most new immigrant nationalities had worked in the local steel mill for more than six months during the year studied; among Slovaks the figure was just over 50 percent, and for Ruthenians, 60 percent. This the Commission considered quite stable, calling "regularity of work is the general rule."[34]

Long hours were the rule when work was available. The twelve-hour day prevailed in the steel industry through World War I, and it was also the norm in iron mining when demand was especially high. There, complained one Slovenian miner, the foreman "drives us ... like cattle." Another Slovenian miner reached into U.S. history for a comparison: "We must work like former slaves in the South."[35] In contrast, the union contract negotiated by the U.M.W. had ensured the eight-hour day for mineworkers throughout Illinois, a fact which doubtlessly allowed for a considerably larger workforce in bituminous coal mining. The steel industry's defense of the brutal twelve-hour day, as Andrea Graziosi has noted, was a typical if extreme example of the well-calculated practice among industrial employers who had determined, according to cost-benefit analysis, that it was cheaper to dismiss and then retrain new workers than to maintain a larger workforce. In 1913, the steel mill worker labored an average of 66 hours per week. Seven-day weeks of twelve-hour shifts were not uncommon, as were 18- or even 24-hour days. Workers were literally *used up* in the steel industry.[36]

The long hours and the pace of work ensured that accidental injury and death were quotidian events in the mines and mills. A Slovenian correspondent to *Poletarec* pointed out that nothing less could be expected "when everything is so arranged that [a miner] must drive himself if he wants to earn anything."[37] Mining accidents were so frequent on the Iron Range that the Dillingham Commission noted that the state of Minnesota's attempt to keep track of killings and injuries was a woefully inadequate source of information for its investigation, instead choosing to consult mine superintendents directly. Informants on both the Iron Range and in the Midwest's bituminous coal fields attributed the high rate of accidents in part to the difficulty in communicating with the foreign-language workforce. In spite of more difficult geological conditions in the bituminous region, with its softer earth and high water table, death and accident rates were similar. In the period lasting from 1906–1911, 88 percent of all iron miners killed on the Range were from Europe; in 1910 just over 30 percent of all miners killed or injured had been employed for less than six months.[38]

In both the Iron Range towns and Illinois coalfields wives and children lived in fear of the dreaded mine siren which announced injury or death below—its sound would gather children together in school, wives would run to the mine: whose father, whose husband, had been killed or maimed? Meanwhile, the steel industry was becoming notorious for the deadly conditions that prevailed in its plants. In U.S. Steel's South Chicago plant, in the year 1906, 41 separate accidents resulted in 46 deaths on the job. In the same time span, 184 men were disabled "temporarily"—a category described as a 13-week absence from work—while 368 were "disabled permanently." John Fitch, in his important investigation of Pittsburgh's steel mills, found an environment abundant with hazards beyond those that imperiled life and limb—ore and steel dust in the air, great noise causing damage to hearing, severe nervous strain due to the threat of injury.[39]

"Looking north on Green Bay Street." South Chicago, ca. 1911. Source: Breckinridge and Abbott, "Chicago Housing Conditions," 145–176.

U.S. Steel unilaterally set the rules for how injury and death would be compensated, codifying a universal system beginning in 1910 for its workforce. It officially assumed no responsibility for accidents on its premises. According to its "voluntary" plan, U.S. Steel would make no payments for work lost due to injuries lasting for less than ten days, or, after 52 weeks, for serious injuries. Injuries could be diagnosed only by corporation-approved doctors and hospitals. By accepting its assistance in the event of an injury, moreover, workers renounced any future legal claim against the corporation. U.S. Steel adjusted payments based on severity of the injury, length of employment, and whether or not the injured worker had dependent children. On the Iron Range, its employees were required to allow a monthly deduction, of either 50 or 75 cents, for its insurance plan. In case of injury the worker could then receive $25 per month beginning only after the first four days of injury and lasting for no more than six months. If the worker was killed, his family could receive $300, and if he was permanently crippled from working, he could receive $240.[40]

In all three industries, new immigrant workers were paid considerably less than American and old immigrant workers. One industrial study has argued that this was so even when new immigrants performed the same function and were not less productive than their more assimilated counterparts.[41] But here again we see significant differences between steel milling and iron mining, on the one hand, and coal mining on the other. The occupational glass ceiling against new immigrant upward mobility was reflected, unsurprisingly, in earnings. For U.S. Steel's employees, earnings strikingly reproduced the sharp divisions between new immigrants and "American" workers. Measuring based on average earnings in one week, the Dillingham Commission found that increases in pay were possible based on length of residency among Croatian, Magyar, Polish, Russian, Slovak, and Slovenian steel workers, with those residing in the U.S. more than five or ten years earning more in nearly every case. However, even among those residing for ten years or more in the U.S., only a small fraction of each new immigrant nationality earned more than $20 per week; at the high end, about 11 percent of Poles and Croatians. In contrast 43.7 percent of English and 34.9 percent of Irish who had lived in the U.S. more than ten years earned more than $20. Among those who earned more than $25 per week after ten years of American residency, the new immigrant proportion declined to zero in most cases; in the case of Poles and Slovaks it was around 4 percent. But 28.6 percent of English, 21.7 percent of Irish, and 18.9

percent of Swedish steel workers earned more than this maximum figure category. On Minnesota's Iron Range, the relationship between earnings and nationality was even starker. Less than one percent of Finns earned more than the Dillingham Commission's maximum earnings category of $20. The figure was zero percent for Croatians, North Italians, Poles, and Slovenians. It appears that only a very circumscribed mobility was possible for the new immigrants; they were virtually shut out of the highest paying jobs.

U.S. Steel pioneered "welfare capitalism" in the period. Beginning in 1903, the corporation launched a "profit-sharing" system whereby workers in its mills, mines, and transport could use part of their pay to purchase stock in the corporation. Part employee morale program, part public relations stunt, the system had the added, and not incidental, benefit of increasing the corporation's power over its workforce by controlling savings. Workers complained that the system also allowed U.S. Steel to calculate how much workers were able to save from their income, and thereby adjust wages downward. The corporation also donated

South Chicago near the mills, smokestacks looming in the horizon. Source: Breckinridge and Abbott, "Chicago Housing Conditions," 145–176.

money to build churches, parks, gardens, and swimming pools. All of these efforts aimed to improve employee loyalty and present an image to the public of a caring corporate citizen.[42]

The picture for Midwestern bituminous coal miners was more complex, and corporate welfare was little practiced, if it existed at all. One is immediately struck by the fact that daily earnings, in contrast to the steel industry, reflect no discernible pattern of discrimination against new immigrants. New immigrants could, and very often did, earn as much or more for a day's labor as old immigrants or native whites, although English and German miners appear to have earned marginally more than their new immigrant counterparts. No clear patterns of differentiation based on daily earnings emerge among the various new immigrant groups themselves—for example, between the daily earning power of northern and southern Italians. Moreover, period of residency in the U.S. did not substantially improve miners' daily earning power. These broad similarities were owed to two factors. First, there was the leveling effect of the U.M.W. and its exclusive trade agreement

"Pioneer Mine pit and 'A' Shaft. In the distance, Ely." Ely, Minnesota, 1913.
Source: Minnesota State Historical Society photographic archives.

negotiated for the whole C.C.F. Second, the piece rate system, whereby miners were paid by the amount they extracted, encouraged ambitious miners to dig more coal. However, when the Immigration Commission tabulated *annual* earning power, a clear distinction emerged. White native-born workers of native-born fathers earned nearly $700 per year. For North Italians the figure was $542; for South Italians, $399; for Lithuanians, $422; for Poles, $324. We may conclude, then, that the mining industry in the Midwest tended to remunerate equitably for similar work among various nationalities; no doubt the U.M.W. played a leveling role in this regard. However, at the same time it appears that the new immigrants were more likely to be the victims of seasonal unemployment and dismissal.[43]

In both iron and coal mining, workers engaged in extraction—the vast majority in coal and a significant majority in iron—effectively worked on a piece rate system, whereby they earned based on the quantity they could dig in a day's labor. This meant that placement in the mine seam was all important. It also impelled miners to work rapidly and place safety in the balance against pay. This took its extreme in coal mines. There the miner was also oftentimes the timberman, and time spent timbering as a warning system against roof cave-ins was non-remunerated time. In the steel mill, instead, workers earned based on daily set rates, and so had a built-in impetus to conserve themselves for long days and weeks. To guard against that, U.S. Steel and its competitors entrusted enormous power to the foremen—usually the "American" element—and demanded a single-minded drive for efficiency all the way from upper management, to superintendents, to foremen, and down to the workers themselves. In the iron mine the foreman also had enormous power. He could reward or punish, and very often insisted on kickbacks and other forms of bribery when awarding seams in underground mines, while the growing proportion of open pit mines on the Mesabi were run in the manner of the mills. In both the Mesabi Range Strike of 1916 and the Great Steel Strike of 1919, workers focused many of their grievances on the tyranny of the hated foremen.[44]

Much has been written about the importance of the organization of work processes for understanding worker protest and consciousness.[45] Yet in spite of the enormous differences between work in the coal and steel industries, workers struggled in remarkably similar ways in both. To be sure, the organization of work in the steel mills had much to do with the vanishing of the craft unions, but this cannot explain the failure to build industrial unions until the 1930s. Indeed,

A coal breaker near Springfield, Illinois, circa 1910.

point-of-production studies prove much more revealing in understanding the defensive, and largely failed, struggles of skilled workers in the Progressive Era. What, then, unified the struggles of 1914 to 1924 if not the defensive struggle for control of production? In the case of the new immigrants, it appears that the formation of consciousness in the late Progressive Era was shaped and given political meaning by broader sociological factors such as mass immigration, the broader occupational and class structure of the U.S., and the world's major historical changes such as war, inflation, revolution, and depression.

Women's Work and the Industrial Community

Industrial labor created commonalities of life beyond work that contributed to the development of a broad new immigrant identity. Among these were similarities in the communities they inhabited, in housing, and in the economic and social roles played by immigrant women.[46] Intuitively we should expect that the locations inhabited by new immigrants were profoundly different based on the industry in which they labored, the region they inhabited, and whether or not they lived in large cities or small towns. And indeed, differences were significant in terms of population density, diversity of the local population, complexity of the labor and housing market, etc. On the other hand, enough broad similarities underlay these differences to allow us to speak of "the immigrant industrial community." This we could define as an industrial town, company town, suburb, or neighborhood in which one industry dominated the labor market and in which new immigrants of the first or second generation constituted a large proportion of the population. The domination of these communities by single industries, moreover, had implications for local political control and even basic democratic rights including freedom of speech, as the Great Steel Strike of 1919 would later show. This was not the only living circumstance available to new immigrants—one thinks of the great and crowded urban neighborhoods such as Manhattan in New York City—but the industrial community was the typical location of the new immigrant worker, as it was in three industries studied here.[47]

The new immigrant industrial community presents a bleak picture. Contemporary observers oftentimes commented on what seemed to be the overpowering physical presence of industry over humanity. Progressive reformer Mary Heaton Vorst captured this eloquently in her description of the Mesabi Range, written as though she had a bird's eye view:

> The Mesaba range is a crescent of towns and mines flung over sixty miles of pit-scarred country, open pits yawning, open pits half a mile across, red as dried blood, pits so deep that the engineers crawling up their flanks look like beetles. Pits the color of burnt lumber, streaked with rust, streaked with yellow. Around the pits forest fires have left the charred stubs of great trees. Among the burnt stumps are boulders strewn there by glaciers. There are nine beautiful towns and fifty bleak "locations" squatting about the flanks of the mines.[48]

Edith Abbott and Sophonisba Breckinridge offered a similarly ominous description of South Chicago's steel mill neighborhood:

> On the one side, shutting out the lake, are the huge mills behind high paling fence, the great chimneys belching forth dense masses of smoke which hangs over the neighborhood like clouds of darkness and pollute the atmosphere so that no whiff of the air comes untainted from the great lake.... Within these barriers and under this pall stretch out the wide streets, unpaved and unkempt. On either side of these are the dreary succession of small frame dwellings [sic].... The stranger within the gates of South Chicago is overwhelmed with the fact that the world is made for industry, not for men and women and little children; that with magnificent enterprise on the one hand there is a hideous waste of human life on the other.[49]

For workers, housing and social services were superior in company towns like Gary, but management gained further power over the workforce. Where corporate power over housing was less direct services were fewer. The non-company coal mining towns and iron mining "locations" were some of the most impoverished places in industrial America. The U.S. Coal Commission studied bituminous mining towns in Illinois, including the heavily new immigrant towns of Divernon and Thayer near Springfield, and Benld and Livingston in southern Illinois. The towns had no electricity, plumbing or running water. Outhouses were located too close to water sources, and thus drinking water was frequently contaminated. Immigrants—Italians, Lithuanians, and Poles—all kept livestock, and stored manure in their yards to fertilize gardens. This caused severe problems with black flies. There was no garbage disposal. The Coal Commission concluded the situation was hopeless. It made pessimistic "recommendations" based on its survey. For "environment and habits of the population," it concluded little "improvement can be made … until the foreign stock become more assimilated." For "water supply," it argued that it would not be "economically feasible to secure satisfactory public supply." For "disposal of human excrement," "it [was] not believed that any material improvement can be hoped for along this line." For "general sanitary control and disease prevention activities," the Commission concluded that the villages were "too small to … undertake any efficient program along these lines."[50]

In these industrially scarred areas—with the marked presence of gaping open pits, enormous slag heaps, and towering smokestacks—people lived and sought to make the most out of what they had. So Mary Heaton Vorst also noted that steel mill women maintained the white window curtain as "flag of defiance" against the soot that, windswept from the mills, covered everything in its path. According to Vorse, "you cannot go into any foul courtyard without finding white lace curtains stretched to dry on frames."[51] Minnesota's Iron Range towns were renowned for their high taxation of the iron ore companies in spite of the latter's bitter opposition, creating "nine beautiful towns" amidst the environmental wreckage of open pit mining. The tax money paved roads, illuminated streets, built well-equipped high schools, and even allowed for the creation of a paid league of imported Canadian professional hockey players. The United States Coal Commission, meanwhile, noted that new immigrants and Italians in Illinois' coal camps immediately set about making vegetable gardens: "Racial customs and habits are particular evident in the buying of food. Italians, Poles, and other foreigners have their own nationality stores where they can purchase the food to which they are accustomed. The Italian particularly demands a special diet, inclusive of fresh vegetables, spaghetti, imported cheeses, and olive oil. Generally, he grows his own vegetables. Other foreigners as well are universally noted for the fine gardens which they maintain about their homes." The gardens expressed both tradition and necessity, as a means of supplementing a diet limited by low wages and periodic layoffs.[52]

Though in the coal, iron, and steel industries women were generally barred from *direct* remunerative employment by hiring practices and custom, some women in coal mining towns did engage in wage labor in nearby industries. More typically, women played an essential role in the household economy and the community at large. In coal mining towns, "the home economy was so visible in ... that only with serious effort could an observer miss its relationship to the extraction of coal," notes Montgomery, in a description that might just as well have described iron mining towns or steel milling communities. "Gardens and livestock were everywhere. Boarders, husbands, and sons ate huge meals and came home needing to be scrubbed at all hours."[53]

To be sure, at the national level immigrant women, too, found their way in large number into employment, but primarily in the so-called "light" industries. In 1900, approximately 20 percent of the U.S. workforce was comprised of women, and by 1910, eight million women were officially employed, or 23.4 percent of all women. While 31.3 percent worked as domestics, a traditional source of female employment and one in which African American women comprised a large share of the workforce, 22.3 percent of women workers labored in factories, with the garment trades, tobacco processing, and food production predominating. In Chicago, the men's garment industry employed 38,000 workers in 1910, one half being women. Of these, almost all, 98 percent, were foreign born or the children of a foreign-born father, with many of these Poles, Czechs, Italians, and Eastern European Jews. In 1911, the U.S. Census Bureau of Labor reported that half of all women workers in men's garment industry were Italian, for the clothing industry as a whole the figure ranged from one fourth to one third.[54]

But centrally located neighborhoods in large cities offered a different set of opportunities than those in the industrial community, where one of the outstanding characteristics was the disproportionately large male population. This was in part a consequence of the immigration process itself, which usually began with young males who often intended to return home. In the fifty years beginning in 1870, the annual proportion of male immigrants entering the U.S. fell below 60 percent only fourteen times and was never less than half. Between 1900 and 1910, the proportion of the male migration surpassed 70 percent five times. The peak immigration year of 1907 also produced the highest male percentage: 72.4 percent. The difference here with the old immigrants was stark. According to Wyman, "percentages of married men in the meatpacking industry who had wives overseas included Bulgarian, 90.2; Serbians, 79, Romanians, 72.7; Russians 53.2, and southern Italians, 42.4. This compared to Germans, 3.7, Swedes, 1.9, and Irish, .9."[55] The phenomenon of the heavily male new immigrant workforce with families and wives abroad—the latter were sometimes called "white widows" because they were without husbands but did not go into mourning—created what Donna Gabaccia has called an international or split household economy. And Ron Rothbart has noted, in an analysis of three new immigrant–dominated industries, that the frequency of single-living men and boarding houses was in fact but one phase in the strategy of building a household.[56]

Yet women of coal, iron, and steel communities played a significant role in generating income and caring for the workforce. Given the social context of an overwhelmingly male workforce and majority male communities, married women and mothers played a crucial role for the entire community by selling services typically associated with the domestic sphere, such as taking in laundry or selling meals—and, at least on the Iron Range, prostitution was also common. In other words, there was a "fit" between male remunerated labor and female domestic labor, the latter making possible the former. Doubtless the most important manifestation of this was the boarding house, which was ubiquitous in the mining communities and the Calumet steel milling area. Working class new immigrant women housed anywhere from a single extra working man to dozens more, and provided them with beds, meals and laundry. New immigrant women therefore played two essential roles in the economy: not only the reproduction of the next workforce, but the maintenance and survival of the current one. They took on boarders to earn money, but also oftentimes out of a sense of social solidarity with single men of their nationality who were without family.[57]

In its study of Minnesota's Iron Range, the Dillingham Commission noted the seeming anomaly that while foreign born workers earned less in the mines than their native counterparts, their *households* oftentimes reported greater incomes than native households. In fact, among the new immigrants themselves, those studied who earned the least in the mines—the Croatians—showed by far the highest household income. The apparent anomaly is explained by boarding. In one location where 195 families were surveyed, Croatian wives secured 72.5 percent of total family income through taking on boarders. The figure for Finnish and Slovenian households was also quite significant; 27.9 and 34.8 percent, respectively. In that location, only 55 percent of families with a foreign-born head of household depended solely on the income of a mining father or husband. Of the 195 wives studied, not one worked outside of the house.[58]

A very limited representative study of a coal mining community in Illinois carried out by the Dillingham Commission found that the practice of boarding was routine among Lithuanian and Polish mining families, though not among either North or South Italians. But among immigrant workers in the Central Competitive Field as a whole, over one half of all Ruthenian, Croatian, Russian, Lithuanian, Hungarian, Polish and South Italian households took on boarders. While the practice of boarding provided added income to new immigrant families, it also caused serious overcrowding and sanitary problems. One study of South Chicago determined that at least 72 percent of all households surveyed stood in violation of a city ordinance prescribing minimum standards for the availability of air, measured in cubic feet. In Gary, company-planned single family homes were rapidly converted into boarding houses after the town's founding in 1906.[59]

Calumet Hungarians even developed their own vocabulary to reflect the new phenomenon of boarding, based on a corruption of the English word boarding house, which became *burdoshdz* in Hungarian, ethno-folklorist Andrew Vazsonyi has found. Not only did the matron, or *burdosasszony,* manage domestic work, including cooking, cleaning, and healing, she also controlled the power of the purse. Vazsonyi proposes that the *burdosasszony* enjoyed a degree of sexual license with her favorite or "star" boarders, and may on occasion have "fired" her husband. One East Chicago Hungarian steelworker and boarding house owner lamented his fate in verse:

> Why should I fight for you? It makes no sense
> God may bless you with your burdoses [boarders]
> You can sit into the laps of your Pista, Simon, and Sandor...[60]

The boarding house could also be something of a social center for young men and women who came to help care for the boarders. Joseph Mavetz, a Slovenian, remembered his boyhood in a boarding house in Ely, on the Iron Range:

> There were 12 of us kids. And we had four boarders, and they never went to a cold bed. When the night shift came along, they would go to a bed that was just left open by the miners that went to day shift.... A lot of these people that had boarders would

have immigrant—young ladies—come to help with the household, for board and room and occasionally shoes with buttons on them and a skirt—and then come time when they were ready for marriage it was almost an unwritten law that the man who bought the most beer got the bride.[61]

Many wives remained across the Atlantic, as evidence from the Iron Range suggests. Among 1,486 workers aged 20 years or over from eight different new immigrant groups, all nationalities except for the Montenegrins reported approximately half or more being married. The statistics for native-born of native fathers and English miners were comparable. But among the English miners, only 20 percent who had wives declared that they lived abroad, while for Slovenians over 40 percent lived abroad. Among North Italians and Croatians approximately two thirds had wives abroad, and over 80 percent of South Italians had wives abroad. Likewise, in the Midwestern coal mining states the Dillingham Commission found that a large majority of men had wives, but that among new immigrant nationalities anywhere from 20 to 43 percent of these lived abroad. When examining the marriage patterns for miners who had arrived in the five years prior to 1911, the percentage becomes much higher: from 44 to 64 percent. Youth no doubt contributed; in iron mining over 93 percent of the total workforce was 44 years of age or younger, and nearly two thirds were 35 years of age or younger. In coal mining the figures were 83 percent and 60 percent, respectively, and among the coal miners much larger shares of the older age brackets were comprised of old immigrant miners.[62]

Children, too, supplemented the family income. One common practice in South Chicago was for children to sweep out emptied grain railroad cars or grain spills near elevators and return it as feed to homes where "goats, pigs, ducks, chickens, geese, pigeons, and rabbits" were raised, oftentimes housed in basements and attics. In Illinois' coal towns, children were assigned the task of what English workers call "liberating"—but what the coal operators called stealing—coal for family heating from the piles and spills near the mines. Coal mines employed guards called "track watchmen" to fight against the practice. At the Pawnee mine in Sangamon County, the job was "no sinecure," according to the *Divernon News*. "Many women and children have made a practice of climbing onto the cars and throwing down as much coal as they can cart home. In this way they have their entire coal bill. The other day Watchman Walter McTaggert found some women [in the act of taking coal] and he interfered. She proceeded to 'climb his frame,' and in since his chivalrous nature prevented him from fighting with women, he was getting the worst of it when help arrived." McTaggert was literally dragged in to the moral economy of the miner's family—that they had a right to the coal their fathers and husbands dug out.[63]

New Immigrant Workers and Social Distance

As important as the empirical data may be—and it paints an unambiguous portrait of backbreaking, lowly-remunerated labor, and poor living conditions—is to what extent this social distance was commonly felt in the communities and industries in question. To complete the picture, then, two more essential characteristics must be added: new immigrants felt they were confined to the bottom rungs of the occupational hierarchy, in the most difficult, dirty and dangerous work—what Russian immigrants called "black work"—positions from which escape appeared all but impossible; and, second, occupational mobility in industrial labor seemed to be typically the reserve of the "old immigrant" or "American" groups. That both were salient features of the industrial landscape can be demonstrated empirically to a great degree by statistics and by evidence produced by corporate and state observers. There is also abundant human evidence.[64]

These two factors—the relegation of new immigrants to the bottom of the occupational heap, on one side, and the limited advance of sections of the old immigrants or "American" workers, on the other—bridges the gulf separating the purely structural factors of immigration and labor market from the more subjective processes of assimilation among the new immigrants. It is from this essential social inequality that kinds of work came to be known as "hunky work," while other jobs were regarded as "American" jobs. In this way dozens of disparate peoples, arriving from nations as culturally diverse as Finland, Italy, Poland, and Bulgaria, came to be viewed by outsiders as one group, called by the name "new immigrant" or the vaguely-condescending name "Foreigner," or the epithets "Hunky," "Dago," and so on.

The Dillingham Commission investigation of the Iron Range discovered a world rife with racial vocabulary. Investigators noted the relative social advance of the "old immigrants." According to the Commission, "of all the races found on the Minnesota Iron Ranges, the Scandinavians are making the most progress. Swedes, Norwegians, and Danes are moving up in the scale of occupations and are found chiefly in skilled work in the ore mines," while "the English, Irish, Scotch, and French Canadians have worked out of the unskilled occupations and are found holding such positions as foremen, master mechanics, machinists, and steam engineers." Mine superintendents verified this. According to one, "the Scandinavians are making the most progress and are the most desirable men we employ." Another noted that "in the high occupations ... which we class as skilled, the natives, English, Scotch, and Swedes are the most desirable." Yet another commented that "of all the races we employ, the Scandinavians are the best; they are ambitious, progressive, and efficient in every undertaking." One mine captain told a journalist that while U.S. Steel promoted men faster than in other industries, "we don't move any but the American born on to the [steam] shovels or other machines."[65]

The Dillingham Commission concluded that Finns were "retarded" "by their surliness and radical tendencies." The description of Finns as radicals and troublemakers appears again and again. One mining superintendent called the Finns "good laborers but trouble breeders. We refuse work to every one who applies wearing the red button of the socialist organization among the Finns." Another superintendent noted that "for hard physical work the Finns are preferred, but they are a surly, troublesome lot, and among the younger men are many who are anarchists."[66]

New immigrants from further south and east in Europe—the most recent of the new immigrants to the Iron Range—were invariably described as lazy, and their perceived racial characteristics were associated with the word "black," an apparent reference, at least in part, to physical traits. One mine superintendent explicitly juxtaposed southern Europeans with "white men": "The Montenegrins and Italians are shiftless and fit only for the most menial work.... The 'black races' (meaning the Montenegrins, Servians [sic], South Italians, Greeks, and Croatians) can not do the work in three days that a white man can do in one, when working man to man. One trouble with the 'black' fellows is that they do not eat enough." The superintendent of another mine held that "all of the races are good workmen" except for "the Montenegrin and 'black Italians' [meaning South Italians]." He continued, "The Montenegrins come from a country where little work is done by the men, except gambling, fighting, and drinking, and as there are none of their women on the range they work in a desultory manner and make no progress whatever."[67]

Despite the U.M.W.'s organizational achievements, new immigrants also bore many negative stereotypes promoted by union leadership.

One union sympathizer, writing to John R. Commons in support of a U.S. Commission on Industrial Relations (C.I.R.) investigation of the Illinois coal fields, encapsulated the prevailing negative view that technological change had "forced the transformation of our mining camps into transplanted colonies of Austrian and Balkan and Italian farm laborers." After interviewing union leaders, the Dillingham Commission noted that, among a long laundry list of grievances, "native labor leaders" complained of new immigrants' "ignorance," their willingness to work under poor conditions, that they were "tractable and slow to demand an enforcement of the stipulations" of the contract, and that they join the union "fraudulently" in order to gain employment.[68]

These affronts were broadly felt across many new immigrant groups. Celeste and Santina Gambucci, both born in Italy in the 1890s, were interviewed in 1981 but still remembered the discrimination of the Iron Range of their youth. "There was lot people against Italian. There was discrimination *e roba* [and so on]. They don't like Italian people.... They call name and every damn thing," Celeste said. Santina then added, "Dago, wop, they aren't supposed to do that." Celeste continued, "Jobs? They get poor jobs all the time." Lola Nizzi, who grew up in a coal mining town, remembered that "we were coal miners and Catholics and Italians to boot—we had three strikes against us." Jerome Davis, who interviewed "several hundred Russians in mining and steel plants" in Illinois found that the great majority "fear and hate" their bosses. "Even when ignorant of English," he wrote, "they are all familiar with the common epithet [the boss] hurls at them, 'You—Polack.'" Davis believed that the conflation of new immigrant "races" exacerbated the insult to Russian workers.[69]

One observer concluded that by the word "foreigners" "the steel industry means not all immigrants or sons of immigrants, but only the 'new immigration'; consisting of the scores of races from eastern and southeastern Europe." Valentino Lazaretti, a coal miner, remembered the strange formulation of "American": "we had Americans [mineworkers], too ... their ancestry went back two or three hundred years, but they were American, you know. They could have been Scotch. They could have been many nationalities.... Swedish or anything." In an interview taken in 1967, David Saposs, who studied the steel industry in the wake of the Great Steel Strike of 1919, recalled the pervasiveness of this division. He recalled talking to children playing in a steel mill town, who responded to the question "what are you?" with "we're foreigners." "I said, 'where were you born?' They said 'Right here in Apollo.'... If you were east European you were foreigners. If you were German, you were American, because you were north European." At the steel mill in New Kensington, Pennsylvania, as of 1919, no "foreigner" had ever held the position of roller, a fact true also of American-born workers of foreign parentage.[70]

New immigrants were aware of the divide separating them from old immigrants. New immigrant iron miners devised the term "Cousin Jack" to describe the Cornish miners who rose to the managerial positions in the mines. The origin of the name, according to Iron Range folklore, is that a Cornishman could show up at work with his "Cousin Jack" and secure him a good job on the spot.[71] In Illinois coal mining towns a similar term was deployed for coal miners of British extraction, "Johnny Bull." An elderly retired Italian coal miner explained that the British miners gained an inside track on promotion in a peculiar way: they "get these Mason rings, you know they wear them. Someone say, 'What the hell you do with that ring there?' 'I'm a Mason.' They get jobs, good jobs, foreman jobs, see."[72] Salvatore Aluni, born in Italy in 1892 and a veteran of both the 1907 and 1916 Mesabi Range strikes, summed up the felt divisions by describing the "American" opinion of the Iron Range new immigrants: "The American born, they hate all of us."[73] New immigrant neighborhoods and towns were stigmatized, so that on the Iron Range, Virginia with its relatively higher proportion of old immigrants, was known as "the only white city." And in spite efforts to build Gary, Indiana, as a model city, soon neighborhoods developed with such pejorative names as "Hunkyville" and "Hungary Row."[74]

Local patronage systems, often linked to the Democratic Party, accentuated divisions. In Chicago jobs as school teachers, policemen, and firefighters often went to Irish Americans. One Italian coal miner remembered both the political and religious power that the Irish exerted: "The Irish had their church and the tendency of the Irishman was to be a Democrat. After all, it was his party—the priest, the precinct captain—they all gravitated around the church and on Sunday they would hail each other." Italians were not allowed in positions of church; "the Irish retained the leadership for themselves."[75]

The Labor Movement and the New Immigrants

The national bureaucracy of the A.F.L. had been for years one of the most implacable opponents of immigration. Yet some unions actually enjoyed success at organizing new immigrants, including perhaps most prominently the U.M.W. We consider here first the A.F.L.'s position toward immigrants, which found expression in the failures to organize the steel industry, and second the U.M.W.'s success.[76]

From 1904 onwards, declining profit rates triggered a new and well-organized offensive against organized labor. Under conditions in which the economy had already achieved enormous centralization, craft unionism's would-be monopoly of skill and knowledge of production stood in the way of capital's imposition of new technologies and efficiency schemes. In major modern industries where craft unionism once predominated, by 1914 the A.F.L. had been virtually eliminated, as in the steel and meat packing industries, or converted into something approaching company-controlled unions, as in textiles. The life-and-death struggle of craft workers in steel wasn't against the new immigrants, but the technological progress that displaced them. Yet the steel industry craft unions focused their grievances on the new immigrants.[77]

Two industries avoided the crisis confronting organized labor. In the garment industry and coal mining, industrial unionism prevailed, and grew rapidly until after World War I. On the surface these two industries could not appear to be more different. However, certain factors allowed industrial unionism to take root in each. Despite the vast centralization and capitalization of the economy as a whole, in garment manufacture and surprisingly enough in coal mining, startup costs for small scale competition remained low. With a small investment an owner could open a small garment factory—perhaps not much more than a sweatshop—in an urban setting or begin caving for coal in Illinois. This is what Carter Goodrich had in mind when he complained of coal mining as a "cottage industry."

Sections of both the garment making and coal mining industries discovered a potential ally in the labor movement, which sought in both to enforce "protocols of peace" that would potentially allow for union growth in exchange for assistance in the enforcement of the wage structure on recalcitrant owners. The U.M.W. in the C.C.F. was "the economic policeman for a highly competitive industry." Industrial unionism had another advantage over craft unionism. It was not organically hostile to the implementation of new technology or efficiency schemes *per se*, since the ultimate goal was to organize an entire factory, mill, or mine, rather than to protect this or that branch of labor therein. Indeed, particularly in the case of the garment industry, both the International

Ladies Garment Workers Union and the Amalgamated Clothing Workers Association promoted themselves as industry's partners in the rationalization of production. The seeds of corporate unionism were thus present even at the inception of industrial unionism—as were rank-and-file oppositional movements against collaboration. But in their heyday, the U.M.W. and garment unions proved the most effective forces for the rationalization of their respective industries; capital was incapable of carrying forward the task on its own, unlike in the steel industry, where financiers wielded the axe of rationalization.[78]

As part of the C.C.F., the coal mines of the Midwest were almost entirely organized by the U.M.W. by 1914. The Interstate Join Agreement of 1898, the pact between the U.M.W. and the major coal operators of the Midwestern states of Illinois, Indiana, Ohio and western Pennsylvania, heralded a period of growth and stability for the union and was widely credited among rank-and-file members with significant increases in wages and as a means of asserting a degree of participation in production. In particular, the union had come to play an important role in establishing employment practices and even managing and disciplining the workforce. It was theoretically necessary for new immigrants to join the U.M.W. before they could secure work in the mines. According to the Dillingham Commission, "the tendency is, therefore, for the immigrant at first to regard the membership fee in the union as the price paid for his job and to enter the union without any real sympathy with the work of the organization." But federal investigators concluded that the new immigrants soon became supportive union members, while the union itself became a tool for Americanization:

> This change is especially marked among the North and South Italians, who were formerly considered the worst offenders. Some employers even assert that the North Italian and Lithuanian are more difficult to deal with and more insistent on their rights than the immigrants of past periods, such as the English and Irish. The general feeling among the older immigrants and employees is one of dissatisfaction with conditions produced by the races of recent immigration and the constant effort is being made to bring them up to the standards put forward by the labor organization.[79]

Another observer, Edith Abott, thought of the process of Americanization in the U.M.W. as largely unconscious: "The union has no program which it labels 'Americanization.' It is, however, in many places almost the only unifying force. None of the local unions ... are organized along racial lines and practically the only places where all nationalities meet is in the mine and at the union meeting. The union theory seems to be that some way, somehow all the immigrants can learn

English if they want to.... In many places it has already been said the mine and miners' union are the only meeting-places of the adults, as the school is the meeting-place of the children." The union and the mine would do what neither church nor fraternal association could do—bring the different groups of miners together.[80]

Though in some Illinois U.M.W. locals Italians actually took positions of authority, this was not the case in Sangamon County, where, according to sub-district President John Clark, immigrants counted for 80 percent of the workforce, and Italians by themselves 90 percent of his own local. Yet elected union officials were native English speakers. At the national level, no Eastern or Southern Europeans were present in significant offices until after World War I.[81]

The entry of new immigrants into U.M.W. unions in Illinois was made more complex by standardized hiring practices. Prior to becoming underground or "practical" miners, workers who were not themselves the sons of miners were required to either go through a long period of apprenticeship or make a payment. The normal U.M.W. fee prior to 1910 was $10, followed by a six-year period of apprenticeship. This could be shortened to four years coupled with an examination before the Miners' Examining Board, a state bureaucracy developed in Illinois at the request of the U.M.W., or upon the payment of $50. Alternately, a miner could prove upon entry in the Illinois coalfields that he had been a practical miner elsewhere in the country. These measures, which were designed to maintain an experienced labor force, keep out non-union labor, and in no small part keep out new immigrants, amounted to what Weinberg has called an effort to make the union "a kind of conservative job trust for the most privileged, skilled and 'Americanized.'" However, the system did little to stem the tide of new immigrant workers into the state. Yet it did ensure that the vast majority of new immigrants entered the U.M.W. once they had entered Illinois' coal fields.[82]

The C.I.R. interviewed a number of Illinois "union men and officials" in 1914, among them a few immigrants. The results of this survey demonstrate the confidence that union members had in the U.M.W. and its exclusive Trade Agreement to overcome divisions between the English-speaking and the immigrants. Indeed, the U.M.W. even took several affirmative steps toward welcoming new immigrants, including translating the union constitution and by-laws into several different languages and occasionally providing translators for union meetings. For some time, the U.M.W.'s national newspaper included Italian and Slovak sections. At the same time, survey responses testified to a level of ongoing hostility toward new immigrants in spite of the U.M.W. and the Trade Agreement. A typical feature of Illinois locals was what the Dillingham Commission called "racial segregation" along what we would today call ethnic lines. According to the Commission, one might find in a given location "a Slavic local, an Italian local, and an American local [with] Americans and older immigrants in the third." The commission noted that though "the segregation of these locals is not absolute ... the separation of the races, as above outlined, is substantially maintained." Integration had its limits.[83]

One American U.M.W. member reiterated the longstanding negative interpretation of the new immigrants. "Immigrants," he wrote, "through ignorance and carelessness, incur great risks ... not being sufficiently intelligent to protect themselves and assert their rights. The Union would be much stronger if only English-speaking workers were employed in the mines." Yet Duncan MacDonald, the Secretary and Treasurer of the Illinois U.M.W., pointed to a diametrically opposed sort of problem with the new immigrants. "Immigrants, as a rule, are anxious to join the union," he asserted. However, "some trouble is caused by the obtuseness of the immigrants and their tendency to suspend work when a grievance arises instead of observing the procedures of the Agreement." Another informant put it this way: "Although there is prejudice against immigrants from Italy, Austria-Hungary, and Russia, on the part of the English-speaking race, still their attitude is not openly unfriendly as long as they can control the situation, but if the first mentioned immigrants try to show their power in any measure, they are usually forced into submission."[84]

In other words, far from new immigrants being unable or unwilling to stand up for their rights at the workplace and thereby undermining American workers, the opposite tended to be the case: the immigrants struck too quickly and in so doing undermined the Trade Agreement. Frank Farrington, then still the member of a U.M.W. Executive Board from Illinois, expressed this ambivalent attitude, as well. "The immigrants have had no material effect on the union in Illinois. The immigrants are compelled to join the union and can be disciplined and assimilated," but he added, "through ignorance they have some times violated the Agreement." In summing up union leadership's attitudes toward the new immigrants, the Dillingham Commission noted that the U.M.W. was in general opposed to the entry of the new immigrants, but out of necessity organized them upon entry into the C.C.F., and often valued their contributions to the union after organization.[85]

Prior to 1914 union organization and common struggle, it seems, served as a significant lever for new immigrants in Illinois coal mining to advance their interests and as a medium through which they cooperated with more assimilated workers. The union and the union contract, furthermore, allowed for a certain degree of occupational mobility— at least in the limited sense that new immigrant workers could perform the same tasks in a given mine that native workers performed in another. On the other hand, the absence of unionization on Minnesota's Iron Range and the Calumet steel region served to entrench divisions between new immigrant and "American," between the unskilled and the skilled. The old craft unions in the steel industry, like the Amalgamated Association of Iron and Steel Workers (the Amalgamated), had an entirely different perspective. To preserve skilled labor, they fought against industrial reorganization. This approach had resulted by 1910 in an active membership in the Amalgamated of just 6,500 members.[86] As organizations representing American workers, the craft unions defended the old division of labor in the mills, which helped to cement the stark segregation of American versus immigrant, skilled versus unskilled and semi-skilled.

The A.F.L. launched no serious effort to organize the iron miners of Minnesota. Neither the impetus of the defense of craft privilege nor the opportunity for industrial unions to contribute to the rationalization of industry existed on the Iron Range. Even more than the steel industry, large-scale Minnesota iron ore production was recent, with production from the Mesabi Range taking off only in the late 1890s, so from the outset there was no residual union presence. And unlike coal mining, iron mining was a highly capitalized and concentrated enterprise, with all of its production falling under U.S. Steel's empire and a few other large concerns.[87]

Conclusion

In choosing years to begin their studies, historians take on certain risks. Inevitably the roots of changes can be traced continuously back further and deeper. In the case of tracking the crucial changes that would forever alter the relationship of new immigrants to American industry, however, 1914 was the decisive year. Developments over the previous two decades had reshaped the American workplace and the population. New immigrants had seemed a world apart, separated by distances measured in space, culture, and occupation. The overwhelming majority took positions at the lowest rungs of a U.S. industrial hierarchy, so much so that distinctions between skilled and unskilled work also typically played out along an "American-foreigner" divide. And indeed, broad commonalities of experience—not only in work, but in the immigrant industrial community—had drawn new immigrant workers from a wide range of backgrounds into an increasingly cohesive section of the working class. These similarities did not extend to the immigrants' encounter with trade unionism in the steel and coal industries. In the former, dying craft unions made little effort to organize the newcomers. But in the coal industry, where the U.M.W. played the critical role in regulating competition in the C.C.F., new immigrants entered the U.M.W. with little difficulty, and quickly constituted themselves as a militant part of the union.

For years the prevailing common sense interpretation of the new immigrants had been that they were birds of passage, ignorant, and incapable of serious organization. Already by 1914, new immigrants had begun to challenge presumptions about their isolation and passivity. They successfully organized into the U.M.W., along with the major garment unions, and in certain cases the I.W.W. A series of militant strikes in which new immigrants predominated heralded a new period in which they would take center stage as actors in the ensuing decade-long historical drama, which would conclude in the de facto prohibition of new immigration. Through their migration and labor, new immigrants had helped to radically change U.S. industrial society. Now this new world, so much of it forged in steel and powered by coal, was to be put through the crucible of war. In 1914, new immigrants and American industry stood on the brink of enormous change.

Chapter 2

"A war of coal and iron": 1914–1917[1]

The onset of World War I in Europe set into motion major changes for new immigrants. The war effectively cut off immigration. Then, as recession turned to boom in 1916, workers showed a new strength and combativeness that was reflected in a surge in strike activity.[2] This affected all sections of the working class, but it was the great industrial struggles and the radicalization of the new immigrants that would take center stage. New immigrant workers came into conflict not only with corporate power and the state, but even the old organizations of the working class. A contemporary observer, the socialist William English Walling, called this the "reaction against the rule in trade unions and in Labor and Socialist parties, of the skilled, 'the aristocracy of labor.'" To Walling, it "constituted nothing less than a revolution in the labor movement."[3] The relationship of these tendencies to the war was not incidental. The war accelerated the polarization of society. As the new immigrants became more militant, so the power of corporations grew through preparedness and the war years, emerging in the postwar as the triumphant "corporate state." At the same time, the buffering reform efforts of anti-corporate Progressivism waned.

The period of mass immigration roughly coincided with a boom in the U.S. economy that lasted, with only brief interruptions, from 1897 until 1913. This period of economic growth came to an end in 1913, and was exacerbated through 1914 and the first half of 1915 by the economic dislocations caused by the eruption of hostilities in Europe. Then, beginning in 1915, the war in Europe began to lift the economy toward unprecedented heights of production as American commerce sought to meet the demands of the Allies and elsewhere elbowed into markets formerly dominated by the belligerent powers.

As industrial demand took off in the second half of 1915 and accelerated through 1916, unemployment declined. Labor's strength versus business and industry improved, and pent up grievances and demands found increasing expression in strikes. This served as a critical contributing factor to the emergence of America's longest and most intense strike wave, which was to begin in 1916—the largest strike year to that point—and not end until 1922. The strike wave was important not only for its challenge to the hegemony of big business, but to the old workers' organizations—the A.F.L. and the Socialist Party. As Montgomery aptly put it, "between 1916 and 1922, when levels of strike participation soared far above those of any other period thus far in the country's history, workers' demands became too heady for the A.F.L. or even the Socialist Party to contain and too menacing for business and the state to tolerate."[4]

Major demographic changes contributed both to the radicalization of the new immigrants and the upsurge in strike activity. The onset of World War I severely constricted immigration from Eastern and Southern Europe—it fell by 80 percent between 1914 and 1918—and began to draw north black, southern white, Mexican, and Caribbean workers.[5] European immigration was curtailed due to military operations on land and sea, the mass conscription of working age men into armies, and the heightened demands for employment within Europe to meet ramped up industrial requirements. The constriction of immigration and return migration contributed to a changing understanding of the meaning of work, family, community, and nation among new immigrants, lessening the characteristics of the immigrant workforce that had caused trade unionists to think of them as "birds of passage," content to tolerate poor conditions and low pay in order to save up for an eventual return to the old country.

These economic and demographic changes combined with another crucial change for new immigrant workers. Immigrants began to follow events related to the war in Europe very closely. Established states, new nationalisms, and old world radical groups competed for their loyalty. The stakes were high: numerous new and independent nations might arise as a result of the war that had consumed the German, Austro-Hungarian, Russian, and Ottoman empires. Socialists, syndicalists, and anarchists made appeals to the new immigrants condemning the war and pointing to it as a vindication of their various perspectives. The S.P., in particular, experienced a rising tide of new immigrant support. This coincided with declining support among native-born Americans.[6]

Together these changes—economic, demographic, and political—set the stage for a growing tide of new immigrant labor militancy and radicalization. Previously thought of as unorganizable and apathetic, by 1916 new immigrants had earned an entirely new reputation as dangerous and militant radicals. As the late Rudolph Vecoli put it regarding Italian immigrants, "during these years, Italians underwent a dramatic transformation in reputation, from being vilified as servile wage cutters and strikebreakers, to being hailed by 'Big Bill' Haywood as the vanguard of the revolutionary proletariat." Gone was the image of the passive immigrant worker.[7]

The Transatlantic Roots and Character of Immigrant Radicalism

Like the new immigrant communities themselves, radicalism was a transnational creation. Ideologically, it had powerful roots in the various "sending" countries of Europe and maintained, in every case, close relationships, both through communication and personnel, with the homeland. Among several new immigrant groups it appears that the first generation of radical leadership was already seasoned prior to emigration. Once established this leadership was infused by newer arrivals and political refugees. Yet the typical rank-and-file new immigrant radical was "made in the U.S.A." New immigrant radicalism, in contrast to old country radicalism, had to articulate a response to the work, social, and political conditions of the new country.

The disputes within immigrant radicalism can best be understood in relationship to struggles within the American radical movement rather than those of the old world—even if it may be true that these conflicts were peculiarly American expressions of similar discussions taking place in radical formations in Europe. The debates within the S.P. over "political" versus "economic" demands found echoes within the new immigrant radical communities, and when the S.P. condemned the I.W.W., the rift that opened soon split every immigrant radical community.

American radicalism had developed within its ranks three strong tendencies. There was the revolutionary-syndicalist I.W.W., with its emphasis on "direct action" "at the point of production," organization of the entire working class regardless of race or nationality, and simultaneously a tendency to disavow the political process—and, as would be revealed in World War I, the power of the state. These characteristics eventually separated the I.W.W. from the S.P., but within the latter there were also two major tendencies. The politically dominant faction, grouped around Morris Hillquit of New York and Victor Berger of Wisconsin, inclined toward critical support of the A.F.L. and openly embraced parliamentary reformism. The left wing of the S.P. stood closer to the I.W.W. on the question of the labor movement, and though it could not abide by the I.W.W.'s rejection of the political process, it found the reformism and "opportunism" of the right wing increasingly difficult to sustain.[8]

Within the S.P. the new immigrants increasingly represented a left wing social force. The reformist, gradualist, and trade unionist approach of the right wing held inconsistent appeal, not surprisingly, for workers that had limited access to the franchise and whose presence in the U.S. was opposed by the A.F.L. Here the new immigrants' outlook was informed by their countries of origin, with so many immigrants coming from states where there could be no talk of parliamentary gradualism, where trade unions faced sharp legal restrictions, and where revolution was openly proclaimed the first order of the day. For these same reasons, the I.W.W., which had originally been based on American and old immigrant hard rock miners of the trans–Mississippi West—first and second generation Cornish, Welsh, Irish, Scottish, and English miners with a rich tradition of trade unionism—discovered that it could also attract new immigrants, some of whom had gained exposure to revolutionary syndicalism in the old country. The appeal of the I.W.W. to new immigrants was countered effectively only by left wing socialists. The eruption of World War I intensified these rivalries, as the parties and trade unions of the Second International—with the exception of the Russian and American parties—one after the other rallied to national defense.[9]

It has been noted that new immigrant radicals, particularly the socialists, were practically segregated from the American movement headed by Eugene Debs, Berger, and Hillquit. This is at once true but also an over-simplification. It was the case that new immigrant socialists, organized in "foreign language federations," operated at a distance from the mainstream of the American socialist movement—a distance preserved by language and, to a degree, loyalty. However, this did not spare the foreign language federations from the struggles and vagaries of American radicalism, particularly the split that emerged between the S.P. and the I.W.W., which reverberated in similar splits among new immigrant radicals. New immigrants followed events within the S.P. closely; Debs, in particular, was broadly admired. At the same time, the various new immigrant radical formations in the U.S. were impacted by developments and controversies in the radical movements of Europe. In any case, the foreign language federations, along with a plethora of radical newspapers and periodicals of all stripes, had created by 1914 a complex new immigrant radicalism.[10]

The Finns, in spite of the fact that they were not one of the largest new immigrant groups, counting some 300,000 among the first and second generation in 1910, had the largest radical movement. Scholars have estimated that as much as 25–40 percent of the entire Finnish American population was engaged with one or another variety of radicalism in the nineteen-teens.[11] There are several explanations for this, best taken in combination. Finns gained their first acquaintance with socialism in the Russian Empire. A significant number of socialist-minded Finns immigrated as veterans of the 1905 Russian revolution, where many had participated in Helsinki and as migrant workers in Vyborg (*Viipuri*) and St. Petersburg. The Finns were highly literate. In the latter half of the 19th century, the nation passed through an exceptional period of national and religious awakening, promoting what William Hoglund has called an intense "associational spirit" that featured a strong tendency toward anti-clericalism. These characteristics combined with the stark reality of Finnish settlement and occupational patterns in the U.S., where the majority worked in the iron and copper mines of the Lake Superior area or the steel mills of the Great Lakes.

In 1912 the Finnish Socialist Federation (F.S.F.) boasted 225 chapters, with 11,000 members, four daily newspapers, numerous weekly and monthly periodicals (among them a women's weekly which circulated between 2,500 and 5,000), a college with 123 students, 76 club houses or socialist "halli," 80 libraries, and an income of $184,128.83 for a total property valuation of over $5,500,000. A 1918 study counted eight "socialistic" periodicals that together circulated to more than 30,000 readers. Finnish socialists crafted a rich cultural life, creating musical organizations, sewing circles, athletic, lecture and debate clubs, socialist "Sunday schools," and literature societies. In Virginia, Minnesota, the second largest Range town, they built a three story opera house. Finns developed a large socialist-affiliated cooperative movement that competed successfully with small town merchants in the northern reaches of Minnesota, Wisconsin, and Michigan. Yet in spite of its size and reach within the Finnish immigrant community, the F.S.F.

was one of the most isolated of the language federations, and relative to its size Finnish radicalism contributed little ideologically to the broader current of American radicalism. The Finns' isolation was composed of the social distance that they and all new immigrants occupied from presumptions of middle American society, an enormous linguistic barrier, and the fact that the majority of Finnish settlement in the U.S. took place in remote regions.[12]

In terms of its overall contribution to American radicalism, the Jewish Foreign Language Federation was probably the most significant of all of the new immigrant radical groupings. Its influence was comparable to that of the Germans among the older immigrant groups. The Jewish section of the S.P. was large, well-funded, and equipped with an active press whose center of gravity rested in New York City. After 1905 an increasing number of Jewish immigrants came to the U.S. with a certain exposure to a radical variety of socialism that had gained considerable ground in the old world in the face of the Jews' persecuted status in Russia's Pale of settlement.[13]

While Finns and Yiddish-speaking Jews had respectively the largest and most prominent radical communities, radicalism was widespread among numerous new immigrant groups. Socialism appealed to a relatively large number of Latvians and Lithuanians. When appraised in connection to Finnish and Jewish radicalism, this suggests the importance of the late czarist Russian empire as a hotbed of revolutionary ferment. As with Finns and Jews, Latvian and Lithuanian radicalism was bolstered by the arrival of political émigrés in the wake of the Russian Revolution of 1905. In spite of their very small population, the Latvians joined the Finns in 1906 in founding the first foreign language federations of the S.P. The Lithuanians were a much larger immigrant group than the Latvians, with a major presence both in the Calumet region of Chicago and the coalmining districts of Illinois. One Lithuanian socialist publication, the weekly *Keleivis* (Traveler), published in Boston, boasted a circulation of 23,000 at its peak. Another, Chicago's *Naujienos* (News), claimed in 1916 to be the world's first daily newspaper in the Lithuanian language. A small influx of Estonian radicals arrived after 1905, establishing a socialist newspaper in 1909.[14]

Relative to the enormous size of its population in the U.S.—as many as 3,000,000 first and second generation in 1910—Polish radicalism punched under its weight, especially in comparison to its Jewish and Baltic immigrant neighbors. This stemmed in part from the relative strength of nationalism and Roman Catholicism among Polish workers, which in turn arose from the legacy of national partition by Prussia, Austria, and Russia. Nonetheless, a number of socialist and labor newspapers and magazines that collectively circulated in the tens of thousands had a significant reach in the U.S. Like the other Baltic peoples, the socialist ranks were infused by émigrés fleeing czarist repression after the Russian Revolution of 1905. A generational split occurred in 1907, when the young émigrés founded a newspaper, split from the old socialist group, and affiliated as a foreign language federation with the S.P. in 1908 (P.S.F.). The P.S.F. claimed 1,870 dues-paying members in 148 locals in 1912, while its newspaper, the *Dziennik Ludowy* (People's Newspaper) claimed a circulation of 8,000 in 1913. That figure was about half the circulation of the leading Polish Catholic newspaper and a third of the leading Polish nationalist organ. Cygan concludes that "a socialist subculture infused a large part of the literate, secular Polish-American community." This subculture, even if formally adhered to by only a relatively small number, influenced a substantial number of unaffiliated Polish workers.[15]

South Slavs pioneered first an anti-clerical and then socialist fraternal organization to rival those sponsored by the churches. Led by Slovenians, the socialists organized libraries and cultural events in Iron Range towns and in Chicago. By 1906, Slovenian socialists had started *Proletarec*, which circulated on the Iron Range and in Slovenian steel mill communities. The newspaper included a page published in Serbo-Croatian as a means of reaching out to other South Slavs. Croatians and Serbians organized newspapers of their own with limited success beginning in 1907. In 1910 the Slovenian, Croatian, and Serbian socialists unified their efforts in the South Slavic Socialist Federation (S.S.S.F), which affiliated with the S.P. the next year as a foreign-language branch. An opposed minority faction formed its own foreign language federation and affiliated with Daniel De Leon's Socialist Labor Party (S.L.P.), which maintained significant membership and newspaper circulation through the nineteen-teens. The S.S.S.F experienced rapid growth in the years leading up to World War I. That the various South Slavic groups amalgamated under the term "Jugoslav" is indicative of the complex interaction of radicalism and pan-nationalist movements possible in the period.[16]

Russian immigrants also developed an elaborate radical political presence. In terms of the organization of workers, the most important group was the anarchosyndicalist Union of Russian Workers (U.R.W.), variously referred to as "Russian Workmen's Association." According to one investigator the U.R.W. had "branches in every large industrial center and many small mining and manufacturing communities." According to a U.S. military intelligence report, the Russians had established at least fifty such locals by 1917. The Russian socialists, for their part, organized branches across the country and published two significant newspapers, *Pravda* and *Novy Mir.* The latter, founded in 1911, claimed within a few years a circulation of 14,000 and was at the center of struggles between transplanted Mensheviks and Bolsheviks. *Novy Mir* would eventually be taken over by the latter, with figures no less significant than Leon Trotsky and Nikolai Bukharin editing its pages prior to their departure for Russia in 1917.[17]

The Italians, like the Poles, were somewhat underrepresented, especially if one goes by the rank-and-file membership levels in the Italian foreign language federation (F.S.I.). In contrast to the Russian empire, Italy maintained a weak liberal democracy in which socialists and syndicalists could generally participate above-ground. Particularly among socialists, there were therefore many fewer political refugees; the cadre of the *Partito Socialista Italiana* remained for the most part in Italy. Anarchism, which had significant support in Italy but was losing ground to socialism, faced greater repression, and some notable leaders fled to the U.S., including Luigi Galleani. Anarchism had significant support among Italian workers in the U.S., even in remote areas such as the Illinois coalfields. This perhaps explains in part the great number of pro-anarchist newspapers, even if their circulation numbers were tiny.[18]

Yet in spite of itself, Italian American radicalism cast a long shadow. In the S.P.–I.W.W. split, the F.S.I. went largely as a bloc over to the I.W.W. taking with them the weekly *Il Proletario,* which engaged in debates in equal measure with "reformists" and the anarchists led by Galleanni. On the Iron Range, Italians strongly supported the I.W.W., while in the coal mining towns of Illinois, significant support persisted for socialism, anarchism, and the I.W.W., cohabitating uneasily with radical miners' membership in the U.M.W. Chicago, for its part, was a bastion of Italian socialist support. Among all of the new immigrant groups, furthermore, Italian radical leaders arguably had the greatest impact beyond their own nationality, primarily as agitators, orators, and strike leaders. Among the prominent figures were Joseph Ettor, Arturo Giovanitti, Carlo Tresca, and Anthony Capraro. Ettor, it was reputed, could address an audience in not only Italian and English, but in Yiddish, Hungarian, and Polish. Moreover, these radical leaders showed a marked ability to react rapidly and intervene in the frequent new immigrant labor struggles of the period. Italian immigrants came to constitute, in these years, "the backbone of the class struggle in all of the industrial East of the U.S."[19] Vecoli has described the growing influence of radicalism among Italians in the U.S.:

> Between 1910 and 1920, Italian immigrants coalesced into a working class imbued with a militant class consciousness. Led by talented organizers—socialists, syndicalists, anarchists—they mobilized powerful radical movements that played decisive roles in strikes. They also formed unions, cooperatives, and cultural organizations, and they found their voices in song, theater, oratory, and popular manifestations.... Inspired by a revolutionary elan, Italian workers were not only seeking liberation from economic oppression, but also redemption from ethnic injury.[20]

As was the case with Poles, the relatively small number of Italians who joined radical organizations was belied by the remarkable influence Italian radicals exerted over workers when strikes came.

The strivings of new immigrant workers toward industrial unionism pushed the leadership of ethnic radicalism, whatever its particular affiliation, to the left. The tensions and splits within American radicalism contended with what appeared to contemporaries a new and powerful social force. Not surprisingly, these tensions found their clearest expression within the largest formation of new immigrant radicalism, that of the Finns, but they were felt in every new immigrant community. The F.S.F. was split over the question of the I.W.W. in 1914, two years after the split within the S.P. The majority, derogatorily styled "parliamentary opportunists" by their Wobbly opponents, sided with the S.P. Yet two factions within the majority were already evident as early as 1913, once again mirroring the development in the American party of "left wing" and "reformist" factions. Meanwhile, the pro–I.W.W. minority—"the impossibilists," their rivals called them—was able to gain a good share of the F.S.F. holdings, including *Työvaen Opisto* ("Work People's College"—which would soon become the national I.W.W.'s training center) in Duluth, Minnesota, and founded their own competing daily newspaper, *Industrialisti*.[21]

The Hungarian-American left had already been split over the question of whether to affiliate with the S.P. of Debs or De Leon's S.L.P. The latter carried the majority of Hungarian socialists in a split that occurred in 1904. Then a second split occurred in 1912, when the majority of the Hungarians associated with the S.P. stood with the American party in its rejection of the I.W.W. They carried with them a daily newspaper, *Elore* ("Forward") which reached circulation of nearly 10,000, while the smaller I.W.W. faction created their own newspaper.[22] Meanwhile, among Italians, the F.S.I. took the vast majority of its membership and its influential newspaper, *Il Proletario*, over to the I.W.W., leaving what started as a rump F.S.I. grouped around the newspaper *La Parola dei Socialisti* in Chicago.[23]

Region played a role. Just as the population of Minnesota's Iron Range was almost all imported from Eastern and Southern Europe, so radicalism in the region grew almost entirely out of the new immigrant communities. In Chicago and the coal mining areas of Illinois, on the other hand, an organized socialist movement already existed prior to the entry of the new immigrants. This was especially true of the coal mining towns of downstate. There was a significant and growing socialist presence in the coal fields of Illinois, especially in the central and southern regions, from 1914 to 1916, with a number of local offices won or fought for closely. Local elections oftentimes featured "old immigrant" socialists, but new immigrants also ran for office and seem to have been a central constituency of local socialist politics in the years, so much so that in one downstate county, the local Catholic churches organized efforts to forestall what they saw as the growing influence of socialism among immigrant miners. While the S.P. claimed, in what was almost certainly an exaggeration, that one third of American coal miners were socialists, in Illinois, the development of the U.M.W. was without a doubt influenced by socialism. One historian has called Illinois ("District 12") "the center of U.M.W. socialist power." Three of the most prominent figures in the Illinois U.M.W.—John Walker, Duncan MacDonald, and Adolph Germer—were socialists and campaigned as such in the U.M.W., where they confronted a powerful rival in Frank Farrington. They also launched attacks on what they perceived to be the conservative national bureaucracy of the U.M.W. Walker very nearly won the presidency of the U.M.W. in 1912.[24]

Leading Illinois U.M.W. socialists acted just as aggressively as the conservatives like Farrington in enforcing the Trade Agreement, which led them at times to a similar policing role over the new immigrant coal miners as that carried out by the conservative union leadership. Within the U.M.W. the socialists fought for a rhetorical allegiance to the demand for public ownership, but this did not affect their practice as trade unionists in the least, a fact well-appreciated by the Illinois coal operators. Moreover, while it was clear that the U.M.W. socialists represented a left wing tendency in the union, within the S.P. they allied with the conservative tendency dominated by Berger, in which the trade union struggle for better wages was viewed as paramount. Germer even joined with Berger and the A.F.L. in favoring immigration restriction, a position that seemed to stand in conflict with the success that the U.M.W. enjoyed with new immigrants.[25]

War, Nationalism and Immigrant Radicalism

The eruption of war in Europe may have "destroyed the illusion of the Melting Pot," but divisions between states in the old world did not produce a mirror image among immigrant groups in the new. In Iron Range towns, placards were posted by the representatives of the belligerent powers calling young men to military service. But one informant told a local newspaper that among the various Balkan nationalities there "was little national prejudice" among "Austrians, Hungarians, and Servians," even if sympathy tended to be with Serbia. He also stated that few men were going back, "but if they are it is to preserve their property and dwellings." Another newspaper, *The Eveleth News*, found "great interest" among new immigrant miners in the war, but that few were "leaving to take up arms." The newspaper proclaimed that "Eveleth has among its residents subjects of all the powers engaged in the war but no race feeling has developed here." "Austria," it added, "seems to have little sympathy from her subjects in this city, and few, if any, will return to the old country to take up arms. On the other hand Servia has many staunch friends here and many will, if possible, return to take the part of the weaker power. Many so-called Austrians are really against the Austrian government in the struggle and will be enlisted on the other side." This evidence suggests that the war was working in a subtle way to promote a Yugoslav identity among the Iron Range's Slovenians, Croats, and Serbs. In Ely a "Jugoslav" library club and "National Home" was organized.[26]

Similarly complex national pressures were at play in the Illinois coal towns and in Calumet. The peoples of the constituent nationalities of the Russian Empire roundly hated the Czar's war, a sentiment shared by the Poles, whose homeland was divided amongst the Hohenzollern, Hapsburg, and Romanov dynasties. In Illinois coal towns, Polish miners signed up to fight for independence as soon as the war broke out. Polish nationalists toured the U.S. calling upon the largely proletarian population to act "as the fourth part of Poland."[27] Depending on which way the war went, it was readily evident that a number of new states might result. Magyar community leaders, however, found themselves in a quandary. Opposed to Austrian domination of Hungary, they nonetheless raged against the accusations of the rival nationalist groups, the Slovaks, Czechs, Romanians, and Yugoslavs, who stood to benefit from the dissolution of the Hapsburg Empire. After U.S. entry, the Magyar nationalists worked assiduously to demonstrate loyalty to the government, but like the Germans and Austrians, they were perceived to be a dangerous population, perhaps doubly so due to their abundant presence in mines and mills. These strands came together in the "Dumbla Affair," when the Hapsburg ambassador confessed of a plan to stir up industrial unrest among Hungarian workers.[28]

But nationalism was not simply an alien force that acted upon new immigrants in the U.S. To a great extent, like radicalism, it was also generated among them, "above all by the hostility and contempt which they as 'Hunkies' encountered 'in the promised land.'"[29] In other words, national feeling was inseparably bound up with class feeling. Moreover, it is very difficult to categorize nationalism without historical contextualization as "reactionary" or "conservative." It represented both a centripetal and centrifugal force among new immigrants.[30] Poles, Italians, Bulgarians, and so on, became in the U.S. for the first time "nationals," as provincial loyalties were lessened by common work and social experiences and linguistic similarities. At the same time, nationalism could provoke differences and rivalries among new immigrants. Puskás has captured this duality in her description of nationalism among emigrants from Hungary:

> It was in the course of emigration that people from the villages rose above local patriotism and solidarity.... Isolated in the midst of a prejudiced and antagonistic environment, depending on each other, the emigrants discovered the cohesive power of a group solidarity based on ethnicity; it was this that became the instigator of their ethnic awakening, and even nationalism. At the same time, conflicts in the new environment increased tensions among the various ethnic groups from Hungary. Their new situation and the unresolved ethnic problems of the old country ... developed the consciousness of the Magyars, Slovaks, Ruthenians, and Croatian emigrants."[31]

The complex international situation also caused difficulties for the nationalist Poles, reflecting the fact that the nation was divided among three belligerent "great powers." Marshal Josef Pilsudski organized a militia attached to Austro-Hungarian armies to fight against Russia, which many Poles viewed as the greatest enemy. But strenuous efforts were also made by pro–Russian Poles. Early on, the majority of immigrant nationalist leaders, prior to U.S. entry into the war, oriented toward the anti–Russian Pilsudski. However, the proximity of the pro–Russian group to the chambers of state power in Paris, London, and eventually Washington, and even more importantly the fact that the U.S. would soon enter the war against the Central Powers, moved most immigrant Polish nationalists toward a pro–Russian group that championed a Poland created largely at the territorial expense of Germany and Austria.[32]

The war in Europe impacted new immigrant radicalism in two quite contradictory ways. On the one hand, it appears to have generated greater support than ever among new immigrant workers, if membership numbers in the language federations of the S.P., voting statistics, and newspaper circulation numbers are taken into account. Simultaneously, the war upset the tenuous balance that had come to prevail within the leadership of the various currents of immigrant radicalism. This combination of growth on the one hand and destabilization on the other was a paradox only on the surface. Radical currents and their leaders began to be put to the test of demanding times. One aspect of this was the growing militancy of new immigrant workers. But that was not the only trial. All of the unresolved questions about loyalty to the nation—new and old—the nature of the state, and the role of politics were now to be forcefully raised by historical events.

The editor of the Wobbly-linked F.S.I., Edmondo Rossoni, soon came out as an unabashed advocate of Italian intervention on the side of the allies in World War I. Shortly Rossoni and a militarist faction would leave *Il Proletario* and the F.S.I. altogether, which had joined the S.P. and the Italian anarchists in rejecting the war and Italian participation. These splits echoed processes underway in Italy, where the majority of the P.S.I. joined the Russian Social Democrats as the only significant European socialist parties to oppose the war, only to see a minority, led and inspired by Benito Mussolini, embrace nationalism and the war aims of Italian imperialism, which centered on expanding Italy's sphere of influence in the Balkans at the expense of the Hapsburg and Ottoman empires. Indeed, Rossoni soon made his way back to Italy, where Mussolini eventually placed him in charge of the fascist trade union movement.[33]

The expansionist aims of Italian nationalism would by war's end run up against Yugoslav radicals' desire for a strong independent state, an aim that was more pronounced among some elements within Yugoslav radicalism than others. A section of the S.S.S.F. dominated by Slovenians under the leadership of Etbin Kristan, began to petition the U.S. government for intervention on behalf of the allies. This position was rejected by the Serbo-Croatian section, and the S.S.S.F. was effectively split in two. Among Lithuanians, Chicago's socialist newspaper, *Naujienos*, which was busy selling subscriptions to the city's millworkers and downstate coal miners, did frequent ideological battle with nationalist newspapers. Lithuanian socialists appear to have had an orientation to the broader struggle of Russian Social Democracy. In Chicago, in 1915, Lithuanians commemorated the tenth anniversary of the Bloody Sunday massacre in St. Petersburg.[34]

The great majority of Polish socialists in the P.S.F. supported the war, viewing it as a chance for Polish independence. They organized together with secular and even Roman Catholic groups to support with money and volunteers the efforts of Pilsudski, in his Austrian-supported war on Tsarist Russia. After the fall of the Czar and Pilsudski's entrenchment in Warsaw, the Polish socialists felt free to support the possible U.S. entry on the side of the allies. Significantly, a number of left wing Polish socialists supportive of Rosa Luxemburg's anti-war and anti-nationalist outlook began to openly challenge the leadership of the P.S.F. This group demanded that the S.P. issue an ultimatum to the P.S.F. demanding that it drop support for Pilsudski's war aims. The S.P. Executive Committee did so in July 1916, and the majority of the P.S.F. left.[35]

Even the Russian Anarchists of the U.R.W. felt the pressure of nationalism. After war erupted in Europe, a leading Russian anarchist, Prince Peter Kropotkin, sent an open letter to immigrant Russian workers calling on them to enlist in the Allied armies to defeat Germany. The U.R.W.'s newspaper supported this line, which provoked a rebellion among chapters across the country, and subsequently a division between what a flummoxed U.S. military intelligence agent described as "Anarcho-Syndicalists" and "Anarcho-Communists."[36]

Nationalist currents cohabitated with a wider embrace of radicalism among immigrant workers. The S.P. witnessed a sharp growth in new immigrant support beginning in 1914, a tendency that coincided with a gradual drawing down of native support. What had been a rump Italian F.S.I, attached to the S.P., for example, saw the number of its supporting sections grow from 41 in March 1914, to 71 in April 1915. When Eugene Debs came to speak on the Iron Range in 1915 at a May Day event sponsored by the F.S.F., over 4,000 attended to listen to the icon of American socialism. In Chisholm, on the same day hundreds of Finnish and Yugoslav socialists paraded behind both red and American flags. In Divernon, Illinois, a Lithuanian socialist and former coal miner ran for village president in 1915, gaining about 20 percent of the votes cast. Large local audiences turned out in the Illinois coal towns to hear socialist speakers such as Debs and Germer.[37]

The cooperative movement also gained considerable ground during these years, as a means of responding to hardship and to counteract the power of local businessmen hostile to unions and radicals. Finnish immigrants had already built up an extensive consumer cooperative movement on the Iron Range that was tied to the F.S.F. In some cities, Slovenian and Italian workers followed suit. One impetus to cooperative organization for the Finns had been that local store owners had cut off credit to striking miners during the 1907 Mesabi strike. It also served to economically unite those Finns who attempted to farm the cutover timberlands of the Iron Range with those who remained in the mines. Similar pressures were at play in the widespread development of cooperative stores among coal miners in Illinois. And it was not uncommon in Illinois for miners to attempt to own or operate mines cooperatively. In Sangamon County in 1914, 17 African American miners pooled their resources to open a mine capitalized at $1,000. But by the middle of 1915, the Illinois U.M.W. had gone on record against cooperative mines. Not only did the mines potentially pit cooperative owners against new-hire union workers, but they stood outside of the C.C.F. trade agreements, and were thus viewed as potential competition.[38]

Setting the Stage: Economic and Demographic Change

The first economic impact of the war was the depression of 1914–1915. The downturn that had already emerged in 1913 was exacerbated by war-related economic dislocations. The war required a rapid conversion of European economic production from domestic to military consumption, which triggered a temporary decline in the value of a number of commodities, including coal and iron. It interrupted shipping, as merchant marines were shifted to military use and as continental Europe became much more difficult to access, which cut against U.S. industry's ability to immediately compete in its rivals' old markets.

The depression hit all three industries. Price per ton of coal, iron, and steel fell off sharply. In the fiscal year of 1914–1915, in the state of Illinois alone 139 mines were closed completely, while many more were worked at a minimal level in order to prevent the mines from flooding. In one Illinois coal town, Divernon, the local mine closed indefinitely in March 1915 after working irregularly through the normally busy winter season. This threw 415 men out of work. Meanwhile, borrowing a tactic that Carnegie had used in the 1890s, some larger coal interests used the downturn of 1914–1915 to buy up mines at fire sale prices. Peabody Coal, for example, significantly expanded its operations—it bought several mines in Sangamon County, Illinois, alone—positioning itself for the expected turnaround.[39]

The Lake Superior district produced 37 percent less iron in 1914 than it had the year before, and about a third of the tonnage that was extracted sat piled in heaps next to the mines. The human toll that followed hit every town on the Range. One Finnish immigrant, who had showed up on the Iron Range in the midst of the depression and was unable to find work, committed suicide, asking in a note found in his pocket that his savings be sent to his family rather than used for his own funeral expenses. Other workers turned to political methods, holding mass meetings demanding work. Iron Range municipalities used financial largesse raised through taxes on U.S. Steel to hire men during times of recession for busywork. In Chisholm, with a population of approximately 7,000, in June of 1914 some 600 men were employed in the "Streets Department." The workforce of U.S. Steel declined sharply. In the summer of 1914 the *Chicago Tribune* cast a nervous glance in the direction of Calumet, warning that unrest would result from unemployment. The tell-tale sign was that the smokestack, "sentinels for a community as large as many a great American city," had ceased sending up their exhaust.[40]

Then in 1915 the war began to turn the river of economic depression back. In short time, the U.S. went from being a net debtor to a creditor nation, as it became banker to the allies, and the center of world finance migrated during the war years from London to New York City. Just as significantly, agriculture and industry—the bases of the export economy—found an insatiable demand in Europe to feed, clothe, and equip the warring armies, and at the same time began to cut into European export markets all over the world. Industrialists hoped to gain access to foreign markets. But they feared that their domestic labor market would be constricted by the departure of immigrants.

The *American Coal Journal* salivated over the possibilities. One coal trader happily noted that the war involved "every important coal producing country in Europe" and he looked to foreign trade as a means of widening profit margins driven down, he held, by "advancing wages and introduction of safety devices." Another coal executive predicted that "the present war in Europe will make an unprecedented demand for American coals ... provided, of course, the war continues." Continue it did, with U.S. industrialists warming their hands over the conflagration. By the autumn of 1915, *The American Coal Journal* was celebrating the decline of the British export trade, choked off by a shortage of labor, strikes and a bureaucratization that required all foreign sales to be approved by the government. The British were not unaware of the U.S. threat. Lord Rhondda, also known as D. H. Thomas, "the Welsh coal king," noted that in the event of an Allied victory, "it would be the competition of the United States and not of Germany which would be likely to prove most keen." The most typical U.S. bituminous coal, "Pocahontas" coal, was similar to Welsh coal chemically, he noted, but was produced for one third the cost.[41]

What was true of the coal industry was true of steel and the U.S. economy as a whole. By 1913 the U.S. had become the world's largest producer of steel, and had entered the ranks of the steel exporting countries. However, in 1913 the great majority of steel produced in the U.S. was consumed domestically—some 90 percent. In contrast, Germany,

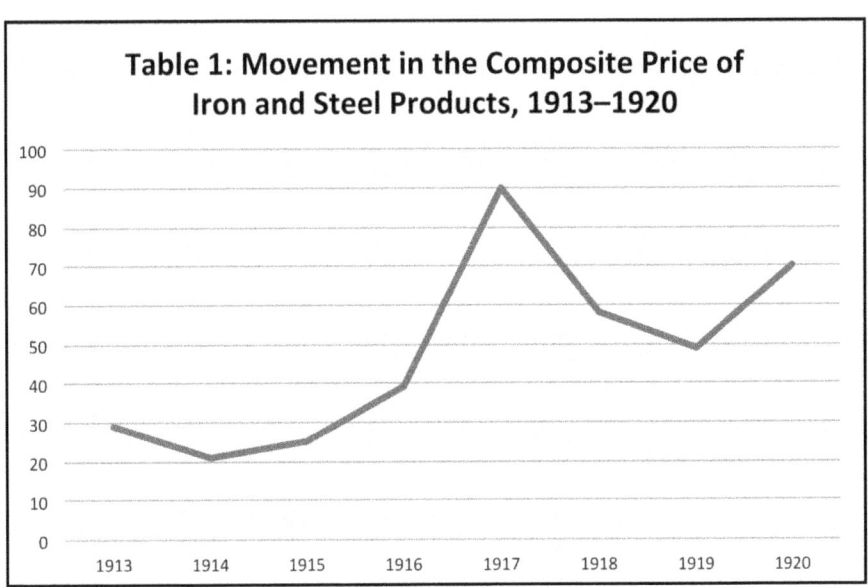

Source: Vanderblue and Crura, *The Iron Industry in Prosperity and Depression* (Chicago: A.W. Shaw, 1927): 8.

the world's leading steel exporter, exported 30 percent of its production, and Great Britain continued to export considerably more steel than the U.S., as well. The recession of 1913–1915, however, announced that the domestic steel market had reached its point of saturation. Significant growth of market and sales could only come overseas, and only at the expense of the other major steel producers—and belligerent powers—Germany, Great Britain, France, and Belgium. This same possibility held true in all fields of manufacturing. In Montgomery's memorable recounting, the barons of industry in the National Manufacturing and Trade Association (N.M.T.A.), assembled at a national convention in 1915, celebrated the arrival of war: "So happy were the convention delegates, reported *Iron Age,* that at the banquet they had all joined vigorously in singing 'It's a Long Way to Tipperary,' and then 'Die Wacht am Rhein.'" By autumn, Montgomery adds, "*Iron Age* had already concluded that the vital question of the hour was not which side was winning the war in Europe but how American industry might emerge from the conflict as master of all the belligerents." American industrialists stood ready to make a fortune. In 1916, U.S. Steel's profits were triple what they had been in 1912.[42]

The return of prosperity was soon in full swing in the iron, steel, and coal industries, and would shortly have an invigorating impact on workers' struggles. Early in the year records were being set for future orders of steel. It took some time for the changing conditions to even out the slack in commodity production created by the stockpiling of materials that had no buyers in the depression years, but by the summer of 1915 in iron and steel, and the autumn of the same year in coal, the recession in employment had ended. "To replenish the low supply of raw materials, the fleets of the ore boats on the great lakes are being rushed back and forth between the ore shipping points of Minnesota and Wisconsin ... [while] additional men are being put to work in coal mines that were temporarily shut down," one observer commented. The recovery thus bound more tightly together the iron, coal, and steel industries in the Great Lakes economy.[43]

The second immediate effect of the war was to largely dry up the immigration of Eastern and Southern Europeans due to military operations on land and sea and the generally heightened demand for manpower in Europe. For the same reasons, return migration was also sharply limited. Coupled with nearly full employment after 1915, this end to mass transatlantic mobility contributed to a new level of stability in new immigrant communities and changed attitudes toward work among immigrant workers. At least temporarily removed was the prospect of making money quickly and returning to the old country.

Some industrialists feared that there would be an exodus of immigrants to serve in the militaries of their native lands. The evidence for this appears mixed. With the mixture of optimism and bunkum typical of small-town boosterism, an Iron Range newspaper declared, "On the Mesabi alone are 10,000 men ready to take up their permanent residence in the United States. All thought of returning to the Old Country has been dissipated by the war." The *American Coal Journal* feared that just the opposite was the case, citing a "general exodus of foreign miners from the Illinois coal fields ... to take up arms for their respective countries. A big percentage of miners in the Springfield District are of foreign birth and are on Army reserve lists in their native countries.... Among these are hundreds of Austrians and Russians." Written in 1914, it seems more likely that the new immigrants were leaving the coal fields because there was little work to be had. In any case, by 1916, workers were coming to Illinois coal mines "from all directions."[44]

The extent to which the end of return migration was decisive in the upsurge of new immigrant labor militancy during World War I, is open to debate. Brody and others may have overestimated its weight versus other causes, believing that the essential factor was the cutting off of the avenue of escape for birds of passage. It certainly was a factor, although the ending of transatlantic mobility dovetailed with a maturation of new immigrant communities in the U.S. that had been underway for many years. This was measured not just by developing forms of radicalism, but with the building up of an elaborate network of community institutions such as fraternal benefit societies—ubiquitous among the new immigrants—churches, innumerable cultural forms such as opera and theater, and the new immigrant press. It was also related to the growth of the female population and the gradual evening out of disparities in sex ratios—always more advanced, not surprisingly, among new immigrant groups who had been in the country longest—as well as the growing demographic weight of what sociologists call "the second generation," or the children of the immigrants. New immigrant workers with families were, unsurprisingly, the least likely to move.[45]

There can be no incontrovertible proof that demographic and community stabilization *necessarily* lent itself to the growth of militancy and radicalism, but there is abundant suggestive evidence that it was an important contributing factor, most obviously in the way that immigrants presented the justice of their own struggles. This perhaps explains in part the growing tendency toward community-wide labor struggles of new immigrant workers, in which wives and children figured prominently. In any case, the two factors in stabilizing new immigrant communities—the ending of migration and the maturing of the communities—complemented one another. By 1916 they coincided with a general labor shortage, which increased workers' ability to make demands on employers. New immigrant workers protested in two ways: through strikes, or the more traditional mode of "voting with their feet," and switching jobs.[46]

The end of European immigration also directly affected the racial composition of the workforce. The implications were not lost on the major African American newspaper, the *Chicago Defender,* which also hoped that many of the "illiterate foreigners" who had "crowded out Afro American laborers" would now depart for military service. "It may now dawn on the American manufacturer, the American captains of industry, and the American controllers of commerce," it wrote, "that the Afro-American is the most dependable laborer." If the *Defender* was uncharitable to the new immigrants, it was correct in anticipating the "revolution" in labor that the war heralded—the coming Great Black Migration, for which Chicago and its steel-making suburbs would be a principal destination. However, because industry did not rebound from the depression of 1914 until 1916, the movement of African Americans to the North would not begin in earnest until 1916, accelerating through 1917–1919, so that in a span of four years as many as 75,000 black southerners had moved to Chicago alone. Chicago's black population doubled between 1915 and 1920, and then more than doubled again between 1920 and 1930.[47]

New Immigrant Labor Militancy and the Mesabi Range Strike of 1916

Prior to 1914, major strikes in which new immigrants dominated or played an outstanding role had already taken place. In their form—the level of militancy, discipline, and solidarity that they exhibited—these strikes very closely resembled and presaged those that would emerge in the period from 1916 to 1922. Now those characteristics of the immigrant populations that had seemed to make them so passive—immigrants' insularity, cohesiveness, etc.—turned outward in labor struggle proved to be potent characteristics of solidarity.[48]

In the seven years preceding World War I, many labor struggles had taken place in the garment and textile industries with new immigrant women workers—especially Jewish, Italian, and Polish—playing a leading role. These strikes came as a shock to contemporaries, not only because they shattered all notions of their passivity, but because it placed immigrant women in violation of the conventional nostrums of "manly trade unionism"—a frequently deployed phrase—and bourgeois Victorian "ladylike" behavior. Among these monumental strikes were the Chicago garment workers' strike of 1910, "the Uprising of the 20,000" garment workers in New York City in the wake of the Triangle Shirtwaist fire in 1911, and the I.W.W.–led textile strikes in Lawrence in 1912 and Patterson in 1913. There had also been notable conflicts in heavy industry led by new immigrant workers—on the Mesabi Range in 1907, in the steel mill town of McKee's Rocks, Pennsylvania, in 1909, and the famous Copper Country strike of 1913 on Michigan's Upper Peninsula, where dozens of new immigrant children—mainly Italian and Finnish—were smothered in a Christmas Eve stampede. These strikes appeared to represent a departure from earlier immigrant strikes, which some scholars have compared to peasant rebellions. Prior to 1907, strikes of new immigrants erupted spontaneously, were extremely militant—often violent—but tended to focus on particular short-term grievances, and then dissipated just as rapidly.[49]

The Mesabi strike was one of the first major new immigrant strikes to have departed from this pattern. It erupted spontaneously, but soon found leadership in the radical Western Federation of Miners (W.F.M.). Finns, Slovenians, and Italians figured prominently, and the W.F.M. sent in foreign-language organizers to provide leadership. The Finnish socialist halls in the small towns of the Range provided the strike's nerve centers. However, after a bitter struggle the strike failed. After that, strikes on the Iron Range tended to be spontaneous, short, affected only one mine, and focused on single grievances. A strikingly similar pattern prevailed in American steel mills, and in spite of the presence of the U.M.W., strikes of Illinois coal mines fit this same mold. Major national or statewide strikes were not the norm when coal miners were under contract. But local unions and their labor forces sang to a different tune. In a two-month period lasting from April 1 to March 31, 1914, the U.S. Commission on Industrial Relations (C.I.R.) recorded 44 different strikes of Illinois coal mines. Of these, 21 strikes lasted one day or less, and 15 more lasted a week or less, with only eight lasting more than a week. Most of these strikes erupted over a single issue having to do with the question of workers' control—matters related to the actual running of the mine, such as the acquisition and cost of provisions, or the removal of disagreeable managers.[50]

The upsurge of labor struggles, in which immigrants figured prominently, was part of a trend that spanned the Atlantic. In the European countries, the outbreak of World War I interrupted a strike wave that had emerged earlier. In the years from 1910 to 1914, Italy, Russia, Germany, Britain, France and a number of other countries were all gripped by significant strike waves, with Italy's "Red Week" in the latter year taking on near-revolutionary proportions. Indeed, if one views strike activity in a number of European states, what becomes clear is that World War I actually interrupted a growing crescendo of labor militancy, which then resumed at a much higher level in the war's aftermath—and in Russia in 1917.[51]

In the U.S., by 1916 a strike wave was on, spurred on in part by declining unemployment and inflation. The strikes were offensive in character and were highly militant. In May of 1916 the *Iron Age* wrote that strikes in the steel and metal industries were "rampant" and called the "explosive nature of the labor situation" a factor in futures trading. The trade journal indicated that wages were at the heart of the matter. Violence and the threat of violence were quite typical, as workers openly defied injunctions, arrests, and other forms of legal authority. In East Chicago, a strike at a war armaments plant anticipated in its contours many strikes to come. There a new immigrant-led struggle was challenged by guards and strikebreakers, which led to a melee in which one was killed. Strike leaders were arrested and "spirited away" to another city so as to avoid mob rescue. The owner of the plant accused the workers of a pro–German plot.[52]

The strike wave was announced in the steel industry through spontaneous eruptions, such as a militant strike of Pennsylvania Westinghouse steelworkers in May of 1916, in which hundreds of workers intervened to free an arrested leader before he could be taken away to prison, and the Youngstown steel strike of 1916. In the latter case, investigators revealed the incomprehension that surrounded the new immigrant strikes: "East Youngstown's 'hunkie' town, was a scene of riot and wholesale burning during [the] strike. But what caused that strike and what moved those 'foreigners' to violent outbreak are still unknown to the good Americans who live on the hill top.... The employment managers, welfare workers and mill officials who try to make it their business to know at least a little something of what is going on in the 'foreigner's head,' say frankly they cannot follow him."[53] In Illinois, the period beginning in 1914 saw a surge in the number of wildcat strikes unsanctioned by U.M.W. District 12. These were relatively spontaneous affairs, at least in the sense that they either lacked, or took place in opposition to, union authority. But on closer examination, labor histories of workers' struggles in the period reveal that behind strike activity stood a potent combination of long-term grievances and the growing influence of a militant minority of workers.[54]

The I.W.W. made significant inroads among immigrants on the Iron Range for several reasons. Here, as in the western frontier mining boom towns where both the I.W.W. and its predecessor, the W.F.M., had been born, modern capitalism had sprung up virtually overnight, and with less of the buffering layers of middle classes separating labor from capital.[55] Second, the Iron Range miners, through direct migratory and employment patterns, had contact with successful W.F.M. and I.W.W. organizing efforts among both the western hard rock mines and among the field hands of the Upper Midwest, both centers of strength of the I.W.W.[56] But the I.W.W. appeal on the Iron Range should more appropriately be considered the continuation of a new form of its activity east of the Mississippi River, where it had found a receptive audience in overwhelmingly new immigrant industrial communities, such as had been the case in Lawrence, Patterson, and McKee's Rocks.

The miners' grievances against U.S. Steel's Iron Range subsidiary, the Oliver Iron Mining Company, were many and deep. Miners bitterly resented the power of the foreman and superintendent in hiring and firing. The system resulted in endemic corruption, as miners were often compelled to bribe their superiors for their positions in the mine through the garnishing of their wages or other favors. This was an especially onerous tax for miners with families, such as the husband of Italian immigrant Melanina Degubellus. "Most of the married men were cheated because they could not grease the wheel, as they would say," explained Degebellus, who was born in 1894.[57] Her husband, an anarchist, became a supporter of the strike and even housed Carlo Tresca on his tours of the Iron Range. Savlatore Aluni, born in 1892 in Italy, recalled that these grievances, coupled with Oliver's hated spy system—which paid informants among the miners to finger agitators—added up to something much deeper. "Well, hatred—there was terrible hatred," he said. "They were terrible people when they began here. They had what they call 'black list'—had stool pigeon—if you say something against the mining people or you're talking about union, they report and you got fired and you couldn't get a job no place." The foreman and the spy—these were the two enforcers of U.S. Steel's corporate power.⁵⁸

The blacklist after the 1907 strike had resulted in a sharp decline in the number of Finnish miners, who went from comprising 20 percent of the workforce to 7 percent. But the new recruits who replaced them became subject to the same system. "After the strike of 1907 lots of Slovenians, Montenegrins, they got from the Balkan. They put them to work, kill them like flies," Aluni remembered. "They blacklisted the Finn ... they couldn't get a job—the Finns—because they were the head of the first strike. I remember the first strike. I was here in 1907."⁵⁹ Andy Johnson, who as a ten-year-old boy tried to help a newly-arrived Finn find a job in a mine, remembered the experience painfully: "I went into the office and asked the guy, I told him that this man was looking for a job. So the clerk at the office says what nationality is he. Well that surprised me. I was ten years old. I said he is a Finn. We don't hire any Finlanders.... So I turned around and walked out. John, the guy that I was with he was asking me.... What did he say? What did he say? I couldn't get the words out of me." Blacklisted in large numbers, the Finns nonetheless remained a major component of the workforce and continued to play the leading role in Iron Range radical politics.⁶⁰

The 1916 strike began on the east end of the Mesabi Range in the city of Aurora in the second week of June. Within two weeks it had swept across the entire Iron Range, as far as Bovey near Grand Rapids, Minnesota, and involved some 15,000 miners. In the strike's first days, hundreds of miners, their wives, and children marched from Aurora to neighboring east Mesabi towns, and gathered in mass meetings at Finnish socialist halls, which once again served as nerve centers for the strike. From there the strike spread to the western Mesabi Range towns of Chisholm, Hibbing, and beyond. Whereas the 1907 Mesabi Strike had been disproportionately led by Finns, in 1916 South Slavs and Italians were equally prominent. Interethnic alliance was powerful on the Iron Range in the 1916 strike. No evidence exists that any one particular nationality was used to break the strike, as had been the case in the 1907 strike when Montenegrins were imported for the purpose. Aluni remembered in particular the cooperation of the three largest new immigrant groups on the Range. "Finnish, they were quite a progressive people," he recalled, "I remember that the Slovenian people were pretty much I.W.W., some Italians, both sides, so I'd say it'd be fifty-fifty of all nationalities."⁶¹

The extent to which the I.W.W. had prepared the strike or merely reacted to it has never been clearly determined. Minnesota A.F.L. officials took the former position, although they had steadfastly refused to initiate any organizational drives among the miners (state officials had toured the Range earlier in 1916 to attract local craftsmen to various affiliate unions, but had stayed away from the mines and miners). Indeed opponents of the strike attributed the entire affair to "outside agitators" of the I.W.W. and insisted that Iron Range miners were content, but that they were being prevented from returning to work by violent Wobbly threats. This is an unlikely interpretation. The support for the strike among rank-and-file miners was overwhelming, enough to shut down the entire Mesabi Range within two weeks. A strike of such magnitude and solidarity could not simply have been smuggled in from other parts. In relation to charges of I.W.W. violence, Wobbly leaders who toured the Range, including Carlo Tresca, Elizabeth Gurley Flynn, and Sam Scarlett, counseled miners against it, precisely because they anticipated that any violence would be attributed to the I.W.W. The serious incidents of violence during the strike were initiated by local authorities, the state militia, and the army of mine security that U.S. Steel recruited—even though the strike's two fatalities were pinned squarely on the I.W.W. and strikers. To be sure, new immigrants committed acts of violence as well. In some of these instances, women took the initiative in beatings and public humiliations of strikebreakers, just as they led the large labor marches that punctuated the strike. In a couple of instances, homes of workers who crossed picket lines were dynamited. And miners certainly did attempt to defy local and state authority. In Chisholm and in Eveleth, hundreds of new immigrants gathered to secure the release of miners who had been arrested.[62]

However, it would also be a mistake to presume that the I.W.W. simply dropped in to take leadership over a spontaneous eruption of working class militancy. The I.W.W. had a large organizational presence on the Iron Range through the split in the F.S.F., which resulted in the significant I.W.W. paper *Industrialisti* and control over the Work People's College (*Työvaen Opisto*), both based in Duluth. There were significant numbers of I.W.W. supporters in all the Iron Range towns, and debates between the Wobblies and their opponents in the F.S.F. were common. In the strike rank-and-file miners forced cooperation among the competing leadership. Prior to the strike, Finnish Wobblies had asked the I.W.W. to send organizers to the Range, and in particular leaders who could speak Italian and the South Slavic languages. But evidence from elsewhere in the country suggests that the I.W.W. held a strong appeal to Italian and South Slav workers in the U.S., with both groups having Wobbly newspapers (there were Wobbly papers written in three South Slavic languages: Slovenian, Serbo-Croatian, and Bulgarian.) And unlike the F.S.F., the F.S.I. had gone over to the I.W.W., taking with it the most important radical Italian newspaper, *Il Proletario*. It appears likely that Tresca had contacts on the Iron Range, as he made his way there rapidly and found accommodations with Italian miners.[63]

The miners faced long odds. Not only did they confront the immense economic power and financial reserves of U.S. Steel, but thousands of hired "gundogs," as the Finns called the steel trust's private security force, in addition to the active opposition of local, county, and state governments. English-language newspapermen publicly baited and printed the names of local strike leaders. Many small businessmen refused striking miners credit. Salvatore Quinto remembered the force of this opposition: "They had all kinds of gunmen they brought up here. The Federal Government was against the people. State government against the people. County government against the people. Our own city police worked with the gunmen and arrested and clubbed the strikers." Indeed, Quinto himself was clubbed and arrested. The solidarity of the strikers remained largely unbroken through September, but with slack season approaching, U.S. Steel was able to wait the miners out.[64] In the wake of the strike's defeat, Oliver's blacklist exacted its revenge. This was the fate of Degubellis's husband: "He worked 18 years for the mines and then because he brought up Carlo Tresca they blackballed him ... he never got rehired—him and other Italian boarders we had. He was an anarchist."[65]

Nonetheless, the strike had shown that Iron Range miners were capable of great solidarity and impressive feats of organization—the rapidity with which miners themselves spread and organized the struggle is perhaps most striking. Furthermore, the I.W.W.'s leadership of the strike pointed to the impasse that the mainstream labor movement, the A.F.L., had reached on the Iron Range and that new immigrants were ready to fight under a radical banner. Taken together with the I.W.W.–led strike in 1913 McKee's Rocks, the meteoric performance of the I.W.W. on the Iron Range seemed to hold serious implications for the steel industry as a whole. In the event of a large steel strike, would the I.W.W. provide leadership? The I.W.W.'s growing influence in new immigrant communities seemed to point in that direction.

In contrast, the enormous C.C.F., containing Illinois, was solidly organized by the U.M.W., including the new immigrants. Yet the U.M.W. had to contend with a growing mood of militancy among miners, which manifested itself in local strikes and worker loyalty to the local over the international union. In interviews with the C.I.R., immigrant coal miners from Springfield expressed support for the U.M.W. and its Trade Agreement, but upon questioning they affirmed that their primary loyalty was to the local in the matter of striking. Joe Petrouth matter-of-factly told the C.I.R. that he "had to join the union before I could get a job." Petrouth told investigators that he read and understood union proceedings and the Trade Agreement, but that he couldn't "remember what the agreement says about striking," concluding that if "everybody says strike I have to strike too." Another Lithuanian coal miner from Springfield made similar comments: "I haven't read the agreement and don't know whether or not it says not to strike. If the members of my local say to strike, then I have to strike." A third Lithuanian miner, Tony Caspar, who had worked in a Scottish coal mine before making his way to Illinois, summed up a very bread-and-butter attitude toward the U.M.W. in response to a questionnaire posed by the C.I.R. It is worth quoting at length:

> I like the union; it helps me in every way. In strike times it takes care of me.... The Lithuanians laborers at the unions where I am employed put me on the mine committee because they could explain their grievances to me and I could take them up with the foreman. I don't know much about the agreement except what my friends tell me. It is only printed in English and I can't read it. It states how much money we shall receive for working in the mines and tells us what to do when the company doesn't furnish rail. The agreement is sure a good thing and so is the constitution.... I don't think the agreement says not to strike. If the company don't give what the miners like, I have to strike.

The U.M.W. had achieved a high degree of organizational cohesion, but as Caspar's comments make clear, in the minds of many workers, solidarity trumped contractual obligation. Prior to 1919, this was expressed primarily in struggles between miners and individual operators.

Moreover, the U.M.W. faced both support and opposition from the left. In the Illinois coalfields, the I.W.W. had won a small following among new immigrant miners, many of whom no doubt "bored from within" their U.M.W. locals. Frequent letters from Illinois coal miners to *Il Proletario*, the Italian-language paper of the I.W.W., provide a glimpse of some of this oppositional sentiment. Suggestive is a letter from a miner from Cedar Point, Illinois, who was campaigning among his coworkers for a general strike: "Miners attacked the 'yellow unionism' of the 'fakers' of the U.M.W., they fought against not just the sanctity but the whole notion of labor contracts, and they denounced the control of local unions by smalltown petty office-holders."[66]

Conclusion

Nineteen-fourteen set into motion a chain of events that accelerated an earlier movement among new immigrants toward labor militancy and radicalism. The war in Europe altered the economy first by deepening the depression that had emerged in 1913, and then, beginning in 1915, by promoting an economic boom. The war also sharply constricted immigration and return migration to Europe. The combination of demographic stabilization and economic boom helped prepare the strike wave that lasted from 1916 until 1922. A Lithuanian letter writer to *Naujienos* captured this transition. Nineteen-fifteen, he wrote, "was the worst year for us. We walked from factory to factory, ragged and hungry, and begged the capitalists to be kind and have mercy on us by giving us jobs, but instead of giving us jobs their hired servants split our heads with clubs." But 1916 was different, "an opportune time to win our fight, and we will probably never have such an opportunity again."[67]

The Mesabi Range strike of 1916 provides an example of the sort of labor struggle that would typify the coming years. From the perspective of U.S. Steel, which had successfully rooted out the craft unions from the steel industry, it was ominous that the strike was led by the I.W.W. On Minnesota's Iron Range, labor militancy—the bread-and-butter struggles of new immigrant workers—intersected in explosive fashion with Wobbly radicalism, which had been developing over the previous years in new immigrant communities. The strike went down to defeat, but it was not the first or the last shot in the developing contest between rank-and-file workers and their employers. Taken with the broader industrial strike activity from 1914 to 1916, it pointed toward a convergence of labor militancy and radicalism among new immigrants.

However, the intervention of world history had not finished with the eruption of war in Europe in 1914. In 1917 and 1918 the historical context of immigrant labor in the coal, iron and steel industries was about to be radically altered again, first by "preparedness" and then U.S. entry into World War I, which led to intense loyalty and Americanization campaigns and powerful efforts to keep workers behind war-related production, and finally by the Russian Revolution, which impacted and changed both new immigrant and American radicalism.

Chapter 3

Securing "the industrial forts of America": 1917–1918

For new immigrant communities, the years 1917 and 1918 were punctuated by two seminal events: U.S. entry into World War I in April and Russia's October Revolution. Both intensified rapidly changing economic and political situations and brought to white heat a number of competing ideological claims on the new immigrants. Among the suitors were American nationalism, old world nationalism fired by the growing likelihood that a number of new states might emerge from the old empires, and various working class ideologies and organizations.

The war quickened the economic recovery that had begun in 1916. Commodity production and finance continued to equip and fund the Allied powers. By the time the U.S. entered the war in April of 1917, full employment had been reached. Acute labor shortage and inflation characterized the 17 months of U.S. involvement. Industrial production and demand for labor increased to unprecedented levels just as millions of workers were taken out of the workforce to fight. Yet the hostilities in Europe had already severed industry from its traditional supply of labor. This acute labor demand coupled with internal factors in the U.S. South—political, economic, and ecological—set in motion the Great Black Migration to the North, changing the racial composition the industrial labor force for decades to come. Mexican and Caribbean immigration also served to fill the void.

In this context, the intense American nationalism of the war was not merely a hysterical overreaction, but aimed to keep new immigrant workers in production behind the war effort and off the picket line.

Yet in spite of the efforts and loyalty of the A.F.L. leadership, workers struck in enormous numbers in 1917 and 1918—over one million each year—including a largely new immigrant general strike of coal miners in Springfield, Illinois. At the same time the influence of radicalism continued to grow. It was in response to the threat of convergence between labor militancy and radicalism that government and corporate officials aimed the unprecedented demand for Americanization.[1]

Americanization tendered a bargain to the new immigrants. On one hand, it seemed to offer a path toward inclusion in the polity. On the other, this potential inclusion required certain exclusions on the part of the new immigrants. Radical visions of a new social order were not part of the bargain. Equally as important, the ways that new immigrants attempted to redress social grievances arising from the mines and mills—long solidarity strikes, strikes for worker control, and whole-community labor struggles—could not be tolerated by the new American nationalism. Redress of social grievances could come only as part of national salvation—the victory of the U.S. in Europe. In the meantime, workers could challenge injustices only through "good trade unionism" of the A.F.L. This entailed deference to contractual obligation and the greater good of victory abroad, a vision of organized labor that came very close to enjoying officially-sanctioned status during the months of U.S. involvement.[2]

In essence the whole project of Americanization aimed to eviscerate working class struggle and to temporarily blur the sharp social and racial divisions that characterized the Progressive Era. However, as Gerstle and Barrett have noted, this language of Americanization did not vanish in half-lives hermetically contained by their designed aim.[3] Workers and unions appropriated the language and harnessed it to their own uses. Whatever its purposes, the language of U.S. nationalism could not paper over, not even during the war years, sharpening social divisions. The continued labor militancy of the new immigrants most clearly expressed this failure. Hence, the Janus-faced character of Americanization—always conjoined to a shrill and oppressive nationalism that brooked no opposition or disloyalty, real or imagined, and which was increasingly directed against the new immigrant communities; a nationalist reaction that grew in tandem with the very labor militancy it failed to offset. Increasingly the period's labor struggles were associated with "foreigners" while political radicalism, such as that espoused by the S.P. and the I.W.W., were portrayed as "Bolshevist" imports from abroad, despite strong American pedigrees in both cases. As the U.S. prepared for entry into World War I, labor strife, socialism, and "foreignness" morphed seamlessly in the public eye.[4]

The melting together of radicalism, worker militancy, and "the foreign" aimed to make illegitimate workers' struggle. Yet looking beneath the hysteria, was there actually any basis in reality for such claims? Were new immigrant workers, tens of thousands of whom were indeed engaging in militant strikes, actually operating under some degree of foreign radical inspiration? In general, accounts have looked upon the frantic calls of foreign "Bolshevism" advanced by the mainstream press, the state, and business elite of the period as a forerunner of McCarthyism, and that working class struggles were carried out over purely bread-and-butter issues.[5] According to this outlook, the hysterical response to the strike wave was out of proportion to whatever popular support radicalism might have had in the new immigrant communities and beyond.

Yet radical working class ideologies, even forms of internationalism, exerted a significant influence in new immigrant communities. The appeal of the Russian Revolution on new immigrant workers was significant. Indeed, the association of labor militancy and political radicalism with immigrants had three mutually-reinforcing bases in reality. It was readily apparent that immigrants provided the backbone of the period's major strikes. Second, labor radicalism generally, and revolutionary socialism in particular, enjoyed an apparently widespread and growing appeal among new immigrants. Third, the Russian Revolution seemed to reaffirm the foreign and dangerous nature of socialism and worker militancy.[6]

Despite the Russian Revolution's obvious significance even in the U.S., most analyses have focused on its impact on either foreign policy questions or the ways in which the leadership in the S.P., the I.W.W., and the A.F.L. reacted. Scholars have shown the revolution's seismic impact on both foreign policy and worker organizations, but have tended to view the Russian Revolution as a shock from without that registered primarily at the upper echelons of the state and labor. Yet the U.S. was simultaneously experiencing its largest labor upsurge to date. This chapter therefore seeks to shift focus by considering the Russian Revolution's influence on new immigrant workers, and in turn the ways in which new immigrant radicalization and strike militancy impacted the organizations and leadership of the U.S. working class, an act which played out in the shadow of American entry into the war.

Labor Turnover and Industrial Organization in War

Three related problems characterized the labor situation during 1917–1918, all stemming from a situation of virtual full employment, economic boom, and the need to mobilize industry behind the war effort: strikes, labor turnover, and the rising cost of living. The labor shortage allowed workers to either strike or "vote with their feet." A prime impetus to both forms of labor protest was the spiraling cost of living, as wage increases and massive corporate profits were shifted onto consumers.[7]

While over one million workers struck in both years, it is difficult to get a sense of the level of labor turnover. This is true for a simple reason. Prior to World War I no thought was given to labor turnover as a "problem." On the contrary, labor turnover or worker mobility—of which mass immigration was a central component—was the unstated labor market policy of industry. This policy presupposed an enormous and expandable pool of labor. In fact, more than policy it was the "common sense" approach to the labor question. It was not viewed as a problem because the interchangeability of lower-skilled workers was the basis of the second industrial revolution, scientific management, and the technological trappings of Fordism. Only under conditions in which the labor market seemed to have reached a finite state, brought on by the war's ending of the new immigration, and in which workers rather than employers seized to their own advantage labor market turnover, did eyebrows begin to be raised. In fact, labor productivity actually *declined* by 10 percent between 1915 and 1918, unusual in times of economic growth. Accordingly, labor turnover became one of the central concerns of the Wilson Administration during the war. The Department of Labor discovered, for example, that for three Chicago meatpacking plants with a large immigrant workforce to maintain employment of 5,219, they were compelled to hire 17,418 workers for the year beginning June 1, 1917.[8]

The Council of National Defense (C.N.D.) studied the problem, conceding that the prevailing industrial viewpoint had been that it was "cheaper to lay off a man than to pay him to do nothing." It now appears astonishing that a government agency could report, as if it were a new discovery, that "lay-offs represent a real loss ... in hiring and breaking [workers] in." Yet seasonal layoffs and multiple jobs were a typical feature of new immigrant life. Though many industrialists thought that layoffs were only temporary, the C.N.D. concluded that "permanent and temporary lay-offs shade imperceptibly into each other." In order to determine turnover rates, researchers concluded that the best measure was the percentage of the total average annual workforce terminated or quitting in any given year, which revealed "the average turnover for a considerable number of factories [and mines] in different industries and different localities in a year of normal prosperity will be found to approximate 100 per cent." In some the number of workers leaving employment in a year actually exceeded the average workforce size, thus producing a turnover rate of over 100 percent. The C.N.D. pointed to the obvious costs to employers in this world of rampant labor mobility, while its proposed remedies pointed toward the social elements of the Fordist economy that was then still in the pains of birth: "Regularizing employment"; "Adjustment of the length of the working day"; "Adjustment of wages"; "The necessity of the centralized employment department"; "Getting in touch with good men"; "Physical tests" and "Mental Tests" for "Sizing up applicants."[9]

What, if anything, did the widespread labor turnover of the war months reveal about immigrant workers' consciousness? At a bare minimum, it demonstrated both dissatisfaction and a recognition that the times made possible job changing. But in the context of the patriotic atmosphere generated by the war, changing jobs was implicitly a political act. Perhaps the reason that labor turnover appeared as a topic of interest for business and governmental authorities for the first time during the war years arose from the atmosphere of loyalty created by war propaganda. Labor turnover not only cost money. In a period when consistent industrial production was considered indispensible to the war effort, it suggested disloyalty.

To ensure as much labor peace and stability in the workplace as possible, the Wilson administration experimented with a labor regime that bore many of the trappings of the sort of social contract that would come to characterize the Fordist economy that endured from the late 1940s through the 1970s. This was characterized by increasing wages, a neutral predisposition toward A.F.L.–style organized labor, and governmental adjudication of labor disputes. This social contract was to be put in place and monitored by several new bureaucracies: the C.N.D., designed to subordinate industrial production to the war effort; the War Industries Board, designed to implement rationalized production methods; the President's Mediation Committee, designed to study and head off labor disputes; and the Fuel Administration, designed to monitor production and distribution of coal.

The Wilson administration well understood that for the war effort the coal industry would be of decisive importance. Furthermore, due to the industry's history of union-management collaboration, it also offered something of an ideal test case for industrial relations writ large. On October 6, 1917, the U.M.W. and operators of the C.C.F., in a joint meeting with Wilson's Fuel Administration, hammered out an agreement whereby workers secured a ten cent per ton wage increase and a .75 cent to one dollar increase for day laborers. The *quid pro quo* in the government's intervention in the coal industry to secure "industrial peace"—the wage conference was precipitated by a series of summer wildcat strikes throughout the C.C.F.—was that prices paid to the operators would have to at least outstrip the costs of higher wages. (Disastrously for the long-term health of the U.M.W., another element of the *quid pro quo* was that the union would desist with unionization efforts in the low-wage Appalachian region during the course of the war.) This pact, which was magnified across the industrial economy, ran ashore on the rocks of inflation and the resistance of workers. Inflation was further exacerbated by the enormous economic demand generated by the warring states of Europe and the U.S. military. In this way, in spite of wage gains, workers, along with the middle class, had to foot much of the bill through increasing prices for basic commodities, such as coal for heating, food, and clothing. Price increases gobbled up wage increases, and then some, and the attempted pact with labor slowly transitioned from being an avenue for industrial peace to a destabilizing force, even during the war years. Though the infant social contract was stillborn, it did not prevent the government and unions from striving to lessen strike activity—so long as the war lasted. But in the coal fields, these efforts brought the unions into conflict with miners.[10]

By the end of 1917, some 8,400 Illinois coal miners had joined the military. Inflation gobbled up wage increases, reducing miners' pay by 20 percent in real terms between 1914 and 1919.[11] U.S. coal companies hoped that World War I might clear the way toward the level of consolidation and recapitalization that had occurred in the steel industry and other sectors of the economy after the merger craze of the 1890s. Though during the war years the operators enjoyed a period of unprecedented profit, in their aim of consolidation the coal men were to be disappointed. The C.N.D., founded in 1916, provided a mechanism for industrial interests to voluntarily comply with state management in numerous industries in the interests of subordinating domestic

Table 2. The Cost of Living, Using 1900 as the Base Year.

Year	Index
1898	100
1913	137
1914	139
1915	136
1916	149
1917	179
1918	218
1919	247

Source: Paul Douglas, *Real Wages in the United States, 1890–1926* (Boston: Houghton Mifflin, 1930): 140–143. These statistics are considered the most reliable, although Douglas did not count rent in calculating inflation.

Table 3. Wages in the Bituminous Coal Industry, 1913–1919. Real Wages Based on 1890–1899 Base of 100.

Year	Days Worked Average	Daily Wage Average	Annual Wage Average	Real Wages
1913	232	2.72	631.04	121
1914	195	2.78	542.15	122
1915	203	2.90	588.70	129
1916	230	3.26	749.86	134
1917	243	4.02	976.86	137
1918	249	4.86	1,210.14	136
1919	195	5.63	1,097.75	139

Source: Paul Douglass, *Real Wages in the United States, 1890–1926*.

production to military need. For the coal industry, the voluntary subcommittee springing from the C.N.D. was the Committee on Coal Production (or Peabody Commission), headed up by Illinois' leading coal operator, Francis Peabody, and including nine other significant operators along with former U.M.W. head John Mitchell, as well as a few governmental and consumer representatives. The Peabody Commission worked feverishly in early 1917 to organize the operators and to work out transportation bottlenecks in the distribution of coal.[12]

Even so, during the war the coal industry, perhaps more than any other, came under scrutiny for "profiteering." This was no doubt due to the fact that millions of consumers were dependent upon coal—usually anthracite—for heating. Inflation affected families and small industrial consumers disproportionately. Larger industrial consumers—railroads and steel plants for example—either controlled their own mines or exercised an ability to defuse inflation through annual contracts. Therefore the extra costs of production were shifted onto the small-scale industrial consumers, who saw coal prices go up by between 200 and 400 percent from 1916 through 1918. This price increase engendered a public backlash against a supposed "coal trust," which made industry attempts to consolidate politically unpalatable in Washington. Indeed, the coal operators became a target for the Wilson Administration to augment its "Progressive" and "trust-busting" credentials, even as Wilson shelved most anti-trust activity. Thus, in 1917 the Wilson administration shifted gears from toying with the idea of encouraging operators' efforts at cooperation—which the U.M.W. enthusiastically supported—to launching high-profile cases against "price-fixing" of coal. Indeed, that Wilson found the coal industry such an easy target stands testament not to its monopolistic nature, but on the contrary to its relative weakness and disorganization.[13]

Sections of big business and industry were committed to what we might call a "cheap coal policy." The production of cheap coal was an organic process in the so-called "captive" mines, owned by vertically integrated railroads and big industrial interests who consumed all their own coal. But for the thousands of small independent mine operators, it was the constraints placed upon them by rival sections of business and finance that prevented the industry, even during World War I, from following the trail of monopolization blazed by U.S. Steel two decades earlier. The needs of the U.S. Navy for cheap coal also contributed to the policy in the war years.

A third factor was at play. The decisions of government leaders—Federal Trade Commission (F.T.C.), the Wilson Administration, and the Congress—to effectively bypass the Peabody Commission demonstrated a tacit recognition that the chaos in coal production could not be resolved by the "jawboning" and panels of important men that were the stock-in-trade of Progressive Era corporatist reform. Nor could it be left to the market, given its importance to industry and the war effort. Something much bigger and bolder was required. The government would take over pricing, the operation of the mines, and the transportation arteries—railroads and waterways—that distributed the nation's leading fuel. This was accomplished through the Lever Act of 1917. To be sure, this was negotiated with the coal operators on a "cost plus" basis to ensure profit. Nonetheless, *Coal Age*, the industry's leading journal, condemned the measures spelled out by the F.T.C.—eventually enshrined in the Lever Act—as "extraordinary and revolutionary." Indeed, the war measures for the coal industry came close to the nationalization of the industry. It all begged the question: if in fact the coal barons stood as an impediment to rationalization, and if in the midst of a national emergency only the federal government could play the role of rationalizing the industry, then why not just nationalize coal and the railroads altogether? Through the logic of war mobilization in the coal industry, the Wilson administration had inadvertently given new impetus to a left-wing rallying cry of the U.M.W.: public ownership. Among coal miners, the demand for nationalization had great purchase.[14]

The coal industry provides only one vivid example of a federal government set on mobilizing and organizing the productive forces behind the war effort. It was more or less true of the entire economy, during a moment that "locked the administrative structures of business and government tightly together."[15] In the steel industry, the operation went more smoothly. For U.S. Steel, the war afforded escape from the anti-trust scrutiny of the federal government. Rather than reversing the trend toward monopoly, the war—as was the case in the coal industry—led to a sort of *de facto* mega-monopoly under the supervision of the federal government.[16] The War Industries Board fixed prices for all iron and steel production, guaranteeing profit to steel makers along the way. "National unity" and "mobilization" thus eviscerated the anti-corporate characteristics of Progressive reform. And indeed, no major indictments against large corporations were handed down during the war years; a pending case against U.S. Steel was ultimately resolved to the corporation's benefit after the war. The chief characteristics of progressivism, which in the years prior to U.S. entry had found difficulty cohabitating in one movement, could now be unified with terrible force—reform of bureaucracy and government, the application of scientific organization and rationality to economic and social problems, the decisive agency of educated professionals in leadership, an effort to ensure social peace through concessions to the working class, defense of the overall interests of capitalism, and a patriotic zeal animating all efforts.[17]

While the government coordination of industry during the war aimed to ensure profit, and thus appeared to be a reversal of the anti-trust credentials of the Progressive Era, it also lent inspiration toward nationalization. As Edwards puts it, "in effect, the corporations were granted a crucial five- or six-year period in which they were not only permitted but actually encouraged to coordinate their policies." On an even more fundamental level, as the examples of coal mining and even the steel industry show—in the latter the federal government "undertook the allocation of orders and the distribution of products according to urgency and need"—the federal government under the Wilson administration had in effect taken a mighty step toward an entirely different principle of social organization. The wartime organization of production, distribution, consumption, and finance could only take place effectively if the entire process were taken out of the hands of the industrialists. This appeared to be the negation of the free market. Or, more precisely, it had stripped the market principle to its essence—domination and profit.[18]

Loyalty and Immigrants

As even the discussion of labor turnover reveals, the labor question was irrevocably bound up with the question of loyalty. The mobilization for loyalty under the banner of "Americanization" represented the unified stance of the newly-minted Progressive Era corporatist state to what was in fact a real threat to the project of U.S. hegemony abroad. The "internal" threats to U.S. involvement was the combination of pacifism, ambivalence, and isolationism that characterized a large majority of the population and the electorate as the Wilson administration attempted to push the nation toward a war footing. This largely inchoate anti-war feeling was if anything stronger in the older immigrant groups. The two largest national groups in the U.S., the Germans and the Irish, respectively, had obvious reasons for not wishing to be involved—the former as the likely "enemy" nationality, the latter as a nationality hostile to the likely U.S. ally, Great Britain. Nor could the hypocrisy of a war for "democracy" abroad be lost on African Americans, comprising close to 15 percent of the nation's population—another suspect population and soon-to-be-target of federal surveillance—who were the victims of a quasi-colonial racial caste system in the South and of segregationist and occupational repression in the North. Farmers, then still the majority of the population, tended to be hostile to U.S. entry, in spite of the short-term economic benefits that could be accrued by feeding and clothing a large army.[19]

The majority of new immigrants from Eastern Europe, including Jews, could at least be tempted by the possibilities presented by nationalism and liberation from the oppression of the "prison camps of nations," to borrow a term from Lenin—the Russian, Austro-Hungarian, German, and Ottoman Empires. And for the Italians, the largest new immigrant group, *la patria* fought on the side of the Allies. Thus, there should have been no *a priori* assumption, based on nationality, that new immigrants were less loyal to the war cause than much more "Americanized" segments of the population. Why did the new immigrants suffer so much wartime repression?

The basic question was not merely that the new immigrants spoke other languages or that they didn't seem to be entirely dedicated to the new country, but that they held "the industrial forts of America," as the prominent Americanizer Frances Kellor put it upon visiting Chicago in 1916 during Wilson's preparedness campaign. There were many new immigrants, of course, but their potential power went far beyond their numbers. Illinois steel and coal, for example, were crucial to war production, but most of the labor in both industries was supplied by new immigrants. In South Chicago of the Calumet region—if anything, the industrial fortress *par excellence*—with a workforce dominated by new immigrants, only 346 immigrants had been naturalized in the five years leading up to 1917. Kellor was alarmed, meanwhile, that in the nearby coal mining town of Streator, immigrant miners had struck and interpreters had to be brought from Chicago "to learn what the trouble was about." Americanization was an ideological antidote to counter class divisions coming to a head in the strike wave that, due to the enormous growth of the new immigrant section of the working class, increasingly refracted along national lines. The *Chicago Daily Tribune* articulated the gravity of the problem, arguing that "if we fought a war to prevent a geographical division," referring to the Civil War, then the country should make "mighty effort to prevent a more insidious and fatal division"—emerging from the mines and mills.[20]

The effort involved in monitoring, disciplining, and propagandizing the new immigrant groups in the U.S. was indubitably one of the most far-reaching and coordinated bureaucratic mobilizations of expertise and government-corporate cooperation in history. It involved federal, state, and local governmental agencies coordinating propaganda, police, espionage, and military groups at every level, all controlled from the upper echelons on down by corporate experts. The most important of these organizations was the Committee on Public Information (C.P.I.), headed by the progressive George Creel, which was primarily responsible for propaganda efforts. On top of that came new forms of coordinated volunteerism, for example the Loyalty Leagues and the deputized vigilantes of the American Protective League (A.P.L.) who counted as many as 250,000 members in their ranks. Special efforts were taken in areas where immigrant workforces might control critical elements of the industrial economy, Kellor's "industrial forts." Yet, as Weinstein notes, at first repression was most severe in old bastions of native U.S. socialism—the Southwest socialist strongholds of Oklahoma, Kansas, and Texas, as well as small towns. This repression helped to accent the growth of the new immigrant portion of the S.P., and also tended to weaken the leftwing part of the native element.[21]

The Calumet steel area, downstate Illinois coal mining, and Minnesota's Iron Range were all critical industrial fortresses, and special efforts were taken to control them. The C.P.I. recruited a number of professors and language specialists from the universities of Illinois and Minnesota to monitor the foreign language press. These professors worked *gratis*, and apparently zealously, searching for "disloyal" writing. Finding translators could be difficult depending on the language. Solon J. Buck of the Minnesota Historical Society reported to the C.P.I. that he had "followed up several leads in an effort to get someone to read the Finnish papers, but without success as yet." Perhaps so as not to disappoint his correspondent, he did report a pair of English-language newspapers as being "pretty nearly disloyal" or "on the border line."[22]

Fierce repression was doled out to the new immigrant radicals. The most important of these were the Alien and Sedition Acts and the postal restrictions on the radical and new immigrant press. Among other restrictions, foreign language newspapers were required to submit English language translations to the Postmaster General; within several months, several had lost their third class postage rates. The attorney general also took away second class postage rates for anti-war publications. The new immigrant press had either to comply with these egregious restrictions on freedom of speech, or be shut down, as was the case with Italian and Hungarian I.W.W. papers in 1918.[23]

The subordination of the A.F.L. to the state during the war bore directly on the questions of whether or not, or when, to organize the steel industry, and whether or not the U.M.W. would seek to expand its control to non-union areas. Union attempts to maintain industrial peace at the same time created conflict between rank-and-file strikers, oftentimes new immigrants, and union leaders. A.F.L. loyalty was a top-down process, finding its most fervent support in the upper rungs of leadership. The Wilson administration formed the American Alliance for Labor and Democracy (A.A.L.D.) headed by Samuel Gompers, who soon became one of the most zealous and indefatigable supporters of the war. Creel considered the A.A.L.D. "our most important body." In fact, nearly the entire union bureaucracy, only a year or two earlier avowedly anti-war, had by the end of 1917 been converted into a pro-war body that sought, just short of a no-strike pledge, to keep workers in production and off the picket line. Rank-and-file union members tended to be hostile to the war, at least prior to U.S. entry. Simeon Larson captured the outlook of the proto-typical organized worker toward war:

> [o]pposition to the military was deeply ingrained, emotional, a part of its folklore, and based on historical experiences. Anti-militarism was as much a part of the ideology of the working man as craft unionism was an integral part of the American Federation of Labor.... [T]he military were not impartial representatives of all the people but an instrument in the employ of big business to be used for strikebreaking purposes. Memories of the industrial battles of the past, of the union men and women killed by the military, of the Ludlows and the Calumets, were constantly rekindled in the union press as reminder to the workingman of the dangers of an America rearmed.

The task confronting the A.F.L. leadership ran deeper than merely countering pacifism and the persistent will to strike to improve conditions among workers, but to extirpate a deeply held *consciousness* among workers about the nature of the military and war, lessons learned earlier at bayonet point.[24]

Organized labor realized significant short-term gains as a result of its adhesion to the wartime state. The state maintained a more neutral disposition toward labor during the war, and this likely contributed to rapid increases in membership for the A.F.L. State agencies intervened to arbitrate labor struggles in an effort to avoid strikes that might damage the war effort, and in many cases they offered rulings or guidelines that responded favorably to workers' demands. Wages grew substantially during the war, both for union and non-union workers, although commodity inflation consumed these gains and then some. However, far more important in determining the growth in wages, union membership, and the successful conclusion of strikes were the efforts of workers themselves and the favorable conditions of full employment caused by the war. The working relationship the A.F.L. enjoyed with the state was a secondary, if still important, factor. Moreover, most of the gains made by labor during the war would be rolled back within a few years of its conclusion.[25]

War and the Russian Revolution: American Radicalism's Ground Zero

> The war brought further mass desertions—this time primarily from the right-wing elements, who were finding the struggle for socialism far more difficult and dangerous than the program of reformist gradualism had made it appear. At the same time, the war, and then the Russian Revolution, also brought a new influx of foreign-born workers who swelled the membership of the language federations and provided a new base of support for a reinvigorated left wing.... This new left wing, armed with the great ideas of the Russian Revolution, fought far more effectively than its predecessor.[26]

The S.P., in particular, benefited from its opposition to the war—at least prior to U.S. entry. This was based on an influx of new immigrants. After watching its membership and electoral fortunes stagnate from 1912 through 1916, the S.P., in the wake of its firm and overwhelming opposition to war declared at its St. Louis convention in the Spring of 1917, witnessed a rapid growth nationally, even as some right wing elements supportive of Wilson dropped out. It was not alone, however. Dubofsky has estimated that the I.W.W. grew from 40,000 to as much as 100,000 from 1916 to 1917, while Montgomery states that fully one sixth of all strikes in 1917 were carried out under the I.W.W. banner. The A.F.L. had also entered a period of rapid growth, with new immigrants comprising a large proportion of the new members.[27]

In Chicago's spring municipal elections, the local branch of the S.P. took more than one third of the vote, its highest ever tally, while "new members joined the party in droves." Weinstein notes that the common feature of the growth of the socialist vote nationwide in 1917 was the increase of working class support. In cities with large immigrant populations, such as Chicago and New York City, the S.P. did well—but in 1917 they also did well in middling cities and small towns with small foreign-born populations. The rapid growth of the S.P. in Chicago propelled the local Democratic and Republican slates to prepare a unified slate for the upcoming fall elections.[28]

Within the growth of the S.P., however, two countervailing tendencies played against each other. On one side stood the rapid growth of the new immigrant/working class section of the party, and on the other, the stagnation and decline of the middle class, American and old immigrant portion, which had historically been dominant. Indeed, prior to World War I the S.P. had vacillated between indifference and opposition on the question of immigration. Immigrants had formed foreign language sections of their own accord beginning in 1906, but the right wing, led by Berger and Hillquit, favored limiting mass immigration, a position derived from their orientation to the A.F.L. and skilled workers. The growth of the S.P. resulted from the movement of new immigrant industrial workers into its ranks, in spite of, rather than because of, any official party position on immigration. By 1917, the foreign language federations had come to comprise over half of all membership, increasing from 35 percent before the war, and from almost zero in 1905. The growth of S.P. support in Chicago between 1917 and 1919 was based largely on this new immigrant influx.[29]

In Illinois coal towns the S.P. got its strongest support from Italians and Lithuanians, while the pro-war hysteria weakened the centrist leadership, and caused an open break between Walker, who joined the state C.N.D., and Germer, who criticized the war. In Chicago, the Cook County Socialist Party expressed enthusiastic support for the Russian Revolution. At the same time, it saw an influx of new immigrants into its ranks. The war issue provoked a split in the socialists of the mill town McKeesport, Pennsylvania. While the foreign language federations grew, the "American" section dropped from over 500 to just over 100 after the war. Taken at the national level, the growing support of unskilled new immigrant workers and the growing weight of the foreign language federations—elements who enthusiastically supported the Russian Revolution and tended to view the Bolshevik Party as a model—tipped the scales inside the party to the left, preparing the way for the power struggle that would eventually splinter the party along reformist and revolutionary lines. The growth of the radical left, in other words, was the ideological expression of an underlying social process.[30]

Such a rivalry emerged within the S.P. of Wisconsin, arguably the strongest state-level party in the country, between the German-dominated state party centered in Milwaukee, home base of Victor Berger, and the Finnish socialist chapter of Superior. The "Twin Ports" of Duluth and Superior were the most important urban center of the Lake Superior iron mining and timber milling region, and the link between the Iron Range and the steel milling centers of the lower lakes. They were also centers of Finnish urban life and radicalism. Controversy had already emerged among Superior socialists in 1916 between the Finns, on one hand, and Swedish and American socialists on the other, when the English-language section, with the consent of the Swedish socialists, decided to scrap the traditional May Day parade, already buckling under the patriotic pressure brought to bear by Wilson's preparedness campaign. The Finnish socialists denounced the decision. The city's socialists were divided into three language factions—Finnish, Swedish, and English, with the "old immigrant" Swedes forming a conservative bloc with the latter.[31]

In early 1917 this controversy between left and right, "new immigrant" and "American" simmering in Superior was extended to the state party. Finnish Socialists condemned the qualified war support given to the Wilson administration by members of the S.P. in the State Assembly in a vote, and likewise criticized the tactics which the state party advised in opposing the war. The secretary of the F.S.F. of Superior wrote the state party:

> We have read in the "Milwaukee Leader," that the Socialist members of the assembly have voted aye on [the war] resolution. It is further said, that "Senator Arnold stated the position of the Socialists as follows: 'We are, therefore, opposed to war unless a very good reason exists. But if a crisis should come and result in war you will find that the socialists will be loyal to their country and, as has been the case in Europe, will rush to their country's defense....'" [Y]ou did not mention anything about the principal thing: Opposing the war.

For the F.S.F. Finns, it was heresy to propose that socialists would support the war in any form. They expressed their ideological certitude by demanding to know whether or not state party had plans to "discipline" the offending Assemblymen.[32]

The impact of the Russian Revolution on the U.S. must be told as part of a larger story of radicalization among workers of the period, which should allow for a fuller understanding of the rifts that were exposed in organizations such as the S.P., the I.W.W., and the A.F.L. In the immediate wake of the Bolshevik revolution, it was rather difficult for labor leaders to criticize it—this was especially true of the I.W.W. and S.P., but even many A.F.L. leaders expressed support.[33] The deep impact that the Russian Revolution had on radical Finns was reflected in a letter sent by Arvid Nelson, a leader of the F.S.F. in Duluth and Superior, to the S.P. of Wisconsin regarding the recruitment of speakers for May Day in 1918. With both the I.W.W. and S.P. Finns attempting to anoint themselves as the true Bolsheviks among the Finns in the U.S., Nelson warned the "Milwaukee socialists" to send someone who could "speak left" and pay homage to the Russian Revolution and the tenets of industrial syndicalism, if the speaker wished contented audiences:

> You will satisfy them [Finnish workers] by injecting considerable bolshevism into your talk and the necessity for Industrial Democracy the world over. Some of the Milwaukee comrades, it appears to me, have not struck the right note here because they have dealt too much on the doings of the Socialist administrations in Milwaukee in their speeches.[34]

Here it appears that the Milwaukee socialists' reputation for "sewer socialism" might not have been an exaggeration—at least to an audience of radical immigrant Finns.

For the Finnish American left, the Russian Revolution was ground zero. The revolution was so popular with the left-wing Finnish workers in the U.S. that it was impossible at first for reformist socialists and the I.W.W. to criticize it; radicals of all persuasions hoped that Finland would remain part of Russia. All factions at first sought to cloak themselves in its mantle. But ideologically it was clear that the Russian Revolution most favored the left wing of the F.S.F. and what might be called the "political" wing of the Finnish I.W.W., grouped around the *Työmies* (Worker) in Superior, along with its west coast companion, *Toveri* (Comrade) in Oregon. These newspapers catered to a primarily unskilled or semi-skilled readership of miners, loggers, and longshoremen, whereas the *Raivajaa* (Pioneer), published in Massachusetts, was reputed to have a readership of more skilled workers. Thus, the Russian Revolution immediately attracted away from the I.W.W. leading figures such as Leo Laukki and Yrjö Sirola. Some of these would emigrate to the young Soviet Union. Laukki did so after skipping bond on I.W.W. benefactors in the wake of the infamous Chicago frame-up trials of I.W.W. leadership.[35]

After the breakup of the Soviet Union in 1991, the media-promoted conception has been that the new nations that emerged were the realization of longstanding popular hatred of Russia. However, evidence from immigrants in 1917 and 1918 suggests that this was not always the case. Lithuanian socialists tended not to view the Russian Revolution as an opportunity for independence. They hoped that Lithuania would federate with the Soviet Union, a position that Finns shared prior to 1918. The association of Lithuanians with radicalism after the Russian Revolution was such that a conservative newspaper felt compelled to respond, although acknowledging there was a basis for the stereotype among workers. Noting that Lithuanian workers were being fired "for no apparent reason," *Lietuva* noted the presence of numerous Bolsheviks groups and the formation of a Lithuanian Workers' Council in Chicago. "Lithuanians are accused of being 'I.W.W.' and 'syndicalists' and are therefore undesirable," it concluded.[36]

Likewise, the sentiment in favor of the Bolshevik revolution was so strong among Ukrainians that it was risky business to even suggest that Ukrainian independence should be achieved, as one editor of the leading Ukrainian newspaper in the U.S. discovered in 1918. An editorial he had written calling for independence was met with such anger from readers that he was fired. Rank-and-file Ukrainian workers rewarded the Ukrainian Socialist Federation's support of the Russian Revolution by tripling its membership between 1917 and 1919, in spite of heavy repression. Among the Russians themselves, a number evidently returned to the mother country in between the two revolutions. Many of these were political refugees, and their return was expedited and in some cases even funded by the Kerensky government, operating through Russian consulates in the U.S. The best known of these return migrants were Trotsky and Bukharin, but evidently the phenomenon reached deeply enough that U.S. military intelligence sent investigators to the Pittsburgh area to report on the matter. In fact, the noted contemporary observer of the Russians in the U.S., Jerome Davis, estimated that 90 percent wished to return in the wake of the revolution, and that most were enthusiastic supporters. Even among Russian subject peoples, a number returned. Radical Finns and Jews went back to assume important positions in the new Soviet government. For Italian radicals, it appeared to "augur the uprising of the American working class"—all factions of Italian radicalism at first cheered the October Revolution.[37]

For Polish nationalists, the Russian Revolution simplified matters. Now the defeat of the Central Powers, Germany and Austria-Hungary, seemed to promise the establishment of a free and independent Poland rather than the strengthening of the Russian Empire. In Chicago, the center of Polish life in the U.S., "Polonia in many ways attempted to out–Polonize the homeland." At the same time, the "feverish atmosphere" created by the Revolution inspired left-wing Poles, who predominated in the P.S.F. The seeds had been laid for the movement of socialist Poles in the U.S. toward communism. Their initial enthusiasm for the Russian Revolution, along with that of other new immigrant language federations, increased suspicion on the part of the S.P. conservative-dominated leadership.[38]

Even if the Russian Revolution helped to propel a general leftward movement of new immigrants into the S.P. and beyond, war and revolution also exacerbated divisions within the various radical new immigrant groups. The experience of the Yugoslav radical community amply illustrates the countervailing centripetal and centrifugal tensions over the question of nationalism. Among Yugoslav workers, the Revolution provoked enthusiasm. The S.S.S.F., which had split into Yugoslav-nationalist and predominately Slovenian factions and a left-wing socialist, Serbo-Croatian faction in the year prior to U.S. entry, went through another round of struggle after the war began. At a special congress of the S.P. held in St. Louis the day after the U.S. declared war on the Central Powers, the two factions of the S.S.S.F. were represented separately. After the majority of the congress condemned U.S. entry, the pro-intervention element quit the S.P. But later in 1919, after the S.P.'s right wing, under Victor Berger and Morris Hillquit, succeeded in drumming out the majority left wing, the pro-intervention faction of the S.S.S.F. reentered, joined by a separate Serbian group, and the left-wing Serbo-Croatian faction joined the larger left-wing S.P. on the outside.[39]

To some extent it appears that the Russian Revolution even inspired experimentation with union and strike organization in the U.S. To the extent it did, it was intersecting with the more profound development of a new spirit in labor struggles. This question is posed first by the rapid increase in factory committees during the period, many in open opposition to official union leadership, but even more explicitly by the emergence of workers' councils, or Soviets as they were called in Russian. It is likely the case that the factory committee and the workers' councils were the spontaneously-generated result of workers' struggles in a period of social and economic upheaval, but this does not preclude the possibility of direct influence by international events. The case of the Toledo, Ohio, workers' council is telling. The name—the "Workers, Soldiers, and Sailors Council"—suggests inspiration born in Petrograd. The Council emerged around Toledo's bitter Overland strike of 1919, and provided the city's heavily new-immigrant population a strike nerve center that spread the strike to other industrial units totaling an estimated 30 percent of the city's population. Another workers' council, calling itself the "Soldiers, Sailors, and Marines Soviet," was formed in Pittsburgh, probably in 1918.[40] The gravity of the Toledo situation was evident in a desperate telegram sent from Judge John M. Killits to Attorney General Palmer: "I beg to say that the situation in Toledo with reference to the Overland strike has been quite desperate.... The plant which employed about 13,000 men has been closed practically all the time for four weeks. Two attempts have been made to re-open it, the last assuming the proportions of a riot as a result of which two men were killed and more than a hundred injured, some severely. The local authorities are powerless and have lost all moral authority."[41]

Inside the Industrial Forts

The national planning and cooperation among the business, government, and labor elite played out in the mines, mills, and factories under conditions of labor conflict. In northeastern Minnesota there was no equivalent to the U.M.W. to mediate between state and capital on the one side and the new immigrant workforce on the other. Fears of radicalism again gripping the miners, as it had only a year earlier in the I.W.W.–led Mesabi Range strike, animated the head of the Minnesota C.N.D. to issue a report to the national office in which he called for the arrest and execution of I.W.W. supporters who were most active in the mines, the timber industry, as well as in the wheat fields of western Minnesota. A military intelligence report concluded that the Iron Range port city of Two Harbors, just north of Duluth, where U.S. Steel had major docks, was "over half socialist," and there were fears that the ore transportation hub could be shut down. The agent said that the Iron Range was a "hotbed" of radical activity and that the Finnish "race" in particular "are practically all socialist" and shouldn't be employed in the iron and copper mines except as a "decided minority." Extensive Finnish resistance to the draft was partly based on the memories of conscription in the czarist army. Hundreds of war resisters disappeared into the woods of northern Minnesota. In one case, over 300 Finns were arrested and charged with draft evasion for organizing "neutrality meetings" in the summer of 1917. The *Ely Miner* lamented that Finnish women "amused themselves and cheered the men in jail by singing Finnish socialist songs." "Slacker" immigrants were also the subject of intense scrutiny and repression in the Illinois coal fields.[42]

One of the most powerful state bureaucracies aimed at monitoring and crushing dissent was the Minnesota Commission of Public Safety (C.P.S.). The C.P.S. in Minnesota and various state and local organizations were called into being in 1917 and 1918 to counter the "foreign," "Bolshevist," and "I.W.W." threat, to enforce the draft, but more important, to keep the crucial iron supply in motion. The C.P.S. determined that Finns were the most dangerous national group. It recruited conservative elements from among business-owning and professional Finns and other immigrant groups to promote war aims among the immigrant populations. Members of Minnesota National Guard, recently returned from service in the failed attempt to suppress the Mexican Revolution, were unleashed on the Iron Range, where they sacked and vandalized Finnish Socialist halls and the Socialist Opera House of Virginia, Minnesota. A new building on the campus of the Work People's College burned at this time, likely the result of arson. In Duluth, a young Finnish worker was tarred, feathered, and then lynched for allegedly refusing to buy Liberty Bonds. The federal government arrested five leading Finns of the I.W.W. in northern Minnesota, placing them in the docket of the frame-up trial of more than 100 Wobblies in Chicago. The defendants were tried, and all were convicted, under the Espionage Act. Military Intelligence investigators worked with local postmasters to monitor what sorts of newspaper immigrant miners, especially the Finns, were receiving. But as radical as Iron Range Finns may have been, military intelligence made similar conclusions about Italian, "Austrian," Lithuanian, Russian, Latvian, Portuguese, Spanish, Mexican, and Japanese workers in various parts of the country.[43]

In areas next to all three industries, there was an orchestrated development of ultra-patriotic "vigilante" groups affiliated with the A.P.L. The term is somewhat misleading, in since these groups oftentimes operated with the tacit cooperation of state authorities. Names varied. In Illinois coal mining towns and on the Iron Range, these were called "100% American Clubs." In Gary, it was called the Loyal American League. By August of 1917 there were 25,000 members of the A.P.L. in Chicago alone. In all three places, the ranks of these organizations were dominated by Anglo-Saxon and middle class elements. "Bank presidents, railroad heads, judges, lawyers, and other captains of industry are zealous workers in this national army of detectives," enthused the *Chicago Tribune*. But there was really "only one qualification," the newspaper explained: "red blooded Americanism and 100 per cent patriotic."[44]

The intense patriotism of World War I was primarily a top-down enterprise designed to overcome opposition to the war in the population at large, and to propagandize and discipline the largely immigrant industrial working class. Yet the language of American patriotism and the changed political climate provided a new language for preexisting rivalries on the local level. Within new immigrant groups, intense pressure was brought to bear to rally to the war cause. This too was a top down process in which generally conservative, middle class, and clerical elements, *i prominenti*, working closely with state authorities, organized loyalty campaigns that featured the buying of Liberty Bonds, parades, and other forms of public and patriotic manifestations. Creel was clear about the importance of the contribution of the middle class new immigrant elements. "The loyalty of 'our aliens,' however splendid it was, had in it nothing of the spontaneous or the accidental," he wrote. "Results were obtained by hard, driving work ... *from the inside*, not from the outside, aiding each group to develop its own Loyalty League." According to one Iron Range mayor, nearly every significant nationality group on the Range had started up some sort of loyalty campaign. The

Finnish anti-socialists, the so-called "True Finn" movement, were strengthened by the atmosphere. The Finnish conservatives created the prototypical patriotic organization, "The Lincoln Loyalty League," that would be rapidly emulated by conservatives in fourteen other new immigrant groups. The same Lithuanian newspaper article lamenting the influence of Bolshevism among workers, exhorted its readers in conclusion, "you are either a loyal American or a traitor. It is no wonder that the immigrants of various nationalities are being watched so carefully. Be loyal! Buy liberty bonds!"[45] Of course, these things were contested on the ground. One meeting of the Slovenian Loyalty League in Ely, on the Iron Range, was broken up by heckling countrymen.[46]

Loyalty and Labor Rebellion: The Springfield General Strike

The interplay of intense patriotism and union politics came alive in the Springfield General Strike. Several working class organizations competed for the allegiance of miners. The area was completely organized by the U.M.W., and the S.P. had considerable support. Anarchism and the I.W.W., too, had attracted the support of some militant coal miners. Jack Battuello, who had joined the I.W.W. as a harvest hand in the West in 1916, was one of these I.W.W. militants. He would later play a prominent role in the formation of Illinois' Progressive Miners of America. Battuello recalled that the I.W.W. was "numerically not too great, but effectively out of this world. We put out more propaganda and more newspapers and periodicals—labor periodicals" in addition to bringing in speakers and staging plays in the area of Mt. Olive.[47]

Coal miners tended to oppose U.S. entry into the war. In 1913 the Illinois U.M.W. passed a resolution calling for a general strike should the U.S. attack or be attacked by another country. U.S. entry into the war "was greeted with very little reaction, either pro or con, in the coal-mining communities of the Macoupin-Montgomery district." There was also more vocal opposition. In Spring Valley, Pietro Negri, an Italian I.W.W. agitator, was arrested after addressing anti-war meeting in a series of towns. The war also provided a new venue for old differences to play out. In the town of Staunton, a naturalized Italian coal miner, Oberdan Severino, was indicted under the Espionage Act for improbably declaring, "I'm against the policy of this Government, and I am a Kaiser man hereafter." Severino, a left-winger in his U.M.W. pit committee, offered a different explanation, claiming that he accused a mine manager of being an "autocrat worse than the Kaiser." Severino was tarred and feathered and driven from Illinois by the local A.P.L. Two days of rioting followed his arrest, with disturbances spreading to Mount Olive, where an Italian-owned saloon was attacked. In the midst of the rioting, the conservative and American element in the Staunton mine combined with the local professionals and middle class elements of the A.P.L. to take over the U.M.W. local. In the spring of 1918, a young German socialist miner, Robert Prager, was lynched by a mob of some 300 for allegedly making disloyal comments. Weinberg believes that the crowd was led by middle class figures, but that miners also participated. The lynching took place in Collinsville, which had been the location of a protracted immigrant wildcat strike only months earlier.[48]

Another hidden rivalry in the coal towns was the growing embrace of cooperativism by U.M.W. miners, which had resulted in a doubling of miners' cooperative stores from 25 in 1915 to 50 in 1917. The cooperatives were in part a response to what miners viewed to be the gouging by local businessmen. But from the perspective of the businessmen, the cooperatives posed a serious threat to livelihood. This tended to push the local businessmen into opposition against the cooperatives, and the socialist ideology that undergirded them. Thus, while the Wilsonian rhetoric coupling democracy and paranoia perhaps tipped the scales toward reactionary elements in the unions and towns—conservative unionists, mine operators, middle class business owners—and it certainly fanned the flames of reaction, it also provided a new language through which pre-existing tensions could be expressed.[49]

The U.M.W. like the rest of the A.F.L. and much of the population, looked upon the carnage of Europe in the war's first year with a mixture of incomprehension and horror, and swore itself against U.S. involvement. But when the U.S. shifted onto a war footing through preparedness, and even more so upon entry, the national U.M.W. enthusiastically adopted the nationalism of the war. In the mining communities of Illinois, it was a different matter. The complex national and racial mix of the labor force—Germans, British, and Irish, in addition to the new immigrants and African Americans—ensured that loyalties would be impossibly divided. These national divisions, moreover, did not correspond in neat ways to the political divisions in the coal communities among Republicans, Democrats, Socialists, and Wobblies, or within the mine locals between militants and conservatives.

The U.M.W. state and national bureaucracies' support of the war, and the silencing of antiwar voices, shifted the ground on which these divisions had hitherto played out. Now an alliance among the state and national bureaucracy, conservative Americanized workers, and small businessmen congealed. Their opponents were militants, often new immigrants, and the pit committees—organs of local workers' control. John L. Lewis, interestingly enough, represents almost a perfect embodiment of the former. Of an Americanized Welsh family, Lewis became a local U.M.W. representative in Panama, Illinois, while his extended family members dominated the town politically. Angry Italian miners wrote to *Il Proletario* denouncing what they called "the Panama cabal," not knowing, of course, that John L. Lewis was destined to become one of America's most important labor leaders of the 20th century.[50]

How can we explain the incessant conflict between union locals and the U.M.W. bureaucracy? The union had provided the engine for the rationalization of coal mining due to the industry's chaotic nature and low bar of capital for entry. The coal operators came to recognize and value the U.M.W.'s contribution, and in turn the union raised the working conditions and living standards of coal miners. In this light, it wasn't incongruous at all for socialists such as Germer and MacDonald to work within the upper echelons of the bureaucracy. The union seemed to be, in the most "practical" way, paving the way for socialism. This was the stuff of Bernstein's evolutionary socialism, whose American standard bearer was Berger. It was no accident that the Illinois U.M.W. socialists became Berger's important allies in the struggle that emerged in U.S. socialism against the left wing during World War I, a struggle that was only temporarily headed off by the exodus of the right wing faction in support of the war effort and Berger's German sympathies.[51]

Socialist leadership or not, the U.M.W.'s role as rationalizer of the coal industry at times brought it into conflict with local unions and pit committees, which represented in a less distilled way the interests of local miners. But the U.M.W. leadership, from its perspective, had the task of representing all coal miners. They viewed the Trade Agreement as the means to accomplish that, but the Trade Agreement depended on the health of the industry overall, which in turn depended on the profits of the union operators. This defense of the Trade Agreement forced the parent union to constantly threaten and cajole the locals, which might have an entirely different set of grievances. This could be done sometimes in the most ham-fisted ways, as when Illinois U.M.W. president Frank Farrington wrote to the heavily Italian, LaSalle, Spring

Valley local, which had, like many other locals in 1917 and 1918, carried out a strike in violation of the Trade Agreement:

> If your local charter is revoked your members will be deprived of all the rights and privileges accorded members of the U.M.W. of America and if any of them should meet with death during the period of revocation or before the expiration of thirty days after your charter has been restored, their heirs will not receive the $250 death indemnity provided.[52]

Farrington's injunction was aimed at miners protesting the use of machinery in the mines. Due to increased profits and the higher cost of labor, use of cutting machinery increased across Illinois during the war. But this was no isolated matter. Ten months later Farrington issued a warning to the "Officers and Members, District 12, U.M.W. of America"—the whole state union—warning that "Operators, both individually and collectively, are complaining most bitterly about the frequency with which spasmodic local strikes occur in violation of our Joint Agreement."[53]

During World War I, the U.M.W. interpreted this collaborationist role more broadly, as a defense of U.S. industry and the whole war effort. This became institutionalized by the tripartite Washington Agreement concluded in October of 1917. Carried out under the auspices of the War Fuel Administration, the U.M.W., and the operators, the Washington Agreement included a no-strike pledge in return for wage increases. Such pacts were not unusual; similar agreements were reached in the meatpacking industry and the railroads, among others.[54] The U.M.W. promised that operators could exact a fee of one dollar per day per striker in the event of a wildcat. This forced the U.M.W. into a constant rearguard struggle against recalcitrant local unions, and tempted it to use the language of patriotism to browbeat and whip into line the locals. Again, Farrington to the Illinois coal miners:

> Our Country is at war. Forced into a conflict that could no longer be avoided ... to the cause of humanity.... America's Allies are now badly crippled by a shortage of coal ... it is instead that it shall be made clear to you that practice of shutting down mines in violation of our agreement to force some desired condition, and of suspending work under every conceivable pretext, must be stopped.[55]

From the late summer 1917 through the early winter of 1918, over 40,000 Illinois U.M.W. miners went out on wildcat strikes. In Collinsville, Illinois, a strike of Italians and "Austrians" dragged on in spite of the socialist local president's demand that they return. Yet without larger organization, organs of workers' control such as the pit committees and union locals couldn't offer an alternative to the U.M.W. Even so, the level of the opposition that emerged in 1917 and 1918 points the way toward the larger-scale rebellions that would take place in the war's aftermath in Kansas, Pennsylvania and ultimately Illinois, which led to the formation of the Progressive Miners of America. The mine workforce continued to engage in wildcat strikes in spite of the Trade Agreement—over 40,000 man hours were lost in Illinois coal mines to strikes between only August and October of 1917. Given the context of the U.M.W.'s loyalty, the wildcats in the coal fields seemed to be politically subversive.[56]

The Springfield General Strike of 1917 illustrated the growing working class militancy of the period. The strike began as a rather prosaic action of street car workers in the summer of 1918. What distinguished it from any number of other similar strikes in the period was the intervention and fierce solidarity of the coal miners of Sangamon County, who without any clear self interest at stake, took the side of the streetcar workers. The Springfield Consolidated Railway Company operated streetcars in and around Springfield. Coal miners used the cars to get to and from work, as well as from coal mining "locations" around the outskirts of the city and to visit and shop in the state's capital. It is also likely that unmarried miners' daughters used the streetcar system to commute to work in Springfield, for example at the city's tobacco factory.[57]

The strike began at the end of July in 1917 when street car employees walked out after the Consolidated refused to negotiate with a union committee. Then, in August, workers understood a settlement negotiated by the Illinois Department of Labor to be a tacit recognition of the union, the Amalgamated Association of Street and Electric Railway Employees of America. On August 12, workers who refused to remove union cards from their hats were summarily dismissed. The resulting strike paralyzed the street car system until the Consolidated succeeded in bringing in the state militia to escort replacement drivers.[58]

The strikers won broad support among immigrant workers in and around Springfield, who participated in picketing and obstructing cars. In early September police attempted to stop a large Labor Day parade in support of the streetcar drivers. Violence resulted in the shooting injury of two marchers, one of whom was a miner. The U.M.W. locals responded with a general strike that shut down 18 of the 31 mines in the Springfield area and put 4,200 miners out on the first day. The strike spread, and shortly included most of Springfield's workers. Nicholas Fontecchio, chairman of the General Strike distanced it from radical aims, but that is not the way the strike was viewed by the media or nervous politicians in the state's capital. Before being called off, the general strike had won the right to parade and the dismissal of the special deputies who had been installed to ensure "peace" during the strike. In July of 1918, an Amalgamated Association organizer came to Springfield in an attempt to have the company reinterpret the August 1917 settlement, aiming to have the fired workers reinstated. This failed and a mass meeting was called for July 14, 1918, endorsed by the Amalgamated Association, the Springfield Association of Labor, and the U.M.W. Some 4,000 workers attended, and the dispute was submitted to the War Labor Board, which ultimately dismissed the case as out of its jurisdiction.[59]

The strike demonstrated how easily a small grievance could escalate and enlist the support of far broader sections of the working population. Nothing approaching a clear victory resulted, but the strength of the miners was such that there could be no discussion of firings or other disciplinary action against them. The strike was also unsanctioned by the U.M.W., which was nonetheless powerless to prevent it, or call it off after it had begun. When the immigrant coal miners entered the fray with a general strike, the state was moved to action out of the fear that it might spread beyond central Illinois. In the context of war mobilization, the strike was invested with far more than its local significance.

Conclusion

The complex interaction of U.S. nationalism, sharp economic change, the Russian Revolution, and old world nationalism had multiple effects on new immigrant communities, but combined to spur on radicalism and labor militancy. Full employment brought on by the war and wage policies designed to secure at once profit margins for business and industrial peace triggered sharp inflation. This accelerated labor turnover and created conditions favorable to striking, in spite of far-reaching efforts to keep workers in production. Indeed, in spite of governmental repression and the cajoling of the unions, over one million workers struck in both 1917 and 1918, labor struggles best epitomized by the rash of wildcat strikes—including the Springfield general strike—that took place in Illinois coal country. The corporate elite and conservative trade unionists feared that this labor militancy might become conjoined with radicalism through the new immigrants. Amidst the economic change, immigrant workers began to feel a growing sense of power and a broadly felt desire to author change. The stage had been set for 1919, the largest and most intense strike year in U.S. history to that point.

Chapter 4

"The Revolt of the Rank and File": 1919

In the year after the war, the nation erupted in its largest strike wave to that point, with 4.5 million workers leaving their shifts. The wartime attempt to fashion labor peace for national unity, never successful during the war, was shattered. Workers, politicized through wartime propaganda and the growing influence of radicalism, and suffering under inflation and pent up wartime grievances, demanded redress. Fearful that the compromises and haggling of the war years might be institutionalized by unionists and reformers, business interests immediately adopted a less conciliatory stance. Within the space of two months, both the nation's steelworkers and its unionized coal miners went out on strike; approximately 350,000 workers were involved in each. The strike wave, coupled with revolutionary developments abroad "seemed just the opening volleys of revolution."[1]

The prominence of the new immigrants in all of this was lost on no one; they were "almost constantly restless."[2] Contemporary observers found it difficult to understand exactly what the immigrant workers wanted, but their actions suggested to most that radical change was at the heart of the matter. While witnesses clearly took note of what *The Nation* magazine called the "revolt of the rank and file,"[3] in the same breath labor leaders often spoke of difficulties in organizing the new immigrants, of their "impetuousness"; that they "do not revere the sacredness of the trade agreement. They will violate it upon the slightest provocation."[4] This purported organizational difficulty actually expressed the conflict between the militant mood of the workers and the conservative, "good trade unionist," tactics of the A.F.L.

Caught between the intransigence of business and the rebellion of the rank-and-file, Gompers and A.F.L. were in a hard spot. Should the

A.F.L. simply stand aside, the growing protest of the unskilled workers—especially the immigrant steelworkers—might proceed regardless, but along other channels. This would in turn threaten the A.F.L.'s position as the sole legitimate representative of labor, which had been nearly officialized during the war. On the other hand, should the A.F.L. assume leadership of the cause of the unskilled, it would jeopardize its new cooperation with government and business. The A.F.L. responded to the twin pressures of 1919 by charting a middle course, attempting to organize the unskilled while using methods aimed to sooth the state and public opinion. This strategy can best be seen in the Great Steel Strike of 1919. The vehicle of the A.F.L.'s intervention would be a loose replica of what historians have called "the new unionism"—a more democratically-oriented industrial unionism that focused on the unskilled—which had emerged around the garment trades, gained inspiration from the U.M.W., and achieved short-term success in organizing Chicago's meat-packing workers. The name given the effort was the National Committee to Organize Iron and Steel Workers (National Committee). Yet the A.F.L.'s attempt to first win support from the Wilson administration hampered the National Committee by delaying the strike.[5]

A similar tension emerged in the Illinois coalfields in 1919. There the cooperation between the U.M.W. and the state was shattered by the enormous bituminous strike that wound up consuming the entire C.C.F. John Lewis hoped to avoid such a scenario, and to carry on the wartime collaboration with coal operators and the government. Yet the wildcats that had taken place in 1917 and 1918 continued after the war at a greater level of intensity. Finally, wildcats led by largely new immigrant locals in Illinois propelled the U.M.W. into the strike that began in November, just as the Great Steel Strike started to wane. The timing, at the beginning of heating season, was more fortuitous. The miners' union articulated ambitious demands, including a near doubling of wages and the nationalization of the mines. They settled for far less, and the stage was set for years of conflict in the C.C.F.

No return of the events of 1916 took place on the Mesabi, perhaps owing in part to the efficacy of the blacklist and spying system that U.S. Steel had put in place. However, on the Vermilion section of the Iron Range, a strike gripped Ely. The strike began at the end of September as the Great Steel Strike was just beginning, when a number of Bulgarian miners walked out of a local mine. Once again, the local Finnish socialist hall provided a nerve center and the I.W.W. the banner. The strikers quickly put out a national call "for English or Slavonic speaker" and formulated demands typical of the heady days of 1919; one of these was "freedom for all class war prisoners." Immigrants held large marches behind both red and American flags. New immigrant women, once again, took prominent positions in these demonstrations, suggesting again the whole-community character of the struggles. In one case, a Slovenian woman was arraigned for attacking a strikebreaker with a broom. A Finnish striker noted that in the past the Finns "have been accused of being the most revolutionary ... many have been 'blacked' so they can't work in the mines." Now, he wrote the socialist daily *Työmies*, the Slavs and Italians participated with even more fervor. "I've been in this area for a long time, and never believed workers could be so unified." But the strike did not spread to the Mesabi, as hoped. Isolated and with slack season approaching, the strike faded in November.[6]

That the I.W.W. headed up of the strike on the Vermillion was the sort of scenario that the A.F.L. wished to avoid in the steel industry. Even though much of the immigrant I.W.W. and leftwing socialist leadership had been imprisoned, labor radicalism haunted the National Committee organization drive in the steel industry. Indeed, accounts from the steel industry suggest that "I.W.W." or "Bolshevist" workers had a significant presence in the mill towns. In the lead-up to the strike, the National Committee rooted out some of these radical workers. Then, during the strike, to mollify public opinion organizers presented the struggle as an "American" affair. This did not satisfy. The strike, in the public eye, was portrayed as both a "Hunky" strike and a radical menace.

Even though the I.W.W. and "Bolshevism" cast a long shadow over the steel strike, the government repression effectively limited the ability of radicals to insinuate themselves in the mass struggles of workers. In 1919 the S.P. and I.W.W. were still reeling from the shocks of the Russian Revolution and wartime repression. Yet among immigrant radicals, there was great confidence that events in Europe and the strike wave in the U.S. heralded revolution. They understood state repression as another sign of revolutionary developments. Just as new immigrants were a militant social force within labor struggles of 1919, new immigrant radicals aligned overwhelmingly with the left in relationship to the controversies developing in American radicalism.

Lessons from the Great Steel Strike

The new unionism came not from Gompers but from progressive elements within the A.F.L., such as John Fitzpatrick and the Chicago

Federation of Labor (C.F.L.), in response to the labor militancy of unskilled workers. The C.F.L., partly based on its experience in the meatpacking industry in the preceding years, determined that the masses of unskilled, mostly foreign steelworkers, stood ready to revolt, and calculated that a broad organizing campaign, provided with the correct timing and resources, could succeed. The A.F.L. gave the venture its blessing and encouraged the myriad affiliated craft unions in the steel industry to support it. However, the A.F.L. offered little money and allowed the organizing drive to go forward only under the proviso that all the turf of the 24 craft unions that comprised the National Committee would be preserved. And Gompers sought to keep the faith with Wilson and business interests by delaying, as long as possible, the strike's onset. By pushing the strike back to early autumn—when it was no longer possible to contain the rebellion from below—the strike was handicapped before it began. With the normal autumn and winter slack months in production just around the corner, "the Steel Trust" had to sit out the workers only for a few months.[7]

Labor militancy was percolating in the steel towns even before the National Committee appeared on the scene. Workers, especially the new immigrants, were ready for a struggle. Only this explains their "stampede" into the National Committee. To take one example, in 1919, in Hammond, Indiana, of the Calumet district, a sudden strike of "foreigners" stormed out of a steel plant after a worker had been dismissed. This brought an investigation from the Federal Mediation and Reconciliation Service (F.M.R.S.). According to an alarmed telegram from a National Committee member, "over one thousand" were out on the streets with "more coming out through the gates every minute." The F.M.R.S. representative sent to the scene found a "very serious" situation. "Foreigners were out on strike with all sorts of foolish ideas in their heads" and no one "had any control over them." "Doctrines" were animating them, such as "Bolshevism and Socialism." He feared that the struggle could rapidly spin out of control: "Foreigners was [sic] just about ready to start and take that whole Industrial District on a Wild Rampage and if that happened they will have to slaughter hundreds of them before they are quieted." If the correspondent exaggerated the threat of mass bloodshed, the explosiveness of the situation in the steel-making region was widely perceived.[8]

It was the anticipation of such spasmodic revolts, and out of fear that they might find radical leadership, that gave the impetus to launch the organizing drive. The National Committee effort to organize the steelworkers began early in 1919, and paid big dividends right away; by spring, 100,000 workers had entered. On August 20, a ballot showed overwhelming support for a strike. Yet, the Wilson administration had pressured Gompers, and Gompers the National Committee, to continue to delay. The strike finally came at the end of September, exceeding the expectations of its organizers. Some 250,000 men immediately answered the call; the figure may have reached as high as 350,000 by the high point, in a strike stretching from Chicago to Pennsylvania.[9]

Suppression of freedom of speech, assembly, and the press characterized the Great Steel Strike across its length. This repression, as we shall see, conflicted with basic democratic notions of "Americanization" that trade unions had promoted, and new immigrants had embraced.[10] Repression prevailed in company-controlled towns, but it was also evident in mill towns and neighborhoods where steel factories dominated and the local political elite, with the backing of state and national politicians, proved itself a supple tool in the hands of the steel corporations. This presented a major problem, for the organization of the strike was impossible without meetings and discussion. To take the fight to the steel towns of the Pittsburgh district where repression was most severe, Foster ingeniously organized "flying squadrons" of loyal union workers that would engage in civil disobedience. Even in U.S. Steel's flagship city of Gary, an ordinance was passed at the beginning of the strike outlawing parades. Approximately 2,000 strikers, led by two hundred uniformed army veterans, marched in defiance of the ordinance. The U.S. Army responded under the direction of Major General Leonard Wood, and "Gary took on the appearance of a city of occupation, with machine-gun squads at all strategic points between the mills and the city and infantry patrols scattered throughout the city." Wood used the resulting public notoriety to position himself for a run for the presidency, losing the 1920 Republican nomination to Harding.[11]

But repression was not the only explanation in the strike's ultimate defeat, for it failed to stem workers' support. Surveying the wreckage of their organizing drive from the vantage point of 1920, A.F.L. officials and outside observers attributed the strike's failure to several different factors. The organizational weakness of the National Committee effort and the strike's delay, to Foster, were decisive. Yet organizers also placed much of the blame on the steel industry workforce, criticizing the impetuousness of the new immigrants, the obstinacy of African Americans, and lack of involvement by the skilled "American" element. While it was the case that the strike's failure owed in part to the racial segmentation of the workforce, it was not only for the reasons that Foster and others thought. The racial problem was in part an expression of the larger political and organizational character of the effort. The National Committee's approach to the various components of the workforce grew out of a conception of the organizing drive that took as its starting point appealing to the Wilson administration and public opinion for support, and winning over the skilled workers. This forced the National Committee to hold back for as long as possible new immigrant industrial workers from striking, a deadly delay. Moreover, by insisting on the "bread-and-butter" character of the strike, the National Committee limited its appeal to African American workers, whose economic situation could not be separated from larger questions of social equality.

In spite of the charge of impetuousness, once on strike, according to most observers, the new immigrants proved to be disciplined. Indeed, as far as the public perception of the strike goes, the fact that new immigrants appeared to dominate it contributed to its being defined as a "hunky strike." Yet public opinion had little to do with the strike's rousing beginning, its long ending and defeat, or the response of the state, which from the federal to local government stood from the first in open opposition. Nor did public opinion lessen the solidarity of the new immigrants. In spite of U.S. Steel's efforts to provoke divisions by pitting different nationalities among the new immigrant workforce against each other, there is little to suggest that this paid dividends. However, there is a significant amount of evidence to suggest that something approaching a three-way division had developed among unskilled new immigrants, skilled "Americans" (mostly old immigrants), and African Americans, who moved north to take jobs in industry in large numbers during World War I for the first time.[12]

The National Committee in large measure failed in its efforts to organize black workers in the steel mills. Thousands used the strike as an opportunity to gain employment previously denied them. In his recounting of the steel strike, Foster dedicated attention to the role African American workers played in undermining the strike. Those already employed rarely struck: "in the entire steel industry, the Negroes, beyond compare, gave the movement less co-operation than any other element, skilled or unskilled, foreign or native." Moreover, 30,000–40,000 African American workers had been employed as strikebreakers, many of whom were recent arrivals from the South.[13]

Of course, there was a good deal of history behind the limited appeal the organizing drive held for black workers. Since its inception, the A.F.L., with few notable exceptions such as the U.M.W., had given little effort to organize black workers, either in the North or the South. Some of the National Committee's affiliated unions maintained segregationist clauses in their constitutions and charters. Moreover, blacks faced a number of pressing issues outside of the mills that the National Committee did not address. Among these was a hardening residential segregation, especially in Chicago, which was still reeling from the great race riot of 1919 when the steel strike came a little more than one month later. African Americans had moved to the Chicago area in large numbers during World War I to find work in rapidly growing industries. Many found jobs in the meatpacking industry, while others made their way, for the first time in significant numbers, into the steel industry.[14]

David Saposs, the trade union reformer and investigator of the Great Steel strike, revealed that trade union organizers' own attitudes likely contributed to the failure to organize black workers. "Some of the organizers felt that the Negroes demanded more than economic equality," he matter-of-factly reported. "One Negro was invited to speak in Cleveland [and] instead of confining himself to the organizing and trade union phase launched into a tirade on social equality. Most of the secretaries and organizers, however, felt that Negroes could be organized and if organized they generally do not demand social equality."[15] In the union indifference toward equality, political realities may have played some role. The A.F.L. hoped to maintain its working relationship with the Democratic Party, a party dominated by southern segregationists, including Woodrow Wilson, and northern machine politicians who oversaw and enforced segregation in cities like Chicago. In any case, "bread and butter" trade unionism held limited appeal to black workers. A more politicized trade unionism predicated upon equality in and beyond the workplace was not then in the offing, and so must be consigned to the realm of the counterfactual. For their part, white radicals remained in the clutches of repression and their own limitations regarding the problems confronting black workers, while immigrant radicals were separated by language barriers. Years later, James Cannon, a Wobbly who later became a founding figure in the American communist movement and later Trotskyism, articulated well the problematic relationship between black workers and U.S. socialism:

> The ninety percent white majority of American society, including its working class sector, North as well as South, was saturated with prejudice against the Negro; and the socialist movement reflected this prejudice to a considerable extent—even though,

in deference to the ideal of human brotherhood, the socialist attitude was muted and took the form of evasion. The old theory of American radicalism turned out in practice to be a formula for inaction on the Negro front, and—incidentally—a convenient shield for the dormant racial prejudices of the white radicals themselves.[16]

Such unstated prejudices revealed themselves in the various investigations into the strikes failure.

Interestingly, the Chicago Commission on Race Relations, which interviewed hundreds of black workers and dozens of employers after the riot, found few examples of workplace friction between immigrants and blacks. Most of the damage and violence perpetrated against blacks during the race riot was on the part of Irish-dominated street gangs or "athletic clubs," that were protected by municipal politicians and the police; there were only a few cases of homicidal violence between blacks and new immigrants. Indeed, the new immigrants had by 1919 accumulated their own long history of friction with the old immigrants, and especially the Irish, who dominated not only the police departments and city halls of many urban centers, but also the A.F.L. unions, the church hierarchy, and school teaching. This was a complex relationship, at once antagonistic and pedagogical. In any case, the "inbetween" neutrality of the new immigrants in the race riot found quite a different expression in the great steel strike, where they were between two groups—skilled old immigrants and black newcomers—who showed far less enthusiasm for the strike than they.[17]

In Gary, blacks had come to comprise ten percent of the city's population by 1920. In terms of residential patterns, they were at least partially integrated in the overwhelmingly new immigrant city, the *Gary Post-Tribune* writing that "the negroes have refused segregation and have blanketed themselves indiscriminately over the whole town." A survey from the period found that there was no district of the city that was more than 90 percent black. And a study by Thyra J. Edwards in 1925 concluded that "Europeans, Negroes, and Mexicans frequently occupy apartments in the same building, the Negroes, perhaps, being the only ones conscious that there is anything unusual in such an arrangement." Indeed, relations seemed by and large harmonious. According to a more recent study, "Eastern and Southern European immigrants at first seemed to consider blacks just another ethnic group.... A Greek Orthodox congregation held its first church services in a small building they shared with blacks. Blacks held political and social meetings in various ethnic halls on the south side. Interestingly, in 1916 a young Gary black man joined his Serbian neighbors who returned to Europe to fight in the Serbian army." Their actions suggest that these new immigrants recognized a shared position in the U.S. industrial hierarchy.[18]

Perplexed by the lack of participation on the part of African American workers on one side and the fervor of new immigrants on the other, A.F.L. observers, among them Saposs, began to ponder ways to "educate" both groups on "good trade unionism." This brought a sharp rebuke from one of Saposs's correspondents, William Leiserson. "Besides educating the immigrant workers, education of the American members to understand and respect those immigrant fellow members is also very important, and more important still is the education of the native leaders of the labor movement," Leiserson wrote. "In addition, it seems to me that the tactics of the American labor movement, their practical methods of organizing and training their membership is at fault and needs revision. You could hardly put that under education." Leiserson understood that if the only "lessons from steel" drawn were to pin blame on the workers, without any analysis of the organization drive's methods and politics, that nothing would have been gained.[19]

In spite of the general lack of support from African Americans, more significant for the strike's failure was the lack of participation by skilled white workers, the "Americans" who in fact tended to be the sons of old immigrants—Irish, German, Scandinavian, and British. They were differentiated by skill and citizenship, and often had affiliation with the craft unions in steel. Native workers participated in the strike in small numbers, and often returned to work soon after having struck. In part this was based on the experience and memory of past defeats and a consequent lack of faith in the viability of trade unionism in the steel industry. The lack of native white solidarity might also be owed in part to their privileged position as a "labor aristocracy" in social proximity to the middle class. Native white workers, according to Saposs, tended to consider themselves "too good to belong to a union with foreigners"; they excluded foreign and African American workers from their vision of labor, and so saw joint action as undesirable and even as opposed to their own interests. Indeed, whereas labor leaders interviewed by Saposs increasingly saw foreigners as easily led astray and impetuous, again and again they attributed the lack of native white participation to "individualism."[20]

A number of "American" steelworkers interviewed by Saposs were not shy in their condemnation of the other sections of the workforce. One native white worker attributed lack of "American" participation to diet: "The foreigners, he said, did not have the same problems because 'they could live on cucumbers and black bread,' but American workers needed a good dinner."[21] An electric crane operator combined the superior material reward of skill with the psychological and social rewards of a privileged racial status: "The bosses run after them [the crane operators] and beg them to stay when they get tired of working sometimes and 'don't care if the world don't move.' They have closed cabs on their cranes, and electric motors, and hunkies to bring them water when they are thirsty.' [...] Every nine out of ten men in the mill have cars, he says. 'How about the foreigners? Do they?' 'Oh, the hunkies? They're only cattle.' He says he wouldn't sit next to a hunky or a nigger as you'd have to in a union." Another native white echoed these sentiments: "How would you like to shake hands with niggers and foreigners, and call them brothers?"[22]

Enemies of the steel strike dubbed it an action taken solely by "radicals and foreigners."[23] In responding to this charge, strike leaders could not deny that the new immigrants represented the vast majority of the strikers. Yet Foster, no doubt in a bid to placate public opinion, publicly insisted that the new immigrant workers fought only for the most immediate, physical needs, and their politics were entirely patriotic. The labor-friendly publication *The New Majority* pushed a similar analysis, suggesting new immigrant strikers understood the essentially prosaic and patriotic nature of the strike. "A strike for shorter hours, for better wages—that was truly American," *The New Majority* claimed.[24] This attitude was reflected in the strike organizers' methods, who, according to James R. Barrett, "employed patriotic symbols and language, stressed the democratic quality of the movement, and wherever possible tied their efforts to American war aims."[25] Moreover, Foster insisted that the National Committee had taken pains to organize the native whites. He described the effort in the following terms:

> It has been charged that the unions neglected the American steel workers and concentrated upon the organization of the foreigners. If anything, the reverse is true; for by far the weight of the appeal made was to the English speaking elements. Every piece of literature put out stressed heavily the English language. Of twenty-five National Committee district and local secretaries, only three were born in Europe; of a dozen Amalgamated Association organizers, not one spoke anything but English, and of the crew as a whole, over 80 per cent were American born."[26]

This shows how, of necessity, unions could be an Americanizing force. But Foster's testimony inadvertently exposed the weaknesses of the National Committee in regards to organizing new immigrant and African American workers. An organizational drive and strike designed to appeal to conservative, skilled, native whites would likely encounter other sorts of difficulties among unskilled new immigrants and African American.

Indeed, in spite of Foster's claims, deeper social grievances were at stake for new immigrant strikers. The politicization and radicalization of the preceding years weighed heavily. In particular, the propaganda of war for democracy, and against "autocracy" and "Kaiserism"— also targets of Eastern European nationalism—seems to have been taken up by new immigrants to meet their own ends. In interviews new immigrants frequently compared the foremen and police to "Cossacks," and the steel management to the "Kaiser" or "Czar." Workers also routinely commented on their own or acquaintances' military service in a war for democracy abroad, only to return to steel mill "hunky work." One worker, interviewed by progressive reformer Mary Heaton Vorst, summed up these feelings:

> You know what the first English is I learn? "Damn Hunkie"—that's what I learn.... But when war come, Hunky good enough to fight. You hear what feller say is difference between government in Austria and government here. He say, there Kaiser rule; here mill boss rule.

Another young man echoed these sentiments:

> What makes an American? Wasn't I born here? Weren't all of us born here? Ain't the boys like my brother Joe who volunteered as good Americans, even if they have got "ski" or "ko" to their names—as good Americans as the fellows called White or Smith? ... They said so while the war was on. You remember the poster "Americans all!" ... The man who made that picture ought to work in Carnegie Steel. He'd learn the different between an American and a "damn Hunky" quick enough![27]

Saposs recognized that the "War for Democracy" had failed to live up to expectations for immigrant workers when he asked one, a recently turned veteran, what work he was now doing: "the same kind of work as the other hunkies" was the response. None of this was a matter of workers cleverly "appropriating" the language of American nationalism. On the contrary, it was the failure of the language of nationalism, the very contradiction between rhetoric and reality, that led to a bitter denunciation of patriotism and to militant labor struggle.[28]

Despite the evidence that "American" workers gave the strike little support, skilled workers shouldered less blame in its failure than African Americans. Though Foster was forced to admit that the skilled American is "hard to organize" because he "is individualistic and critical" he still "makes the best type of union man."[29] Interestingly, in the dozens of interviews that Saposs conducted, and in the rest of the primary sources considered here, new immigrants and their leaders rarely decried the lack of solidarity on the part of African Americans, or their role as strikebreakers—although these phenomena are beyond dispute. A rare example came from a "Slavish organizer," who put it this way: "They [Americans] are too proud to strike with Hunkies. They're not too proud to scab with negroes."[30]

But for all the strategic weakness of the National Committee, its methods represented a progressive element within the A.F.L. Much of the A.F.L. remained either openly or implicitly racist towards African Americans, and often maintained a decidedly hostile and reactionary stance towards "foreigners" and anything that hinted of radicalism. Saposs discovered this in interviews with A.F.L. officials. A letter from Jere L. Sullivan, secretary of an A.F.L.–affiliated union and himself an Irish immigrant, indicated some of the reactionary sentiments prevalent within the House of Labor: "[W]hen I went to the other side of the pond I had to learn the language of the country or take what was handed to me.... If you are an American at heart, speak our language. If you don't know it, learn it. If you don't like it, move ... these European trained servants have been transformed into ranting, crazy, Bolsheviki ... we are convinced that the alien permitted to remain in this country, lick up all the cream in sight and then hike back to his place of origin is a menace second only to that of Kaiser Bill," and so on.[31] Saposs summarized a remarkably similar interview with a different head of an A.F.L. union, J.E. Roach, also an Irish immigrant: "Foreigners as a rule do not make good unionists. One of the faults is that they have too many isms. The Jews are the worst offenders. Foreigners should be forced to learn English."[32] As Montgomery has pointed out, the relationship between this sort of unionism and the new immigrants "was very simple: the immigrants had nothing to do with [it], and it wanted nothing to do with them."[33]

In deciding not to strike, some American workers felt that they were defending individual homes and families. They prided themselves that wives did not have to work for wage, while many sought to establish daughters in office or teaching jobs. This contrasted sharply to the role of new immigrant wives and daughters. Immigrant daughters tended to work in factories or as domestics; immigrant wives supplemented family income through taking on boarders and other forms of remunerated domestic activity. Moreover, new immigrant women in the Great Steel Strike often led the labor marches, picket lines, and engaged in quasi-violent acts of community defense. The public-private divide in the American workers' households, culturally informed by middle class notions of domesticity, placed a taboo on such activity. The "manly trade unionism" of the A.F.L. maintained as a basic assumption that wives and daughters would not be involved in public confrontations. This gender distinction, thus, was a cultural characteristic that drew the skilled American workers closer to middle class and even managerial elements. Saposs captured some of this complexity when he recalled of the "aristocratic" American workers that "they had the best looking women as wives. Best-dressed women as wives. The contrast was extraordinary in the way they lived, the way they dressed, the way the women were." But in the end what made this sort of distinction possible was the higher wages paid to skilled American workers.[34]

Even though the National Committee failed in its efforts to unify the three large sections of the steel industry workforce, Foster acknowledged that the most critical factor in the strike's defeat was its delayed timing.[35] However, this "mistake" resulted from the wartime outlook, taken root among trade unionists, that the state could be a neutral arbiter, even an ally, and that it would reward labor for its service to the national cause. Instead labor's advantageous conditions presented by the war—full employment and the life-and-death importance of continuing production—had ended with the signing of the armistice on November 11, 1918, and gratitude for Gompers' loyalty quickly forgotten. While the worker militancy and the political enthusiasm during the war years continued and even redoubled in 1919, postwar conditions threatened to put strikes and unionization drives at a decided disadvantage. This did not appear to be the case right away, however, as the postwar boom continued through most of the first year of peace.[36] Yet the ending of hostilities in Europe promised heightened unemployment as the mills, mines, and factories scaled back production to readjust toward peacetime markets and as millions of working age soldiers returned from Europe. Also, unlike later periods of high structural unemployment when workers' struggles nonetheless experienced a degree of success, such as the 1930s and 1970s, in 1919 U.S. industry emerged from the war extraordinarily rich, confident, and with time to lose. Judge Elbert Gary, head of U.S. Steel, caught some of the spirit of the time in an address to stockholders just prior to the Great Steel Strike:

> Gentlemen, we have in the United States between a third and a half of all the wealth of the world. We have more than a third of all the gold.... We are a creditor nation, holding the notes or securities of foreign countries, perfectly solvent, amounting to nearly ten billion dollars; we have the best country, the largest resources, the best

climate and I may say pretty nearly as good brains. And in the competition with other countries we can take care of ourselves.[37]

To some workers, the reshuffled deck was also apparent. Leonardo Minelli, returning from World War I, could not find a job on the Iron Range: "When I came back, Mr. United States Steel said he couldn't find my name on the list.... I went to the main office. He told me. 'The war is over now ... we don't hire anybody anymore.'"[38]

Yet the A.F.L. and the National Committee continued to operate under the war-born illusion that the state would remain neutral. As Gompers' and Foster's public testimony later revealed, it was primarily in order to placate the Wilson administration that the National Committee carried forward the strike as a "pure and simple" trade union struggle over "bread and butter" issues, when in fact from the perspective of the largely new immigrant workforce it involved deeper social grievances such as democracy in the workplace, and even more radical goals. McKillen has described these "loftier aspirations of workers" as "'workers' control' and the 'democratization of industry.'"[39] To make the strike appear "pure and simple," moreover, the National Committee strained to appeal to the "American" labor aristocracy, who nonetheless like the new immigrants tended to see the strike as something more, and something with which they wanted no part: the establishment of equality with "foreigners" and blacks. This "responsible" approach before the state also caused the strike's delay into autumn. The Wilson administration was able to restrain Gompers, who was able to hold back Foster and the National Committee, who in turn restrained the new immigrants. This broke down only when it was determined the new immigrants could no longer be contained. By then the slack season was approaching and U.S. Steel had been given ample time to prepare.

The Revolt of the Rank and File in the Bituminous Coal Strike of 1919

New immigrant rank-and-file miners revolted in the coal fields while the steel strike was in its latter stages. Although the strike began among heavily-new immigrant locals in Illinois, the "American" portion of the workforce participated as well. This vindicates Foster's assessment that skill and pay, not race or nationality, was the decisive factor in the lack of participation of American workers in the steel strike. The

U.M.W.–led bituminous strike in the C.C.F. showed once again that the war and the attitude toward the state were decisive even under conditions where a union was already organized. The U.M.W. "lost" this strike, settling in the end for a Wilson administration-brokered settlement with the operators that fell far short of miners' demands, although it was not weakened as an organization. As was the case with the steel unions, the U.M.W. ran headlong into a government to which it had given extensive support during the war.

By 1919 anger was growing in the nation's coal fields, based on the effects of growing inflation on stagnant wages and the continuation of the Washington Agreement during peace. Never popular with the rank-and-file, the Washington Agreement was to be voided by the ending of World War I. However, since Congress did not officially ratify an armistice with Germany, the provisions of the agreement remained officially in effect, and the U.M.W., in keeping with its defense of contractual obligation, was compelled to continue its increasingly difficult role as policeman of the miners. Furthermore, as was the case with steelworkers, the ideological pronouncements of the war generated feelings of indignation and injustice as miners' grievances and broad claims to democracy collided with a postwar readjustment that took as its primary aim "normalcy," a stability that would entail the carrying over of "industrial peace" from the war based on the continued assumption that what was good for profit margins was good for workers and the nation.

In Illinois, the growing rank-and-file opposition of coal miners to the Washington Agreement found outlet in the new immigrant wildcat strikes of 1917 and 1918, such as the Springfield general strike. It threatened a torrent by the summer of 1919. The entire Kansas district went out in opposition to the Washington Agreement that summer, and Illinois locals continued to strike against both District 12 and the U.M.W.'s insistence that the no-strike pledge was still in effect. More troubling for John L. Lewis was that this opposition was beginning to express itself in fissures within the bureaucracy itself, as powerful district presidents such as Alexander Howat of Kansas, Frank Farrington of Illinois, John Brophy of Pennsylvania, and other members of the International Executive Board (I.E.B.) sought to place themselves atop the wave of opposition from below.[40]

Illinois coal miners mounted a veritable rebellion against the U.M.W. leadership of both District 12 and the national union. Radicalism showed itself to be, for the first time, a prime factor in the mass revolt, for it was the defense of Tom Mooney, a socialist San Francisco labor leader who had been framed and imprisoned for a "Preparedness Day" bombing in 1916, which triggered the rank-and-file rebellion. Mooney's defense won broad support among workers. The radical new immigrant press followed the case closely. Thousands of coal miners in largely new immigrant coal towns in southwestern Illinois went out on strike in July for several weeks in protest against the Mooney imprisonment, but they were quick to couple their avowed aim of his release with their own grievances against the U.M.W. and the operators. In a mass meeting in Belleville, Illinois—a heavily Italian and Russian local—the coal miners demanded either the renegotiation or the abrogation of the Washington Agreement. But they did not stop there, denouncing the U.M.W. leadership as "beneficiaries" of capitalism and demanding of "the capitalist class" "that all instruments of industries be turned over to the working class." The southwestern Illinois coal miners soon organized "Crusaders" who were dispatched throughout the state to publicize grievances and to link up with the other sub-districts. Once again, new immigrant women often headed up these labor marches. Illinois coal miners created their own democratic councils in opposition to the U.M.W. leadership. This too began in Belleville, but was soon replaced by a statewide "rank-and-file policy committee" that aimed to call a special convention of Illinois coal miners outside of the official channels of the U.M.W. This took place in Springfield on August 19. Delegates representing 141 locals and 57,000 members assembled in the state capital and demanded among other things that "all instruments of industries be turned over to the working class … a thirty-hour week, a pay increase, reform of the contracting system, and transfer of 'the mines to the miners.'"[41]

The strike forced Lewis's hand, though he feared the demise of the labor-capital-government coalition that had provided the venue for his meteoric rise through the union ranks. The I.E.B., the highest governing body of the U.M.W., responding to the welling pressure from below, called for a strike on November 1, 1919, with demands as bold as any in U.S. history, and more striking still in that their formulation represented, by all accounts, the bowing of leadership before broadly-held membership demands. To offset inflation, the U.M.W. called for a 60 percent immediate increase in miners' wages, the gradual nationalization of the coal mines as the natural solution to resolve the chaotic nature of the industry, and the formation of a labor party—an explicit threat to the two-party system.

President Wilson, the erstwhile "friend of labor," and Attorney General Palmer threatened the U.M.W. leadership with arrest, accusing it of violating its no-strike pledge and the wartime-created Lever Act, which had given the federal government de facto control over the coal industry. Coal miners struck en masse on November 1. A federal court issued an injunction on November 8th demanding the miners return to work within four days, and Palmer sent F.B.I. agents to U.M.W. headquarters in Indianapolis to enforce compliance. Lewis backed down, calling miners back, but his order was disregarded by the rank-and-file. The strike, now a *de facto* industry-wide wildcat, dragged on through November. Then in December Wilson threatened to deploy 100,000 troops to ensure the operation of the coal mines. Amidst the threats and a propaganda campaign against the miners, the I.E.B. accepted a temporary compromise of a fourteen percent wage increase. This was a defeat to miners' most elementary economic aims, to say nothing of their loftier goals. The contract satisfied no one, and the stage was set for further struggle within the union and wildcats against the operators. Pressure on the Lewis leadership was somewhat relieved early in 1920 when the fourteen percent wage increase was bumped to 27 percent upon federal investigation.[42]

The I.W.W., "Bolshevism" and the Challenge from Below

Ample evidence from the strike wave of 1919 shows fears of Bolshevism or radicalism among immigrant workers were not entirely based on paranoid fantasy. Even organized labor's more radical representatives faced difficulties with the new immigrant workforce. When Foster and the C.F.L. began their campaign to organize the steel industry, their timing proved perfect in more ways than one: in the first place they found new immigrant workers "stampeded" into the new organization by the hundreds of thousands.[43] Second, A.F.L. leadership deemed it a necessity to proceed with organizing the unskilled steelworkers, lest they turn to a more radical option. Indeed, U.S. military intelligence had determined as early as January 1919, that a strike in Gary was imminent and that it would be led by the I.W.W. and "Bolscheviki," information based on the research of an informant who conducted interviews throughout the city. Nonetheless, the high degree of immigrant militancy even put such a radical as Foster in a hard spot.[44]

The C.F.L. organizers recognized that the I.W.W. and "Bolshevism" held an appeal to the immigrant workers. In 1919 even when the I.W.W. did not exist as a credible alternative, strikes very often "breathed the spirit of One Big Union."[45] Equally as important, it was feared that immigrant workers might gravitate towards such options as the limitations of the C.F.L. organizing strategy became apparent. Thus, David Saposs, both a sympathizer and reformer of the American trade union movement, wrote:

> The upshot of the matter is this: the methods of organization used in the steel strike were old fashioned and became ostentatiously so as the organizers recognized the radical possibilities of the strike and conscientiously believed that anything other than tried trade unionism would be bad for the steel workers in their newly organized state. The cry of Bolshevism was ... a dangerous thing because it advertised to the mass of immigrant steel workers, who went down to defeat under old flags and old slogans, an idea and untried methods under which they might be tempted to make another battle.[46]

If Saposs undervalued the ideological influence of radicalism among the immigrants, his estimation of their gravitation to new forms of struggle was apt. Such insightful criticism of the organization drive was rare.

The National Committee recognized that organization of the new immigrants would depend upon direct communication in the workers' native languages. However, this depended on the unions finding "trustworthy" leaders, a plan that often backfired.[47] When foreign language speakers were used, "often they ... have been talking contrary to instructions, instead of explaining the AFofL idea of unions they will advocate I.W.W.ism or Bolshevism and incite the workers against the AfofL."[48] Another steel industry informant wrote to Saposs that "recently a radical element asserted itself among the foreign workers. Whether they are Socialists, I.W.W.'s or Bolshevists is uncertain. Most of them have been of great aid in organizing the workers of their nationalities and showed real initiative; as a consequence, they were elected officers. Evidently they came in to capture the organization, and bided their time for an opportunity. This came when the A.F.L. unions were unable to show tangible results."[49]

A.F.L. observers expressed an almost obsessive fear and respect for foreign I.W.W. orators and their ability to influence the masses, particularly the Italians.[50] But more than the communicative abilities of immigrant political leaders, the enthusiasm of the workers' at the time explains the "magnetic" success of radical orators. They fed off of receptive audiences. An observer of a Polish immigrant meeting during the

Overland strike of 1919 remarked, "these last two (socialist speakers) spoke very radically and even violently and I noticed that the more violent their remarks, the greater was the applause."[51] Another informant from a steel mill in the Pittsburgh noted the voracious appetite among the new immigrants for radicalism in print: "since the strike they beg for literature and devour any labor and radical literature they can put their hands on. Even in the mill the men who can read English among the immigrants will be indifferent to a Pittsburgh paper, but the *The Call*, *Appeal to Reason*, *The Toiler*, and any other radical paper is eagerly scanned no matter how worn out and blurred the type may be from much handling."[52]

To contain the threat from the left, the National Committee carried out measures against militant workers, in cases barring suspected I.W.W. members or those who expressed "Bolshevist" opinions, and seeing to it that these workers also lost their jobs.[53] In Pullman, the I.W.W. "have established themselves so well that the chairman of the different safety and welfare committees were generally I.W.W. and they were making good headway to form an industrial organization. If this [National] Committee had not come in they very likely would have been in a position to call a strike and tie up the industry such headway had been made. [The National Committee] also got the managers to discharge these I.W.W.s."[54] In Calumet, after the I.W.W. successfully organized hundreds of tank workers, the National Committee entered, and with the help of the local police "were given a hearing." Afterwards, the National Committee made a pact with the company forcing the workers to join the A.F.L. union.[55] In this way, the A.F.L. pitched itself to capital as the only safe alternative to something much worse. Leiserson reported that an A.F.L. official named Quinilivan told a factory owner that his "only safety lay in letting the men be organized into a conservative trade union affiliated with the A.F. of L. The employer answered him that this was the second time that such a statement had been made to him and he was beginning to believe it."[56]

The strike in Hammond, Indiana, in April of 1919—several months before the steel strike—brought forth an urgent telegram from Edward J. Evans, Chair of the Chicago (and Calumet) District of the National Committee to the Federal Mediation and Reconciliation Service regarding the I.W.W. threat. The strike erupted spontaneously after a worker had been dismissed. Yet the I.W.W. was present, according to Evans: "over one thousand employees out on the streets now more coming out through the gates every minute situation very alarming there has been considerable organization work in this vicinity by the I W W had just about counteracted that influence when this happened Will send every international representative possible to try to prevent trouble and ask that Conciliator be assigned immediately."[57]

John Corpi, a Finnish organizer for the I.W.W. on Minnesota's Iron Range, explained to Saposs some of the difficulties the A.F.L. faced. "When the Minnesota Federation [A.F.L.] held its convention in Virginia in 1918, a parade was given in its honor, at the head of which marched the local militia and the private mine guards," Corpi recounted. "This was taken to be an endorsement of the AF of L by the mine operators. Naturally the workers can have little confidence in a labor organization endorsed by the bosses." Corpi then succinctly summed up U.S. Steel's strategy on the Iron Range in the face of the A.F.L. steelworkers' organizing drive: "The steel trust may be fighting the A.F.of L. in Pittsburgh because the I.W.W. is not strong there, but here they are encouraging it in order to counteract the I.W.W." Indeed, in the Pittsburgh district Gompers campaigned for reluctant National Committee officials to launch the strike out of fear that it would go ahead regardless, but under an I.W.W. banner.[58]

The fear and respect that the A.F.L. and the National Committee held for the I.W.W. is astonishing given the historical context. The Wobblies, after all, had been crushed by state repression beginning with U.S. entry into World War I in 1917 and on. Nearly all of their leadership had been, or remained, in prison; their offices and printing plants had been destroyed; their newspaper circulation suppressed. The imprisonment of the Wobbly leadership included many of the outstanding new immigrant leaders. Then the Palmer Raids, which began in November of 1919 as the steel strike began to falter, targeted primarily radical new immigrant leaders, who faced arbitrary detention, abusive interrogations, and deportation.[59] This makes the influence that the I.W.W. continued to exert in the steel mills and elsewhere more striking. If these reports did not pertain to Wobbly leaders, then to whom did they refer? The numerous reports of I.W.W. activity show that radical ideas had taken hold in a section of the new immigrant workforce. Indeed, that the National Committee organizers used the terms "I.W.W." and "Bolshevism" interchangeably suggests that what they confronted was a more general radical challenge.

As the trade unions struggled to assert their own authority over the new immigrants, they looked for scapegoats within the ethnic communities. Beyond the favorite culprits, the I.W.W. and Bolshevism, trade unionists suspected that ethnic leadership, referred to condescendingly as "clan leaders" or "chieftans," were to blame for thwarting A.F.L. unionization.[60] Echoing these trade unionists, historians have often viewed Americanization as a struggle for authority between transplanted Old World "folkways" and corporate structures of ethnic life (e.g., the safeguarding of culture, continuance of the native language, obedience to the church and other social superiors) and the Americanizing culture and institutions of the New World (e.g., trade unions, the workplace, the American state, popular culture, acquisition of English, etc.) This dichotomous tension between "new" and "old" overlooks the times when various forms of authority acted collaboratively to influence the immigrant population—or, as during the 1916–1922 strike wave, when authority of different kinds found its hold on the new immigrant working class tenuous.[61] Mystified by their inability to contain the new immigrants, trade unionists and ethnic "chieftans" each suspected the other was to blame (along with the infamous "few radicals" who misled the workers), while both often forged pacts with business interests in an attempt to contain and regain authority over the new immigrants.[62]

In fact, new immigrants frequently laid intra-ethnic loyalty to social superiors aside during the strike wave. In 1918 Chicago, Italian assistant barbers struck against the Masters' Barber Association, in a long and bitter dispute.[63] In 1919, Italian workers struck against Italian factory owners organized in the Italian Macaroni Manufacturers' Association.[64] According to Dominic Pacyga, leading Chicago Polish language newspapers denounced the meatpacking and steel strikes, but despite this Polish workers participated en masse.[65] In Bayonne, New Jersey, striking Polish workers arranged to have a local Catholic priest fired after he urged them to return to work.[66] After officially opposing the steel strike, a Hungarian newspaper in Pittsburgh found that striking miners responded by simply canceling their subscriptions, and many wrote letters of protest.[67] A wise editor would not make such a mistake, Budimer Grahavoc, editor of the *American Srbobran* ("Serbs' Defender"), pointed out. "One Serbian paper in Chicago came out openly against the strike and has lost most of its subscribers," he explained. "It is now on the verge of bankruptcy." Grahavoc recognized that "practically all" of his readers worked in the mills and mines of America's industrial heartland. As a Serbian war hero, injured five times in combat, he had been sent to the U.S. by the Serbian government with the specific task of keeping Serbian workers on the job and behind the war effort. But learning from the case of his nearly bankrupt competitor, Grahavoc recognized that a full frontal assault on the strike wave was inadvisable:

> One must be foxy in trying to guide the Serbians as they are becoming well informed.... The best that could be done is to indirectly keep as many Serbians from striking as possible. This has been done by appealing to them not to go back on the United States after what it did to help Serbia gain its independence.... Even this indirect effort has had its disapproval. Letters have come in protesting and showing that a strike against capital is not opposing the government.[68]

When ethnic leaders did express opposition the steel strike, it seems to have either been based upon financial support from U.S. Steel, or else arose from a mistrust of American trade unions. Albert Mamatey, President of the National Slovak Society, represented both tendencies. During the steel strike he confronted a momentous decision: oppose the strike and risk alienating over 80 percent of his membership; support the strike and risk losing the generous financial patronage of U.S. Steel. To balance between these constituencies, Mamatey and the National Slovak Society remained neutral, but believed that the new immigrants had been led astray by the "Americans," who were all still at work.[69] The following quotes taken by Saposs from "clan leaders" echo Mamatey's distrust of the A.F.L. and American workers: "The strike was a serious mistake on the part of Slovak workers as they are being deceived by the Americans ... from Gompers down.... They have been against the foreigners and have now organized this strike to discredit them...."[70]; "the strike is a betrayal of the immigrant by the Americans."[71]

Some immigrant leaders expressed both condescension and incomprehension toward the immigrant steelworkers similar to the attitude of some American trade unionists. Saposs summarized the testimony of the assistant editor of the Slovak *Narodne Noving*: "The foreigners, especially the Slovaks, are like children, simple-minded and know nothing about the issues in the strike.... They are so simple they will follow anybody." Compare this to Edward J. Evans, Secretary-Treasurer of the National Committee's Chicago District: "the foreigners in the community are dependent [upon "clan leaders"] because of their ignorance of our institutions and conditions and languages."[72] G. Guntkiewicz, Treasurer, Polish Falcons Alliance of America: "The immigrant workers were satisfied and would not have come out on strike if it were not for fear of violence. They were intimidated by a few radicals."[73] But the supposition that workers followed a few radicals flies in the face of the sheer magnitude of the strike wave.

New Immigrant Radicalism in 1919

The crisis confronting American radicalism in the wake of World War I was multi-faceted. State repression that had emerged during the war only intensified after Versailles in the form of the Palmer raids, the first Red Scare, and a large-scale arrest and deportation operation directed primarily against new immigrant radicals. At the same time, enthusiasm over the Russian Revolution and a desire to transplant revolution to America confronted the reality of a sharply divided left. The unmaking and remaking of the American left that began during World War I accelerated in 1919. Divisions within the S.P. between a reformist right and a Communist-oriented left led to the splintering of the socialist movement. Similar pressures tore the I.W.W. in two between those who embraced left-wing socialism and advocates of direct action. In these ideological battles, the greater part of new immigrant radicalism remained a powerful left wing social force and gravitated toward what was itself a sharply divided and largely underground proto-communist movement. The fact that the U.S. had entered its largest and most intense strike year in 1919, in which immigrant workers figured so prominently, coincided with these developments and seemed to vindicate the revolutionary prognosis.[74]

For U.S. radicalism, 1919 was the best of times and the worst of times. With an element of tragic irony, only a few weeks before the Great Steel Strike of 1919 tipped off, much of the radical left gathered in Chicago in three separate sites. In the months preceding, the right-wing controlled National Executive Council of the S.P. had suspended seven Eastern European foreign language federations—the Russian, Latvian, Lithuanian, Ukrainian, Hungarian, South-Slavic, and Polish—along with the entire Michigan branch of the party. In Chicago, the local socialists in the C.C.S.P. were overwhelmingly left wing, based in large measure on the influx of new immigrants that had taken place in the preceding years. This process continued in 1919, and the C.C.S.P. remained enthusiastic about the Soviet government. The national party, dominated by the Berger-Hillquit National Executive Council, responded on May 24 by temporarily suspending the C.C.S.P. The Finnish, Yiddish, and Italian foreign language federations did not go over to the communist parties until 1921, although they were "almost completely 'communistic' in character." In the meantime, the three remaining federations continued to be a left-wing ballast within the S.P. Their trajectory was never in doubt. Finnish socialist leadership in Duluth, for example, found it impossible to even nominate candidates on the S.P. ticket for local office. An attempt to do so, taken surreptitiously by the leadership on instructions from a Berger associate, provoked a mass general membership meeting that unanimously rescinded the nominations. The smaller right wing element in the F.S.F. actually enlisted itself in the government spying operation against the left wing in order "to prevent the spread of Bolshevik propaganda."[75]

For the far left, the expulsions were entirely welcome, for it seemed to be the prerequisite for breaking with reformist elements, forming a Bolshevik-style party in the U.S., and preparing the way for a revolution, which to many seemed imminent. Out of these expulsions two rival communist movements emerged—the Communist Party, and the Communist Labor Party. Another contender, the Labor Party founded under the auspices of John Fitzpatrick and the C.F.L., also took shape. The I.W.W. carried on as well, though not yet ready to spell out its differences with the Bolsheviks and the Russian Revolution.[76]

In 1919 there were as yet few clear principled differences among all these factions of the radical left, and even fewer programmatic differences. All still formally supported the Russian Revolution, and except for significant parts of the Labor Party group, all had opposed U.S. entry into World War I. Differences developed, but the expulsions and splits came hastily, and workers had no means of following, much less understanding, their origin in politics or social composition. In retrospect, it may well have been an opportune time for the formation of a Labor Party based in the trade unions. The move had big support among critical elements in the A.F.L., including much of the U.M.W. leadership, especially in Illinois, the C.F.L., and the Seattle Labor Council, to name a few. By 1919 the Democratic Party had been somewhat discredited by the war and the failures of Wilsonian liberalism at Versailles, a fact attested to by a popular "isolationist" mood that would persist for two decades. The S.P., however, jealously defended what it perceived its rightful position as the party of the working class. The young communist parties, meanwhile, had proclaimed revolution the order of the day. Had they seized the chance and entered the Labor Party movement, they might have found protection from illegalization and an avenue to reach large numbers of a still restive industrial workforce. In turn, they would have provided the Labor Party with an important and energetic cadre. The young communist movement did not seize the opportunity—which would linger in various less appealing forms for the next four years—while the old U.S. radicalism of the S.P. was dying. Much of the I.W.W. leadership was still imprisoned or had fled. All of this meant that in the greatest strike year in U.S. history, there was a vacuum of radical leadership.[77]

Yet in spite of divisions and repression, as evidence from the steel strike and the I.W.W.–led strike on the Vermillion Iron Range suggests, radicalism was exerting its most significant influence on immigrant workers in 1919. This is also evident from the way the defense of Tom Mooney erupted into a challenge against the U.M.W. leadership by rank-and-file miners, who articulated a socialist program in their challenge. In one mine in southern Illinois, "according to Military Intelligence files ... there were representatives of the Polish communists, Bulgarians of the Socialist Labor Party, the Finnish Socialist Party, Lithuanian Communist Party, and the South-Slavic Socialist Party." We know, furthermore, that large meetings of radical new immigrant groups took place in Chicago throughout 1919: Bulgarian Wobblies; a "Czech and Slovak" workers' council; a "Russian Mass Meeting" in favor of the new Soviet Government, to name a few. Gary became a center of U.S. military intelligence activity during the Great Steel Strike. Radicalism seemed to have gripped Gary's new immigrant groups beginning in the spring of 1919. A pro-communist rally on May 4 attracted a crowd estimated at 10,000. Military intelligence monitored large meetings and rallies in Gary and throughout the Calumet area. Several radical workers, likely active in the strike, were arrested and deportation proceedings begun. An intelligence agent, John Spolansky, found that "I.W.W. propaganda has created a strong revolutionary sentiment" in the places men gathered "now that the saloons have been closed." A parade had been scheduled for May 4 in defiance of a city ordinance banning it, in which marchers were to go forward under the following slogans: "We demand the liberation of political prisoners; We demand recognition of the Soviet Government; We demand immediate release of our Eugene Debs and Wm. Haywood; We demand immediate withdrawal of American troops from Russia; We demand recognition of Martens as the only people's representative of Russia; Long Live the International Solidarity of the Working Class." Thanks to the investigative work of Spolansky, the police, armed with shotguns, arrested the strike leaders before the march, although a crowd of some 4,000 had already assembled. Radical workers in Gary, agents assured the Department of Justice, were planning on a strike against the mills.[78]

The majority of the Finnish Socialist Federation aligned with the communist movements, although it officially remained a part of the

S.P. until 1921, when it left, taking with it the majority of its membership and property. The Jewish Federation entered in the same year. The departure of these two large foreign language federations, who had been a left wing bloc within the S.P., coupled with ongoing attrition, left the S.P. a shadow of its former self. Upon officially embracing the communist movement, the F.S.F. immediately established itself as the largest component of the Workers Party of America (W.P.A.). Its 7,000 members comprised over 40 percent of total W.P.A. membership, and only its donation of $25,000 made possible the launch of the *Daily Worker* as the communist movement's official organ. With its base among miners, the support for communism was especially strong among Finns of the Lake Superior region and the Iron Range. The rump section of the F.S.F. that remained in the S.P. found a regional basis of support among the Finns of Massachusetts. A significant portion of Finns also left the I.W.W. behind as it became increasingly hostile to the Bolsheviks and the Russian Revolution.[79]

Italian American radicals—including all shades of socialists, communists, and Wobblies—created the *Camera del lavoro* ("labor exchange" or "chamber of labor") founded in New York City, while in Chicago a *Casa del popolo* (people's house) was created.[80] The Chamber of Labor was designed to replicate the massive growth of the chambers in Italy, where they had come by 1919 to hold about 2 million members. The Chamber aimed to bring together all Italian workers' parties and unions, and got off to an auspicious start. Cooperation among the incipient communists in Italy and the Italian American communists led to discussion of forming a international labor union for Italian workers. Anthony Capraro, a prominent figure for his leadership of the Lawrence textile strike, corresponded with the two leading figures of Italian communism—Amadeo Bordiga and Antonio Gramsci—on precisely this question.[81]

Conclusion

In 1919, new immigrants led major and protracted strikes that engulfed both the steel and coal industries, shattering forever notions of their passivity. In its place a new stereotype had emerged: that of the radical and dangerous immigrant. The reputation was earned. Radicalism had indeed animated the struggles of new immigrant workers in 1919, as abundant evidence from both steel and coal show. The context of revolutionary struggles in Europe contributed inspiration to this development. Yet at the same time, the organizational structures of U.S. radicalism had been ground down by the twin shocks of state repression and the Russian Revolution, whose impact on the left caused the splitting apart of both the S.P. and the I.W.W.[82]

The defeat and limitation of working class struggles in 1919 mark a watershed in U.S. history. Business interests emerged from the war determined to preserve business' prerogative to control property and production. Industrial unionism survived in the coal industry and the garment trades, but the U.M.W. began a long retreat from its most daring ambitions, which had been imposed upon the leadership by the restive rank-and-file, and which had included the nationalization of the coal industry and the formation of a labor party. The effort to organize the steel industry ended in complete failure, and U.S. Steel would remain for the next twenty-six years the bastion of the ruthless open shop. The failure to organize steel, coupled with the ensuing rollback of union gains in meatpacking, weakened and marginalized progressive trade unionism within the A.F.L. In both the U.M.W. and the A.F.L. at large, conservative sections of the bureaucracies were strengthened by defeat.

Nonetheless, the corporate and political elite had been shocked and chastened by the militancy workers had exhibited in 1919 and the preceding years. The association of radicalism and labor militancy with the new immigrants, together with the new concern about labor turnover, set the stage for a rupture with the previous approach to the labor force that had characterized the steel and coal industries. Now business interests gradually moved toward the social and economic elements of a social contract with the working class that would come to be called "Fordism," which placed a new premium on labor stability and loyalty. It also entailed an end to mass immigration.

Chapter 5

Reaction in New Country and Old: 1920–1924

In 1928, Frank Palmer, a young journalist from Colorado, went to the Iron Range to research claims that U.S. Steel carried on espionage against its employees. What he found, he said, "was so astounding that I found it difficult to believe." The spy network reached deep into the new immigrant communities. A respected Italian mailman from Chisholm, Vergillio Bertone, was paid $125 per month for reporting on the radical and union activities of Italian miners. In one significant revelation, Bertone detailed a 1922 meeting in Chisholm in which Carlo Tresca, the noted Italian American syndicalist, spoke. Tresca evidently allowed Bertone access to the Iron Range subscription list for *Il Martello*, which the latter dutifully turned over to U.S. Steel. Among the Finns, two prominent members of the local of the Communist Party reported on the sympathies of radical Finns. Agent "No. 2," John Lampela, was secretary of a meeting in Hibbing in which a letter from Otto Kuusinen, the leading Finnish Communist in the Soviet Union, was read to local working men. Lampela turned over the names of those in attendance. Dozens of spies from across the Lake Superior District sent in such reports. Immigrants on the office payroll of Oliver made translations from the various languages. Then lists were made of miners who attended union, communist, or I.W.W. meetings, or who subscribed to union or radical periodicals. These names were then turned over to the local mine superintendents, and the workers were fired and blacklisted—or blackmailed into themselves becoming spies.[1]

U.S. Steel's spy system had a chilling effect on labor militancy and radicalism. Radical workers faced blacklisting for what they received in the mail, and even for their conversations with acquaintances. However, U.S. Steel's greater fear was union organization. Worker radicalism, it believed, could be used as a way of targeting workers most likely to lead organization drives. In this way union activity was limited until the late 1930s and the emergence of the Steel Workers Organizing Committee (S.W.O.C.) of the young C.I.O. Although corporate espionage was not new, the communities of the steel industry lived in a state of fear in the post war.[2]

What had changed was the relative balance of strength between business and labor. The position of labor, and especially immigrant workers, had eroded rapidly after 1919. The most obvious economic factor was the recession of 1920–1922, which amounted to a purge of the "excess capacity" that had been built up in the economy during the war years. Industry trimmed its sails as it readjusted to the peacetime economy, laying off hundreds of thousands of workers nationally. Labor struggle did not cease in this period, but the strikes of 1920–22 were conducted defensively, as workers fought, often in vain, to hang on to wartime gains. In the steel industry, after the defeat of 1919, mass layoffs were met with little resistance among the overwhelmingly new immigrant workers. In the coalfields, the U.M.W. fought a series of defensive struggles in the C.C.F.—the most bitter of which occurred in Illinois. While the business recovery of 1923 ushered in what we have come to remember as "the Roaring 20s," in iron mining, coal mining, and steel milling, wartime employment levels would never be seen again. In essence, industry needed fewer workers. The 1920s have been called labor's "lean years," the decade of the "fall of the house of labor," the open shop, welfare capitalism, company unions and corporate espionage against militant workers. It was also the decade of the Ku Klux Klan, prohibition, immigration restriction, and Republican domination of the White House. As one historian has put it, the decade, "did not mark the 'return to normalcy,' but rather the end of any effective challenge to the monopoly of capitalists' new regime."[3]

The two strands of this book—worker militancy and radicalism—that seemed to be near convergence in 1919, diverged once again. U.S. radicalism had been undone and redone. The young Communist movement faced a period of isolation, partly self-imposed, in the early 1920s. Strategies for gaining access to the working class, such as "boring from within" trade unions and launching labor defense campaigns, began to pay dividends only as the decade progressed. Meanwhile, the S.P. and the I.W.W. emerged in the 1920s less relevant than at any point in their previous histories. New immigrant radicalism and labor militancy were in unmistakable decline by the early 1920s, so much so that one eminent scholar, Lizabeth Cohen, in analyzing the 1920s, has portrayed new immigrant communities as a bulwark of conservatism. What had happened? How can this reversal be explained?[4]

Historiography has so far fallen in three channels established decades ago. One has been primarily descriptive: new immigrant labor struggles of the period went down to defeat, with few exceptions (here competing explanations are provided for the defeats), and recovery from these losses would only come during the 1930s.[5] The second has placed emphasis on American nationalism and state repression—arrests, deportations, the suppression of the new immigrant press and freedom of assembly, the smashing of offices and organizations, and the eventual prohibition of further large-scale immigration from Eastern and Southern Europe through the Johnson-Reed Act of 1924.[6] The third has proposed that new immigrant radicalism found itself out of step or in conflict with the development of domestic or "American" radicalism.[7]

These explanations paint an incomplete portrait, overlooking the international component of radicalism's decline. In the early 1920s, new immigrants found themselves caught in a dual reaction, in new world and old. In most states of Eastern and Southern Europe, by the late 1920s, revolutionary movements had failed and fascist, royalist, or military dictatorships had come to power. This was true in Italy, Poland, Yugoslavia, Bulgaria, Romania, Greece, Finland, and the Baltic states. Even the Soviet Union and its Comintern, by 1923, were caught in the ebb tide of revolution, which found expression in the gradual consolidation of bureaucratic power under Joseph Stalin.[8]

The decline of new immigrant radicalism in the 1920s—and indeed that of American radicalism more generally—must be understood as a transatlantic process. Just as old world labor and revolutionary struggles had fired the imagination of immigrant workers and breathed life into their struggles from 1917 through 1920, so the revolutionary defeats suffered in Europe during the early 1920s sapped immigrant radicalism of its vitality and helped prepare the way for the growth of insular nationalism among new immigrant communities in the 1920s. This chapter addresses the dual nature of the reactionary period the new immigrants confronted, analyzing developments in the old world both for context and for their impact on new immigrant struggles in the new, and by analyzing the fierce national reaction confronted within the U.S. itself.

To study the new immigrants in this period inescapably draws us to broader questions: the development and crises of capitalism, the nation-state and national identity that took place during the next twenty-five years of reaction, depression, and war. The mass worker mobility across national boundaries in the period preceding World War I, though economically indispensable, had proven to be a profoundly destabilizing factor for nation-states in the old world and new. In both the U.S. and the "sending" countries, due to its disruption of established cultural norms, immigration had called into question social order. It is not incidental that reactionary political currents in America and Europe that emerged in the 1920s took as their first task shoring up national identity. Meanwhile at the level of political economy, the U.S. effort to limit European migration was a manifestation of a general attempt to refortify the nation-state against destabilizing global pressures—in this case the essentially international essence of its labor force. It was therefore akin to the development of restrictionist trading policies and blocs that developed internationally in the period.

Readjusting Workers in the Postwar

The decisive question for U.S. capitalism at stake in the First World War had been this: Would the American contribution to Allied victory translate into sufficient geopolitical power to effectively pry open the world's markets for the excess capacity of commodity production generated by superior U.S. organization and technique, and thereby make the dream of an "Open Door" a reality for the world? The failure at Versailles, Woodrow Wilson's "ordeal," in fact expressed the failure to reorganize the world economy according to its needs. Britain and France obstinately clung to their colonial trading blocs, forced punitive sanctions upon Germany, turned Eastern Europe into an anti–German/anti–Soviet buffer zone, and carved up the Middle East. Worse, the Russian Revolution had removed roughly a quarter of the world's land mass from the world system and at the same time generated an ideological rival to contend with American liberal democracy. In response, the U.S. joined perhaps a dozen other countries in attempting to strangle the young Bolshevik government through military intervention. The effort failed due to Russian resistance, worker sympathy for the revolution in the West, and American-Japanese rivalry in the Far East.[9]

There would be no vast new markets for the excess capacity of U.S. industry. Coal and steel employment and production peaked in

World War I. In the wake of 1919, a new period of consolidation emerged in the already highly concentrated steel industry. Over 250 steel concerns disappeared through mergers, acquisitions, and bankruptcies.[10] It was only a matter of time, in the war's aftermath, for there to emerge a "readjustment": this came in the form of the depression of 1921–1922. Even prior to 1921, however, the economy cooled as the U.S. military and the warring armies of Europe demobilized, as government production decreased, and as European competition began to take to the field again.

Already in 1919 business leaders were aware that the economic situation had shifted the balance of power with labor in their favor. Nineteen-nineteen may have been the period's high-water mark of labor struggle, but business leaders could count themselves fortunate that the *annus bellicosus* had not come during the months of U.S. participation in the war. Organized labor had paid the state and business a service in keeping conflict in check as much as they had—even if one million workers had struck in both 1917 and 1918. The U.M.W. had tacitly agreed to hold back on unionization in Appalachia, and the A.F.L. did not take the initiative to organize steel until after the war. Would organized labor's patience and loyalty be repaid by a continuance of government-corporate-labor cooperation? Nineteen-nineteen had answered with a resounding "no." The defeats of organized labor in the steel and coal that year paved the way for a broad-ranging corporate assault on organized labor. If workers fought on unfavorable terrain in 1919, the situation was more adverse in 1920–1924. By 1921 the economy was in full recession, which would last until 1923. The strike wave continued through 1922, but these struggles increasingly took on the form of rearguard, defensive actions. While the complete defeat of the National Committee drive spelled the end of serious attempts at organization in the steel industry for another fifteen years, the U.M.W. was forced into a decade of retrenchment and decline, although the militancy of the unionized coal miners never waned.[11]

In sum, the economic situation had shifted the balance of forces very strongly in favor of business. Massive wartime production had nurtured economic overcapacity. In the case of coal, this threatened the industry, which entered a depression 1920, with collapse. Coal production had increased between 1913 to 1923 by 336 million tons; only in the five years between 1918 and 1923 it had increased by 254 million tons. In the same span, more than 1,000 new mines were opened, an expansion of the number of operative mines by more than 10 percent.

However, all of this added supply was suddenly confronted, upon war's end, with falling demand due to demobilization and the growing importance of oil in the energy markets. Decline in demand was reflected in a drop in the average price of coal (from $3.75 in 1920 to $2.68 in 1923) and in the average number of days each miner worked (249 days in 1920 to 179 in 1923.) This was compounded by the growth in the available labor force, as soldiers became miners once again. By 1921, 28 percent of Illinois coal miners were unemployed. Deflationary pressures in coal showed no sign of abating as the national economy began to pick up speed in 1923.[12]

The coal industry in the Midwest, where the U.M.W. had its basis of strength, faced triple pressures. The first stemmed from the normal decline in demand from wartime highs. The second resulted from the growing importance of petroleum to the nation's energy consumption. The third, the U.M.W.'s Achilles heel, arose from competition from cheaper non-union Appalachian coal, whose lower cost structure resulted from higher grade ore, cheaper labor, and the relative absence of regulation. The U.M.W. resumed its efforts to unionize the southern West Virginia coal fields in the aftermath of the war, which brought on the legendary "mine wars." These same factors allowed the operators to launch a counteroffensive against the U.M.W. in the C.C.F.[13]

The defeat of the bituminous coal strike in 1919 shaped the rest of the decade for the U.M.W. The groundswell that year had formulated such breathtaking demands as nationalization of the industry and the formation of a labor party. In spite of his desire to perpetuate good relations with the Wilson administration and the operators, the pressure from below had been such that Lewis could not stand in the way. The defeat of the 1919 strike and the ultimate failure to unionize most production in West Virginia strengthened conservative tendencies in the union. Beginning in 1920, Lewis, the consummate bureaucratic brawler, never elected to a significant office prior to his appointment as U.M.W. head in 1918, pursued the wartime collaboration with business and government cooperation again, but this time via the Republican administrations of the 1920s. (Lewis, as a matter of fact, was a Republican.) Lewis also carried on a bitter internal warfare and repression against militants and radicals in the union. This warfare to some extent mirrored that which U.S. Steel carried out against its workforce. Like U.S. Steel, Lewis built up an espionage network designed to ferret out potential opponents. If anything the intensity of the conflict was greater. Not only did Lewis have to contend with the fierce resistance of locals and constant wildcat strikes over matters ranging from wages to the operators' ongoing struggle to introduce cutting machinery. Throughout the 1920s he contended with well-organized, whole-district opposition, first in Kansas, then in Pennsylvania, and virtually non-stop in his home-state of Illinois. A preferred method was to declare illegal entire U.M.W. locals and even districts and then to cooperate with operators in firing and blacklisting recalcitrant miners. Nor did Lewis find the rigging of elections, intimidation, and even violence beneath his office.[14]

The defeat of 1919 also put a *de facto* end to attempts to organize the unorganized in other regions and put the emphasis once again on the U.M.W.'s role of policeman of the C.C.F., where it expended most of its effort in the 1920s in disciplining its own membership and crushing ideological and organizational rivals within the union. The failure to unionize the South and the West, to nationalize the coal industry, and to build a labor party did not, in the short term, adversely affect the financial and organizational health of the union, representing as it did more than 300,000 workers and thousands of mines across the C.C.F. It did, however, hurt the coal communities of the C.C.F., whose workforces shrunk. By 1921 bituminous coal prices had fallen to their 1916 levels.[15] It is noteworthy that strikingly similar problems would prove the bane of industrial unionism once again in the latter half of the 20th century, as U.S. industry first shifted production to the South, and then "globalized," shifting basic commodity production across the globe to find the lowest costs.

Yet even after the settlements of 1919 and early 1920, the U.M.W. and the Illinois coal miners did not give up collective struggle. In the summer of 1920, Illinois coal miners carried out a wildcat strike that spread to Indiana and soon rattled the Wilson administration. The wildcat began as a strike in the largely new immigrant coal mining area around Springfield, and quickly spread out in all directions. The miners demanded a higher wage adjustment than that established in the agreements of 1919 and 1920. The U.M.W., the operators, and local industries dependent upon coal appealed to the National Mediation and Reconciliation Service (N.M.R.S.) for intervention, and it seemed that the Illinois operators were prepared to adjust the wages of the day men upwards independently of the rest of the C.C.F. The N.M.R.S. was reluctant to condone such a localized resolution for fear that it would spread to the rest of the C.C.F. and the entire industry, and thus reignite inflationary pressures through coal into the rest of the economy. Lewis and the national U.M.W., furthermore, feared that an individually worked out local agreement would shatter the C.C.F. and its Trade Agreement. Lewis, in a telegram to Wilson, prophesized that a partial victory by Illinois coal miners would "result in the dissolution of the interstate movement and the national union will be compelled to accept [the Illinois agreement], which increase will later sweep eastward and of course be applied eventually in the other three states. In the meantime shutdown will occur and confusion will exist."[16] Though unstated, it would also have improved the position of Frank Farrington, head of the Illinois U.M.W., in his duel with Lewis for the national presidency of the union.

The Illinois wildcat attracted the attention of the Wilson administration, with Secretary of Labor Wilson, Woodrow Wilson's personal secretary, Joseph P. Tumulty, and Wilson himself attending to it. Wilson sent an open letter to the hundreds of thousands of U.M.W. coal miners. "It is with a feeling of profound regret and sorrow that I have learned that many members of your organization, particularly in the State of Illinois, have engaged in a strike in violation of the award of the Bituminous Coal Commission and your agreement with the Government that the finding of the Commission would be accepted by you as final and binding," he wrote. The wildcats will cause "great suffering in many households during the coming winter and interfere with the continuation of industrial and agricultural activity, which is the basis of the prosperity which you in common with the balance our people have been enjoying...." "What is of far more importance," Wilson continued, is that "the violation of the terms of your solemn obligation impairs your good name, [and] destroys the confidence which is the basis of all mutual agreements...."[17] In response, in a letter to local U.M.W. presidents instructing them to return miners to work, Lewis asserted once again that Wilson was an ally:

> I am profoundly impressed by the President's telegram. The fairness of his statement must be apparent to every one with respect for constituted authority or the least regard for the public weal.... Up to this time the Illinois Coal Operators have not requested this office to enforce the validity of the wage agreement in that State. I intend, however, in compliance with the wishes of the President, to immediately issue a mandatory order instructing and directing all miners now on strike in Illinois and Indiana to immediately return to work so as to permit the normal operation of the mines.[18]

Yet as Wilson recognized, but Lewis could not admit, the rebellion came from below, beginning with new immigrant miners. The conciliator sent to investigate the wildcats in the area around Springfield,

Illinois, concluded as much: "We have had conference with Farrington and associate resident officers regarding resumption of work ... their position is that they have endeavored to have men remain on the job and that it is useless to attempt to have men resume work unless they first have assurance ... that the day wage question will be reopened and readjusted. They say they cannot prevail on men to return to work."[19]

The wildcats continued through the summer, spreading to neighboring states, and, in certain mines, throughout the C.C.F. In the end, day laborers forced a $1.50 per day raise in much of Illinois and elsewhere in the C.C.F., brokered by the Wilson administration in a meeting in Cleveland on August 13. Nonetheless, or perhaps because of the partial nature of the agreements, the wildcats continued, especially in Indiana, where most production in the state was crippled by the end of the month.[20]

Bloodshed came to southern Illinois in the midst of the strike. In West Frankfort, Illinois, near Cairo, a coal mine employing about 2,000, predominantly "foreign" miners, had been on strike throughout the summer and the beginning of August and had recently rejected Farrington's order to return to work. On August 5 two young men were killed, precipitating an eruption against the foreign miners, especially Italians. Feeding into the violence was sensational news coverage, which claimed that there was an Italian "Black Hand" chapter, and that Italians were engaged in larceny. The media overlooked the wildcat strike of the local coal mine dominated by foreign miners. Italians and other new immigrants were attacked, stoned, beaten, their homes burned, and at least one was murdered in front of his family in what the *Chicago Defender* called "practically a repetition" of the East St. Louis riot of 1917 in which as many as 150 blacks were killed. Hundreds fled the county. "Foreigners of all descriptions have been beaten on sight and the roads leaving West Frankfurt are clogged with fleeing families," the *New York Times* reported. The violence had the effect of driving out from the county the entire new immigrant workforce that had been on strike. The attacks caused a diplomatic spat between the U.S. and Italy, with the latter claiming damages. The events in West Frankfort showed the explosive character of racial and class tensions in the coal fields which had been first exposed in the attacks on Italians and Germans during the war.[21]

Then, in the spring of 1922, some 610,000 coal miners struck defensively against wage cutting, one of the largest strikes in U.S. history and a striking display of worker solidarity. The strike began as a response to Ohio and Pennsylvania operators who had sought to eliminate the U.M.W. Yet as in 1919 and 1920, it was the rank-and-file that catapulted local issues into a much larger confrontation. Pit committees walked out, gained the support of union locals, and the locals in turn forced the hand of the state-level unions, who eventually steered the entire organization toward another showdown with the operators. With excess coal heaped up on the surface, and much of the potential labor force unemployed or underemployed, the operators stood ready. The U.M.W. refused to negotiate with Ohio and Pennsylvania operators separately, sending out the entire union, both bituminous and anthracite miners in Northeastern Pennsylvania.[22]

One by-product of the 1922 strike was the Herrin massacre in "bloody Williamson County" of southern Illinois. All the unresolved questions of the previous years surfaced in the local struggle. The strike of the Illinois U.M.W. miners in solidarity with the locked out miners of Ohio and Pennsylvania showed the fierce solidarity of the unionized coal miners and their shared and pent up grievances. The local Herrin mine operator was something of a maverick; he resisted calls from state and local authorities, fearful of violence, that he cease production at the mine during the strike. The questions of skill and mechanization reemerged as well, as a union of skilled workers, the Chicago Steamshovel Men's Union (C.S.M.U.)—which had been recently expelled but then invited back into the A.F.L.—had been imported to replace the striking miners, along with a number of hired gunmen from Chicago to provide protection. In a protest outside the mine pit against the C.S.M.U.'s strikebreaking, three coal miners fell dead to machine gun fire. The local union miners then armed themselves and surrounded the barricaded mine. The strikebreakers eventually waved white flags of surrender, but the angry miners showed no clemency, brutally torturing and then executing eighteen in an orgy of community violence that lasted for several hours and included women and children. A total of 23 died in the struggle. Williamson County was largely "American," and populated by people from neighboring Kentucky and Tennessee. But reports from the massacre suggest that new immigrants as well as at least one black miner participated. The overwhelming support in the community for the U.M.W. and in opposition to the operator was revealed by local juries which acquitted all the accused on all charges.[23]

The massive strike of 1922 caused coal shortages and soaring prices, and the Harding administration determined to place the crisis of the bituminous coal industry atop its domestic agenda. That none other than Secretary of Commerce Herbert Hoover, "the Great Engineer" and himself a mining man, took charge of a plan to stabilize production and employment in coal stands testament to the impact the 1922 strike. Hoover hoped to stabilize the industry through voluntarism on the part of the operators. Hoover, who called the coal industry "the worse functioning of any industry in the country," proposed the sort of industrial cooperation that would typify seven years later his response to the Great Depression. He favored voluntary and cooperative pricing among regional distributors, which would regulate local competition and in turn pit regions against one another with an eye toward shifting production toward areas where it was most profitable, while lessening productive capacity and employment gradually.[24] According to a U.S. Coal Commission investigator, the basic aim was to rid the industry of the smalltime operators, the "gopher holes and one-man shows" that competed with more capital-intensive operations at times of acute demand. What was needed were more operations along the lines of Illinois' Peabody Coal, the only coal producer and distributor that could make any claim to a true national market, with production in Illinois, Indiana, Kentucky, Arkansas, and Wyoming, and with sales in eighteen states. Such trends were to be given encouragement through the newly-created Coal Distribution Committee. This was supplemented in the summer by passage of a Congressional bill to create a federal fuel distributor acting under the auspices of the Interstate Commerce Commission—again with the primary aim of coordinating the voluntary actions of the operators.[25]

In the short run, Hoover's Committee persuaded some operators to cooperate with the scheme of voluntary price reduction and "priority movement" whereby a more rational system of distribution could be put in place, at least theoretically. However, the Harding administration's efforts failed to reconcile the U.M.W. and the operators, and the strike dragged on through the summer of 1922. Harding blamed the U.M.W., and called on the governors of nearly thirty states to protect operating mines, and then declared martial law, utilizing both national guards and state militias. The strike began to wear out in the autumn, and was called to a halt by the temporary Cleveland Agreement, which resolved none of the sources of conflict between the U.M.W. and the operators—each side felt the other had won greater concessions—much less the larger problems of rationalization and overproduction. The Coal Commission produced an extensive study of the industry in the wake of the agreement, but its recommendations, even less than those coming out of the Cleveland Agreement, had no legal or industrial force, and the resulting reports were not even published. Finally, in 1924 the U.M.W. and the C.C.F. operators, under the largely moralistic tutelage of Hoover, hammered out the Jacksonville Agreement. The U.M.W. made significant sacrifices, freezing the C.C.F. wage scale at $7.50 per day for three years in hopes that capping wages would competitively benefit the C.C.F. These hopes proved futile, however, as production and jobs continued to shift to the non-union Appalachian areas. In the three years of the Jacksonville Agreement, the C.C.F. lost forty-four million tons of production, while Kentucky, West Virginia, and Virginia gained fifty-seven million tons. The basic problem in the C.C.F. remained: "too many mines, too many miners." This problem, the state and the operators agreed, could only be resolved at the expense of the miners. The Lewis bureaucracy was caught in the middle, between the demands of the operators and the government, on one side, and rank-and-file miners on the others. It was prepared to concede terrain to the former, but could still be compelled to represent the interests of the latter. This set the stage for bitters struggles in the coalfields through the 1920s, 1930s, and 1940s.[26]

In essence, the Great Depression had hit the coal industry a decade early. Ironically, the lessons Hoover failed to learn about voluntarism in coal would be repeated at the nation's expense from 1929 until 1934, when Hoover's successor, Franklin Delano Roosevelt, finally launched what historians call "the second New Deal." In spite of the depression in coal, the miners of Illinois continued to fight defensively against loss of jobs and production. As was the case during World War I and 1919, this put the miners more and more into conflict with the U.M.W., and laid the basis for John Brophy's failed "Save the Union" insurgency against the Lewis bureaucracy, and the eventual formation of the Progressive Mine Workers of America and the subsequent "mine wars" of Illinois in the late 1920s and early 1930s. In Illinois the U.M.W. took cooperative steps with mine owners in order to discipline its own membership, which was still not always enough to contain worker aspirations. "L.F.," an Italian miner in Freeburg, Illinois wrote to *Il Proletario* that the local union had adopted a resolution declaring that none of the miners would work on Saturdays, a rule that had been in force for three months: "Who was it who protested this action? The officials of the U.M.W.! However, we didn't listen to them. They said that doing that we violated the contract, etc., etc. And we responded to them that those contracts could be modified, and so it ended."[27]

Reaction: The American Context

The primary target of American nationalism in the 1920s was the new immigrant worker. This was true of the Ku Klux Klan and the American Legion. But anti-immigrant sentiment was increasingly embraced by American industry and by politicians of both parties. This culminated in passage of the Johnson Reed Act of 1924, which marked the *de facto* exclusion of Eastern and Southern Europeans until the 1950s.

The emergence of a belligerent nationalism had deep roots in American soil, as John Higham and others have persuasively argued.[28] Many aspects of American nationalism in the 1920s such as racism, anti-urbanism, anti–Catholicism, anti–Semitism, anti-immigrant chauvinism, anti-modernism, anti-radicalism, and so on, had by the time of World War I their own long and sordid pedigrees. This long-view intellectual approach helps us to understand cultural currents in U.S. history, but not why these tendencies emerged in such force when they did. Other scholars have attempted to explain particular manifestations of nationalism, reaction, and conservatism—such as the Red Scare, the emergence of the Klan, the abeyance of progressivism and urban liberalism, the domination of the White House by the Republican Party, prohibition, etc.—with reference to more immediate causes. These include the jarring changes of modernity—especially in relation to sexual liberation and urban culture, or to the insular and exhausted mood that resulted from Progressivism and Wilsonian internationalism. Indeed, when one adds up the ingredients of the 1920s reaction, it is clear that we are not dealing with any single historical oddity; we have, rather, a period of systemic reaction. Moreover, if we take a step further back from even this enormous subject, we see that the reactionary period in the U.S. during the 1920s was hardly unique—or even, relatively speaking, all that extreme.[29]

The new immigration supplies a means of understanding the 1920s reaction in the U.S. and in Europe. More than any other section of the population, new immigrant workers felt the full brunt of all of the chief characteristics of the post war reaction. The primary factor in the welling up of anti-immigrant sentiment was derived from what contemporaries called "the labor question." It is this element that also connects anti-new immigrant sentiment to the international post war reaction. Prior to World War I, entire sections of American industry—such as iron mining, steel milling, and in many locations, coal mining—were dominated by new immigrant workers. Leading academics, social observers, and the A.F.L., a union primarily of skilled and well-assimilated workers, cultivated an image of the new immigrants as passive, ignorant, and helpless, and because of this, the greatest single danger to "Anglo-Saxon" culture and the standard of living of American workers. Immigrant workers put paid to this myth in the years prior to World War I through strike militancy and a growing movement toward radical politics; but in so-doing, they began to garner a new negative image as dangerous carriers of foreign ideologies.

The movement of new immigrants toward strikes and radicalization, a stream before the war, turned into a torrent by 1916, just prior to U.S. entry. Mobilization for war demanded an exceptional degree of loyalty; American nationalism was elevated nearly to the level of a state religion by 1917. The war, in the domestic context, was used by the government, business, and the trade unions as a means of suppressing sharpening class and racial antagonisms and of rallying the population behind American war aims. Above all else, workers in key wartime industries, such as coal, iron, and steel, had to be kept at work. Yet despite unprecedented propaganda and repression American nationalism in World War I failed to head off the strike wave. Adding to the high-pressure atmosphere of domestic politics were intense gales from Europe—the prospect of independence for new states triggered new and competing nationalisms, and then came Russia's October revolution in 1917, which generated immense interest, repulsion, and enthusiasm across the U.S., and which had an enormous impact on new immigrant communities. Then, immediately after the war, the conflicts that had only been partially repressed surged to the fore in 1919, the largest strike wave in U.S. history to that point and the bloody "red summer" of racial violence. Four and one half million workers struck; massive strikes crippled the steel and coal industries. New immigrants again predominated. Radicalism reemerged, only to be ferociously countered by the first Red Scare. State repression continued against new immigrants in the postwar.

The postwar reaction was, in its many forms, an antidote against the radicalization and militancy of the new immigrants. This was a critical factor in the ending of the new immigration through Johnson-Reed in 1924 and the political shifts that prepared this landmark legislation. It was also true, either directly or indirectly, of other features of the postwar reaction. Americanism, or American nationalism, far from providing a vehicle to advance the interest of workers, as some scholars have argued,[30] was in fact from the beginning used as a battering ram against them. This was true during the war, when Americanism was used to obscure class divisions. It was even more obviously true after the war, when it was used to openly suppress resurgent working class struggle.

In the ideology espoused by the Klan and the Legion we see the unity of several leading aspects of the American nationalism of the 1920s relating to culture, the labor question, and immigration. As in its first incarnation, the Klan was against "race mixing." But this subterfuge for the political terrorization of African Americans was joined by new concerns for the 1920s: now the Klan was anti-communist, anti-strike, anti–Catholic, anti-immigrant, anti-modern, and anti–Semitic. It was for "100 percent Americanism" and the so-called "Nordic races." Yet scholarship on the Klan has underemphasized the role it played in attempting to intimidate new immigrant workers. In summarizing revisionist work on the Klan, one scholar has gone so far as to present the group as largely innocuous social club and even a sort of egalitarian-populist formation.[31] This was not how the Klan presented itself, nor how it was viewed by contemporaries. Though scholarship has largely missed the Klan's connection to new immigrant workers, it has shown that wherever there were large numbers of the latter, the Klan appeared. Moreover, the evidence from the Iron Range, the Illinois coal fields, Calumet, and from secondary literature shows that the Klan was composed overwhelmingly of non-immigrant and middle class elements. The Legion and the Klan frequently engaged in violence, but more significant than the actual violence was its threat—and the protection the organizations enjoyed from authorities, which stood in stark contrast to the repression meted out against immigrant radicals.[32]

Both the Klan and the Legion called themselves "100 percent American" organizations, carrying out parades and other manifestations of militant Americanism. In the Finnish socialist halls of northern Minnesota and Wisconsin, the Legion occasionally entered meetings to intimidate audiences. A leader of Finnish socialists in Duluth, Arvid Nelson, explained to a correspondent that "rounding up communists appears to be the latest fad on the program of the reactionaries" on the Mesabi Range, where "six Finn boys were arrested in Gilbert, Minn."[33] One of the Legion's most spectacular attacks took place in Weirton, West Virginia, where 150 "Red Finn" steelworkers were rounded up, marched to the public square, forced to kiss American flags, and then driven from the town. The men, not coincidentally, were reputed to be "the leaders" of the Great Steel Strike in Weirton.[34] Indeed, the suppression of the steel strike was everywhere "combined with an anti-radical campaign."[35] The Chicago Croatian newspaper *Znanje* warned its readers that "the legionnaires are armed. They usurp the right to arrest people, to disband meetings of foreign workers, to demolish business places, to destroy libraries, and to commit other acts of violence."[36]

The Klan held large rallies in the mining towns of Springfield, Illinois, and Virginia, Minnesota, cities at the heart of coal and iron regions, respectively. New immigrants remembered these events decades later to oral historians. One elderly Italian immigrant, interviewed in 1981 in Eveleth, Minnesota, recalled the Klan rallies in Virginia and the burning of the cross on slag heaps. The Klan thought that "they were the upper class" of the Range towns, he said. Young Celeste Sambucci recalled hurling rocks at the Klansmen with his friends, then boys. Henry Pappone, too, remembered how the Klan burnt crosses on slag heaps, and going with boyhood friends to shoot sling shots at them. In a memoir written in the 1970s, an elderly Italian immigrant from an Illinois coalmining town told of remarkably similar memories:

> This increase in foreigners was not going to pass unnoticed by the old stock American families of the area. Some of the latter joined the Ku Klux Klan.... I can remember stumbling upon a group of them with their white robes and paraphernalia one night. It scared the heck out of me.... They burned a cross on the jumbo [tm: slag heap] one night, but that brought a sharp reaction from the Italians, who knew quite well what the Klan was all about.[37]

Molly Morcum, the daughter of a Slovenian miner, remembered cross burning in her small Vermillion Range town of Soudan. As the Klan burnt crosses in sight of the elementary school while the children were in session, "we'd all look through our windows. We'd be scared stiff. The Masons did it. Small business owners. Those crosses, and the flames would go, and we'd look through, way down, we lived at the other end, and we could see it. It was behind the school here. And it was up high, and here we'd all run. Everybody knew then what was going on.... You know, little kids, how scared you would be. You wouldn't dare go out at night, you'd be really afraid of that."[38]

The Klan operated in areas with large new immigrant populations, but it didn't have free reign there, as the immigrant boys recollections of throwing rocks at the Klansmen suggest. In an Illinois coal town, an elderly Italian recalled, "miners, brickyard workers and so forth, banding together with pickaxes, shotguns and the like, were not easily intimidated. The Klan, some of whom were local people who were hypocritically friendly during the day, quickly abandoned any scare tactics around Roanoke."[39]

In June of 1921, a horrific lynching of two black circus workers took place in Duluth, Minnesota. Much like lynching in the South, the two men were accused of raping a white woman, under charges shortly exposed as bogus.[40] This brought reflection from a Finnish socialist, who wrote to his brother, "They pulled off a lynching bee in Duluth on Tuesday evening of this week.... The whole stunt is what you might call 100 per cent Americanism and I guess it helped place Duluth on the map for some time to come." The connection to "100 percent Americanism" was significant: "They said it was the first lynching in Duluth just as if they did not remember that a poor Finnish workingman met a similar fate there in the hands of a few prominent 'citizens' during the Liberty bond drives. The poor fellow was found hung to a tree with his hands tied behind his back a bunch of war savings stamps in his pocket. And they said he 'apparently committed suicide' after being tarred and feathered."[41]

In the Calumet area and Chicago in 1922 and 1923 the Klan experienced a meteoric rise and fall. Chicago became the largest single "klavern" in the country, with as many as 200,000 in the greater Chicago area joining, and publishing its own newspaper, *Dawn: A Journal for True American Patriots*. There were 500 Klansmen in the Gary, Indiana, chapter at its height, another 2,500 elsewhere in Lake County, Indiana, and there were chapters in Joliet, Chicago Heights, Blue Island, Hammond, and Michigan City. However, Chicago was not friendly terrain. A large majority of the city's population was Roman Catholic, Jewish, African American, immigrant, or the children of immigrants—or some combination of these categories. In Chicago the Klan studiously avoided violence, and some of its largest rallies were held at a safe distance from the city. In response to the Klan, Chicago's Irish establishment and Catholic Church formed an organization called the American Unity League, which invited participation among African American and immigrant groups. It began publishing a newspaper called *Tolerance* that listed the names of Klansmen. The city's large ethnic population boycotted shopkeepers and professionals whose names made the list.[42]

As the oral histories suggest, the Klan was comprised largely of middle class and "American" elements. It was not, in the first place, an organization of dying rural America. In Chicago, over 60 percent of Klansmen were "white-collar workers," with businessmen, salesmen, clerks, and lawyers being the largest represented professions. The numbers of Klansmen defined as "blue-collar workers" were remarkably low:

only 2.7 percent were counted as "unskilled workers," and even less, .9 percent, worked in factories. On the other hand, 7.3 percent of Klansmen were foremen, and the rest of those not white-collar workers came from the ranks of skilled labor.[43] The vigilantes were given practical state sanction, as we have seen, during the war, when they massed into organizations like the American Protective League, whose members also tended to be middle class, shop owners, professionals, and the well-assimilated. In the Great Steel Strike, one of the most important anti-strike organizations was the Loyal American League, an organization "composed primarily of Gary businessmen, professionals, and others from the city's WASP establishment," that attempted to intimidate strikers and radicals. Mother Jones, after visiting Gary, described the league as made up of "little shopkeepers dependent upon the smile of the steel companies." The A.P.L.'s origins were in the war, when it was also a "patriotic vigilante group."[44]

Herrin, Illinois, which had only two years earlier been the sight of the massacre of strikebreakers, became in its wake a center for Klan activity. According to the *New York Times*, the Klan "organizers made no attempt to disguise the fact that the object of the Klan in Williamson was to destroy the strong coal miners' union by spreading the doctrines of religious and racial bigotry." The Klan began to operate openly in Williamson County in 1923, and soon attracted thousands of members. It cooperated closely with state and federal authorities, who granted copious "search warrants" for Klansmen to investigate violations of Prohibition. New immigrants throughout the county, and especially Catholics, were targeted, as well as Anglo-American bootleggers.[45]

Prohibition was inseparable from other major questions of the period, a fact not lost on the conservative *Bulletin of the Italian American Union*. "The Immigration Law, the Naturalization Law, and no less vicious, the Prohibition Law were created, it seems, to strike at the Italian," it wrote.[46] Samuel Gompers and the A.F.L. opposed prohibition, too. His was an opposition that even more clearly suggested the close relationship of the controversy over consumption of alcohol to immigration and the labor question. "Instead of sitting down over his pitcher of beer," Gompers warned, the worker "goes into the streets to meet other men restless and unsettled like himself. They rub together their mutual grievances and there are sparks and sometimes fire." In the same article, Gompers made the improbable claim that "Bolshevism in Russia began in Prohibition," hastening to add that this was a problem especially with the new immigrants: "The apostles of Bolshevism in this country seize Prohibition as a mighty weapon to force into their ranks the foreign-born people of the United State who have accustomed to the use of beer and light wine."[47]

Some new immigrants recognized that they were at the center of powerful political pressures. In an oral history Chicagoan Roberto De Facci remembered how the Sacco and Vanzetti case was bound-up with the Russian Revolution, the presence of new immigrants, and the defense of U.S. industry: "They knew this was a frame[-up]. See in the establishment ... see there was another hysteria period in those days. It was right after the Russian revolution and there are so many ethnic groups that came in after the war they came in the millions, including me, you know? What scared all these people, the establishment, and especially the eastern banker, they were afraid that we would come in with this idea and like an infection, you know what I mean? So they took this as a pretext to kill. This had no more to do with it than the man on the moon. They know it too, somebody ... had to pay the price."[48]

Transatlantic Reaction: The European Context

In Europe, there developed a political reaction even more profound than in the U.S. While revolutionary hopes in the early 1920s remained—Germany again experienced revolutionary circumstances in 1923, as did Bulgaria—1919 had passed, and with it much that had seemed to threaten world order. The left wing maximalism of the early 1920s based on the presumption of imminent revolution—a tendency very much evident in the new immigrant sections of the young U.S. communist movement—stood in increasing contradiction to the ebb tide of working class struggle and capitalist stabilization. This outlook Lenin called "an infantile disorder."[49]

The left receded in Eastern and Southern Europe in tandem with the advance of nationalism, which had been given a great material push forward by the formation of a number of new states from the wreckage of the old empires. Finland, Estonia, Latvia, Lithuania and Poland were born in the Baltic; Austria, Czechoslovakia, and Hungary emerged in Central Europe; and a new Yugoslavia joined Bulgaria, a greater Romania, Greece, Albania, and Turkey in the Balkans, facing an impoverished Italy across the Adriatic. Not only did these states prove inhospitable to working class movements, liberal democracy—as supposedly exemplified by the Western powers—also failed to take hold or collapsed more or less quickly. Among the foregoing list of countries, only Czechoslovakia maintained liberal-democratic and constitutional forms throughout the interwar years. All the states, new and old, based nationalist ideology on irredentist grievances of one sort or another. Moreover, in an economic sense, a proliferation of customs duties and borders further "balkanized" the largely agricultural region. In terms of their social basis, the Eastern European regimes tended to speak for the most socially conservative elements in society—large feudalistic landowners, the clergy, the government bureaucracy, and the military. Fascism emerged as a potent force in a number of Eastern European states from the 1920s onward. Unlike in Italy and Germany, the "native fascism" of the Eastern European states produced no seizure of state power until the onset of World War I. Yet forms of "white terror" and nationalist authoritarian states that emerged certainly held much in common with their bigger neighbors to the West. Throughout Eastern Europe weak and economically backward states based on conservative or reactionary socio-political forces emerged.[50]

Case Studies: Italian and Finnish Radicalism in the United States

Perhaps the most striking example of transatlantic revolutionary hope and then defeat took place not in Eastern Europe, but in Italy, the largest single homeland of new immigrants in the U.S. Of all the victorious Allied powers of World War I, Italy faced the most severe revolutionary crisis. In certain respects Italy resembled Russia. In both nations, a relatively weak industrial capitalism confronted powerful feudal and landed interests on the one side and a relatively small but strategically-powerful working class and a massive and restive peasantry on the other. The social polarization that engulfed Italy in the wake of World War I threatened revolution. The period of 1919–1921 came to be known as the "Two Red Years," and it was punctuated by "the occupation of the factories" in September of 1920, when industrial workers assumed physical control over the most important sectors of economic production. The subject of why Italy's proto-revolutionary experience failed cannot be the subject of this chapter. But the explosive situation did lead, eventually, to the collapse of liberal democracy.[51]

Benito Mussolini and the fascists came to power as an antidote to the working class struggles. Now with the tacit backing of the state, the fascists unleashed a reign of terror on the organizations of the insurgent working class. Street battles, public humiliations, and extra-legal violence soon chastened communists, socialists, anarchists, syndicalists, and the unions. In short order, such organizations were banned altogether and democracy ended. In all its critical elements, the scenario provided a dress rehearsal for the Nazi seizure of power that would come in Germany a decade later.[52]

The fascist movement's gradual consolidation of state power in Italy was a heavy blow for Italian American radicals, who were at the same moment increasingly isolated in the U.S. due to the decline of the strike wave and the anti-foreigner belligerence of American nationalism. The significant presence that Italian syndacalists and socialists had on the Iron Range seems to have disappeared or gone underground by the 1920s; in Illinois, radical Italian coal miners found an arena of struggle in the Progressive Mineworkers of America. The Italian Chamber of Labor, begun so auspiciously in 1919, soon found itself reformulated primarily as an anti-fascist organization, with *"gruppi antifascisti"* formed from its chapters. The defeat of the Italian left put to an end promising direct organizational links that had been created in the previous years. It also promoted nationalist currents in the Italian American community. While some Italian radicals came to the U.S. in flight from fascism, the organized Italian American left declined, and increasingly focused on defensive measures—anti-fascism, defense of class war prisoners in Italy, and the Sacco and Vanzetti case. At the same time, fascism exerted an appeal on Italians abroad. Many went back to Italy in the period. Italian American communists found themselves, according to Anthony Capraro, "isolated from [the] movement in Italy and from the one in the U.S." For some Italian Americans, Mussolini's claims about restoring the glories of Rome, Italy's inflated position in Great Power politics, and its colonial machinations in the Mediterranean and Africa provided a pole of attraction and a sense of national pride for a population that had been subjected in the U.S. to racialized humiliation. Some Italian Americans fought fascism in the U.S., even if it could not be fought openly in Italy. But the decline of Italian American radicalism was undeniable. When Italian American fascists marched to cheers from the crowd in 1924 in a Memorial Day parade in Lawrence—that sight of striking Italian American worker militancy in the strikes of 1913 and 1919—the feeling of defeat was palpable.[53]

If Italy teetered on the brink of a revolution from 1919 to 1922, developments took place in Finland much more rapidly. In November of 1918, a general strike gripped Finland in the wake of the October revolution in Russia, which centered in nearby Petrograd. In elections earlier in the year, bourgeois and conservative parties had gained a majority in parliament. These elements immediately sought to use the opportunity of the Russian Revolution to gain independence for Finland. The provisional government appealed unsuccessfully to Sweden and Germany for recognition; ironically it was the young Soviet regime that first recognized Finland as an independent state, a position that reflected Lenin's policy on the "national question" as well as his hostility to "Great Russian chauvinism." One month after the Soviet Union recognized Finland, however, Red Guards seized control of the government in Helsinki, and soon consolidated power throughout the industrial South, declaring a Soviet Republic. The "white government" fled, and entrenched itself in the North and West of the nation, where it disarmed thousands of Russian troops bewildered by the twin Russian and Finnish revolutions. The white government accused Russian Bolsheviks of intervening on the part of the Red government, thought there was little material support. The whites, however, were assisted by a small contingent of well-trained German troops—only about 10,000—who were able to defeat the Red government after several months of intense fighting. Those unable to flee became targets of the "white terror," with tens of thousands placed in concentration camps where starvation, disease, and firing squads claimed thousands of lives.[54]

Ironically, the sharp divisions between "white" and "red" had been presaged more among the Finnish immigrants in the U.S. than in Finland itself, where the ferocity of internal class divisions had been muted by Czarist control. The "red" socialist and "white" national press in the U.S. fought out a war of words over the events in Finland, the labor press hailing the new workers' state and solidarizing itself with the Bolsheviks in Russia. The Finnish American left expressed incredulity at the failure of the Red government, assigning much of the blame to the limited German intervention. For its part, the white press hailed the victory of the Mannerheim government and Finnish independence, and attracted attention instead to Russian-Bolshevik intervention. Each side, therefore, found its foreign stalking horse.[55]

Though the white government's alignment with Germany in 1918 amounted to a desperation measure as much dictated by geography as political affinity, it had interesting repercussions for early U.S.–Soviet relations. The U.S. could not officially support or recognize an ally of Germany, and the Finnish Red government worked to exploit the situation by installing a diplomatic mission, the Finnish Information Bureau, led by the Finnish immigrant socialist, Santeri Nuorteva. Though Nuorteva failed to gain U.S. recognition for the Reds—much less any sort of assistance—his office's propaganda efforts placed conservative White Finns in the delicate position of supporting a government allied with the U.S.'s main enemy, Germany, at the same time giving an extra boost of morale to those immigrants who supported the Red government. However, after the collapse of the Red government in Finland, Nuorteva's office assumed another role: it became the only diplomatic outpost for the young Soviet state in the U.S. Funding for the diplomatic mission which had come from the F.S.F. was replaced by the fall of 1918 by money from the Soviet Government. In January 1919 Ludwig C.A.K. Martens took over Nuorteva's office, and the latter went to work for the newly-minted Information Bureau of the Soviet Government of Russia.[56]

Finnish radicalism had not written its final pages in the greater drama of U.S. radicalism. The F.S.F. claimed victory in defeat, and announced a "Million Mark Fund" to rebuild the Finnish left—more than the targeted amount of money was raised and sent to Finland in 1920. Finnish workers clubs made many direct appeals to Finnish-American socialists for support through the left-wing press. At the same time they funded the rebuilding of the Finnish Social Democratic Party in Finland, Finnish communists provide crucial resources for the building of U.S. communism. Later, in the 1930s, several thousand Finnish American communists migrated to Finnic-speaking Soviet Karelia in the 1930s, often taking with them all of their possessions in order to help build the "workers' paradise." This so-called "Karelia Fever" tragically resulted in the killing or disappearance of most of the male portion of this migration, as they fell to Stalin's purges in the late 1930s. Newspapers representing the three main currents of Finnish American radicalism continued for decades, and the *Työvaen Opisto* (Work People's College) became the official college of the I.W.W. Yet decline was sharpest for the I.W.W. Most of its best known leaders rejoined the F.S.F. or left for Russia. Its rank-and-file membership remained so enthusiastic about the Russian Revolution through the early 1920s, that the I.W.W. saw a sharp decline when it finally began to openly criticize it. In any case, an overall decline of radicalism among Finns, dictated by events in both Europe and the U.S., had set in by 1919.[57]

Voting with Their Feet: Return Migration

Just as mass immigration had been a formative characteristic of U.S. industrial and political developments prior to World War I, the ending of the new immigration was bound up with economic and political developments transatlantic in scope. Another element of the turbulence afflicting the new immigrant communities in the aftermath of World War I was return migration, which American business interests initially reacted to as another example of the "Bolshevik menace." Former Minnesota Governor A.O. Eberhart by 1919 headed a company specializing in "Americanization." He wrote to U.S. Steel that millions of new immigrants, "[W]ill actually go taking with them billions of our currency.... A shortage of labor will obviously mean high wages, strikes, industrial unrest, and all the attendant evils. The laborers who remain, in the absence of competition, can then dictate wages while the employer stands helpless. Prompt and concerted action is needed by American employers to counteract this mentality warping Bolsheviki propaganda." While fears over the depletion of currency were also raised, the primary concern was a fear of scarcity of labor. Was there any basis to the fears? It seems that among the industries studied there was indeed a sharp spike in repatriation in 1919 and 1920. This was true among most new immigrant groups, but especially among those from the lands farthest east and south in Europe. Most of the returnees were young single men. The most obvious factor in this change was that the ending of hostilities in late 1918 opened once again the major transportation links to Eastern Europe after five years' closure.[58]

Dejection at the American experience and defeat in strikes contributed to return migration as well, an explanation advanced by the new immigrant press. "While they were here," lamented the *Magyar Tribune*, "they were degraded and discriminated against, which accounts largely for their desire to leave." The radical Croatian newspaper, *Znanje*, cited the propaganda against new immigrants as a factor. "It seems that all the wrongs that torture the world are the fault of the foreign worker," it wrote. "This situation is becoming unbearable for foreign workers, and they are eager to leave the country." It claimed that 8,000 Croatian workers had "left for home on account of the steel strike and the bad treatment received from employers."[59] For their part, the business elite were convinced that the repatriation was yet another sign of the Bolshevik menace. Whatever its causes, from 1919 on return migration likely outstripped the number of immigrants entering. More Croatians returned from the U.S. than entered it in 1919, 1920, 1922, and 1924. Among Poles, return migration was called a "fever." One study of Russian immigrants estimated that in 1920 "fully 90% ... would go home if they could," but were prevented from doing so until the spring of 1920 when U.S. government prohibition on travel to Soviet Russia was lifted. By 1921, even though "the difficulties in the way of travel are enormous ... the exodus has begun." Russian immigrants "want to see for themselves" the results of the revolution. The author, who interviewed "Russian workmen all over American in 1920" "met only a mere handful who did not say they wished to return at once."[60]

The case of the Yugoslav immigrants is suggestive. The Commissioner General of Immigration of the Department of Labor calculated the "Yugoslav" category broadly, including not only those nations that comprised the new Yugoslav nation, but also Macedonians from Greece, and Bulgarians. From 1918 through 1924, 16,485 more Yugoslavs left the U.S. than arrived. Even after the Johnson-Reed Act (or National Origins Act of 1924), more Yugoslavs left the country than arrived, in spite of the fact that the law allowed for the reunification of families and, for other non-naturalized Yugoslav emigrants, the door would shut behind them. At the same time, immigration restriction in the U.S. seems to have pushed the stream of Yugoslav immigrants toward Canada and South America.[61]

At the level of the political consciousness of the returnees, we know little, though these masses of young men were leaving one turbulent society and entering another. It is beyond question, given the enormity of the strike wave that gripped the U.S. from 1916 to 1922, that a very high proportion of these returnees would have experienced first-hand industrial struggle in the U.S. Depending somewhat on the nationality in question, a greater or lesser proportion of them may have gained experience in the U.S. with some form of radicalism—through the foreign language federations, through the reach of the radical press, or through the I.W.W. Of course many of the more illustrious Southern and Eastern European immigrants—starting with the Russians Trotsky, Bukharin, and Kollontai—made a name for themselves on return. There were many other figures of some prominence among Finns, Latvians, Yugoslavs, and so on, that made what we might call "an international circuit of radicalism." But what of the masses of young, cosmopolitan men? What role did they have to play in the political struggles that would punctuate Eastern and Southern European history in the coming 25 years?[62]

Puskás, the eminent Hungarian scholar of emigration, has written suggestively on this question. Local authorities in peasant villages resented the democratic mores that had developed among "the Americans": "they have no respect for authority," "they urge people to rebel and emigrate," "they do not want to work," "they are unpatriotic," "they do not go to church," "they spread Pan-Slav ideas," "they praise American democracy and say that there everyone is 'Mister.'" She notes that there were also powerful re-acculturating tendencies working on the returnees, and that many hoped to simply buy land. Nationalism or national self-awareness at least gained through the experience, for "it was in the course of emigration that people from the villages rose above local patriotism and local solidarity." Yet "it is not by chance that research into local history reveals that the 'Americans' ... are always to be found among the local activists during the revolutionary times of 1918–1919." Among Finns, Virtanen has found that returning migrants were crucial in building up socialism in largely peasant Ostrobothnia. Some workers rose to prominence in the ranks of Finnish radicalism, such as the iron miner Oskari Tokoi, who became a leading figure in Finnish Social Democracy only after his ten year sojourn on the Iron Range. Another man, who was a teenage member of the I.W.W., eventually rose to head the Finnish Seamen's Union. A Lithuanian who had lived in the U.S. founded that country's Communist Party, Vincas Mickevičius-Kapsukas.

Conclusion

New immigrant radicalism and militancy had been pushed forward by events and ideologies on both sides of the Atlantic. Now, after 1919, it found itself caught in the vice of transatlantic reaction. However short-lived, its impact should not be underestimated. The American nationalist reaction of the 1920s largely defined itself against the new immigrants. In the decade from the outbreak of World War I in Europe to the passing of Johnson-Reed in 1924, the image of the immigrant became something of a stand-in for the specter of revolution.

The retreat from an open immigration policy dovetailed with the American government's movement toward "isolationism." The relationship was not coincidental. Here the new immigration provides a means of casting light upon international developments in the period. The Great War had resolved none of the basic contradictions of the world order that had given rise to it. The most profound of these contradictions was the conflict between the national state and globalizing economic production—of which mass immigration was an outstanding feature. Governments responded to the war by attempting to solidify the state—the story is well known to economic historians since the various barriers and restrictions on trade helped to set the stage for the Great Depression and World War II. The ending of the new immigration and the nationalist American reaction of the 1920s, then, must be understood as part of a worldwide nationalist reaction, a shoring up of the nation-state against disruptive social and economic forces.[63]

Epilogue: The Nation-State, Immigration Restriction and Fordism

A central question confronting scholars of immigration in U.S. history is why restriction of mass European immigration succeeded only when it did? The coalition of die-hard restrictionists—that combination of New England Anglo-Saxon elite with its fears of "race suicide," the A.F.L. and its defense of "the American standard of living," and reactionary southern and western politicians—had not much changed over the preceding decades. The A.F.L. continued to consider immigration restriction its highest political priority, as Gompers pointed out to readers of the *New York World* in 1924, near the end of his tenure. His language favoring restriction had scarcely changed from the 1890s: immigrants were "hordes of low wage European workers ... brought to America to destroy our standards of living and our standards of citizenship. This is a menace to every American interest." Ranking right after immigration restriction on Gompers' list of critical issues, was the suppression of "Communist propaganda" and the effort to give diplomatic recognition to "the unspeakable Soviets."[1] True, the popular mood had changed, with restriction gaining greater support in the population, a tendency that can be partially measured in the astonishing growth of the Ku Klux Klan. This changing popular mood, however, was not the work of the Zeitgeist, but of the largely middle class reaction against the polarization of U.S. society and, especially, the association of "the foreigner" with radicalism that had been conjured up not out of thin air, but based on the massive strikes, radical ideologies, and foreign revolutions of the preceding period.

A decisive change took place in the boardrooms and executive offices of U.S. industry. Big business lessened its opposition to immigration restriction. Industry had long been the most steadfast defender of open European immigration, a position advocated through the National Association of Manufacturers (N.A.M.). Indeed, it is a testament to the political weight of big business at the time that in spite of mounting popular opposition a relatively lax immigration policy held sway into the early 1920s. A number of factors paved the way for this crucial shift. First, after the enormous production of World War I, the U.S. economy confronted significant overcapacity. The "reconversion" began with the depression of 1920–22. In order to defend profit margins, efficiency would be the order of the day. Furthermore, the mass migration of blacks from the South and the immigration of Mexicans looked poised to fill any acute labor needs for U.S. industry. There had also been, even prior to restriction, a diminution of immigration from Europe. Finally, and perhaps most importantly, the tumultuous labor situation of the war years through 1922, with enormous and persistent strikes and high labor turnover, had pushed industrial and financial interests toward a new labor regime, one much broader than the experiments of the first decades of the 20th century—toward Fordism.

A critical factor in the changed position of business and political leaders toward immigration was the association of the new immigrants with political radicalism and labor militancy. The bitter struggles of the period lasting from 1916 until 1919 were associated with the new immigrants and with either the I.W.W. or "Bolshevism." The Great Steel Strike, which involved 350,000 workers and stretched from Chicago to New Jersey, was simply called "a Hunky strike" carried out under "Bolshevist" influence. It was commonly accepted—and in fact was actually the case—that the overwhelming majority of communists and of left wing socialists were new immigrants. The newly founded communist movement was perhaps 90 percent foreign—and nearly half Finnish.

The Finnish press by itself amounted to about one third of total party circulation, and through its halls and cooperative movement, it continued to be an important source of revenue for the national party. Nonetheless, the Finns held little influence in the national party, and according to Klehr, were perceived as "petty-bourgeois farmers." On the Iron Range, the I.W.W. was totally comprised of new immigrants, and in Illinois the organization had adherents or sympathizers among immigrant coal miners, especially Italians. There was also within the U.M.W. an association of the most radical and militant elements with the new immigrants. The memory of the new immigrants' militancy—

Table 4. National Composition of the Workers Party (U.S.) by Nationality, 1921

Nationality	Members	Percent of Total
Finnish	6,803	44.7
American	1,192	7.8
South Slavic	1,064	7.0
Jewish	1,048	6.9
Lithuanian	1,048	6.9
Russian	877	5.8
Hungarian	359	2.4
Italian	349	2.1
Polish	245	1.6
Scandinavian	243	1.6
Others	2,182	14.2
Total	15,233	100.0
New Immigrant	11,889	78.5

Source: Kivisto, *Immigrant Socialists*, 167.

and the evidence of their radicalism—from the Great Steel Strike was still fresh.[2]

In sum, business arrived at the view that its traditional source of labor, Europe, was the very source of class conflict and radicalism. Indeed, during the Great Steel Strike, both "American" and African American workers proved to be more reliable. In some quarters it was presumed that southern Americans, white and black, would be more amenable to corporate needs and less receptive to "foreign" ideologies. To this must be added the changing employment patterns favored by American industry. As Bruno Ramirez has pointed out, mass immigration was the prerequisite to the reorganization of American industry in the first two decades of the 20th century. The steel and coal industries provide prime examples of this, as I show in my first chapter. But new problems resulted. Both skilled and unskilled employment declined relative to the rise of semi-skilled labor through mechanization, which presupposed a more stable and loyal workforce. Management in the steel industry had been aware of these problems early on, and from the first years of the 20th century had experimented with company welfare schemes, model towns, employee stock ownership, and so on, to limited results. Instead, corporate welfare, relative stability of employment, and the promotion of employee loyalty would become the hallmarks of the Fordist economy beginning in the 1920s.

The critical element in all of this was the question of labor turnover, which had become a major issue during the war.

Immigration restriction was bound up with changes to employment patterns in the U.S., both in terms of a rapid increase in worker productivity that took place in the 1920s, and more generally to what might be defined as the prevailing "social contract" between employers and workers. The connection between immigration restriction and developing managerial techniques was not lost on contemporaries, although it was not always clear what was cause and what was effect. "Restrictions on immigration brought about by the war and legislation," wrote one sociologist, "have led employers to conserve the skill and strength of their labor and to put a considerable investment into training and improving it." The characteristic developments of managerial reform in the 1920s—corporate welfare, professional personnel management, and scientific management—had their roots in the late Progressive era, when they were largely concerned with the problem of the new immigrant worker.[3]

It is appropriate that Ford gave its name to an entire economic epoch of labor-management relations that was being fitfully born in these years, supplanting an earlier, and fittingly nameless period that was perhaps best represented by U.S. Steel. The auto industry had been among the hardest hit by labor turnover in the nineteen-teens. The impetus for all of Ford's early sociological work, and even the "five dollar day," were bound up with his concerns for Americanizing his largely immigrant workforce.[4] It should come as no surprise, then, that it was Ford that pioneered a new form of management predicated on the technological advance of the assembly line. It was in Ford's plants that corporate welfare reached its pinnacle, but Fordism went beyond that. It was also based on the notion that workers could aspire to be consumers like the middle class, and that workers might work at one factory and for one employer for their entire career, based upon a bond of mutual loyalty and understanding. What was being authored in the early 1920s, in other words, was a new social contract between capital and labor. The Italian Marxist Antonio Gramsci early detected the elements of a new social order in Fordism that extended from its mass production methods far beyond, giving shape to a new social order. This would be contingent, Gramsci thought, on the disciplining or absorption of organized labor in exchange for a higher standard of living for workers.[5]

Until the 1920s, these schemes were largely failures. Scientific management never gained any traction in either the coal or steel industries, while U.S. Steel's experiment with corporate welfare was revealed as a failure when it was put to the test by the Great Steel Strike of 1919. Management experts concluded that the schemes failed because they were too limited in their scope. They had been exposed by the labor unrest and turnover of the preceding years. What was required was something much broader. As one manager put it, "We employers who feel that management is to become a true science must begin to think less of the science of material things and more of the science of human relationships." This new approach came to be called the American Plan. The central goals of "promoting higher productivity and reducing labor turnover, industrial strife" and unionization, according to Montgomery, "included systematic hiring procedures, a large staff to handle workers' grievances on and off the job, and employee representation plans to encourage a sense of participation by the workers in the execution of company policies," as well as, finally, scientific management and corporate welfare.[6]

Edwards, considering the case of Ford, argues convincingly that ultimately the search for order arose out of the implementation of new technology; this he calls the search for "technological control." Foremen, with their power over the shop floor, their right to hire and fire, had remained strong at Ford through the nineteen-teens. It was the reorganization of work that eventually made the foreman less powerful as machines came to supplant the foremen in directing the actual physical organization of work: "With foremen holding less responsibility for the direction of work, they needed less power. Their power of arbitrary dismissal had been essential as long as the battle between workers and bosses was a directly personal one. But this power was costly; by 1914 so many workers were fired or quit that five hundred new workers had to be hired each day to replenish the fifteen-thousand-person workforce; the payroll office maintained records on nearly one hundred thousand persons previously employed at Ford."[7]

The corporate control at the heart of Henry Ford's labor regime was shattered by the Great Depression, when the state and organized labor reasserted a degree of control over the relationship between the industrial worker and industry. But this new labor regime, which would last until the 1970s, did not represent a rejection of Fordism at its most elemental level—the stability of the workforce—as opposed to the wide open regime of rapidly moving labor that had characterized the era of U.S. Steel's corporate preeminence. For the latter, in its heyday, an open immigration policy was needed. But the lessons of World War I compelled a decisive section of the U.S. corporate elite to embrace workforce stability and abandon the open immigration policy. What had those lessons been? Business interests had not forgotten the militancy and radicalism of the nineteen-teens, or the problems of high labor turnover in a situation of nearly full employment.

Interestingly, our own time bears much greater resemblance to the pre–Fordist labor regime. Highly transient immigrant workers have once again come to play a major role in the labor force. In addition, industrial production and even service industries rapidly disperse and relocate around the world. Workers no longer expect to work one or two or even three jobs in their career; they fully expect to move, usually multiple times. The forces of globalization have ultimately subverted the Fordist economy and the social contract that undergirded it.

The new immigrants, through their militant labor struggles and radicalization, provided the prime impetus for these developments. Though many of their labor struggles went down to defeat, and though the immigrant component of radicalism was weakened by the transatlantic reaction of the 1920s, their experience holds valuable lessons for workers today. Immigrants now comprise a critical component of the working class in most countries, and their transnational lives link them with workers in their homelands. Just as occurred in the 1920s, immigrant workers have provided a political lightning rod for social tensions building up in a number of nations—tensions that arise, once again, out of the globalization of economic production. Immigrants will undoubtedly play a significant role in labor struggles in the coming years, as the massive protests of Mexican and Latino workers on May 1, 2006, perhaps presaged. As was the case in the nineteen-teens and 1920s, labor and radical formations in the immigrants' new lands will face difficulties in reaching this section of the workforce. However, history suggests that immigrant workers must play a role in labor struggles and radicalism that equals their indispensable role in the global economy.

Chapter Notes

Introduction

1. http://ddr.lib.drake.edu/cdm4/item_viewer.php?CISOROOT=/ddarling&CISOPTR=l157&REC=1.
2. Robert K. Murray, *Red Scare: A Study in National Hysteria, 1919–1920* (Minneapolis: University of Minnesota Press, 1955); William Preston, *Aliens and Dissenters: Federal Suppression of Radicals, 1903–1933* (Urbana: University of Illinois Press, 1994); John Higham, *Strangers in the Land: Patterns of American Nativism, 1860–1925* (New Brunswick, NJ: Rutgers University Press, 1988).
3. Joseph McCartin, *Labor's Great War: The Struggle for Industrial Democracy and the Origins of Modern American Labor Relations, 1912–1921* (Chapel Hill: University of North Carolina Press, 1997); Joan M. Jensen, *The Price of Vigilance* (Chicago: Rand McNally, 1969); Charles S. Maier, *Recasting Bourgeois Europe: Stabilization in France, Germany, and Italy in the Decade After World War I* (Princeton, NJ: Princeton University Press, 1975).
4. Aristide Zolberg, *A Nation by Design: Immigration Policy in the Fashioning of America* (Cambridge: Harvard University Press, 2006); Michael Robert LeMay and Elliott Robert Barkan, eds., *Immigration and Naturalization Laws and Issues: A Documentary History* (Westport, CT: Greenwood, 1999); Mae Ngai, *Impossible Subjects: Illegal Aliens and the Making of Modern America* (Princeton: Princeton University Press, 2004); Sumner H. Slichter, *The Turnover of Factory Labor* (New York: D. Appelton, 1919), and "The Scope and Nature of the Labor Turnover Problem," *Quarterly Journal of Economics* 34 (Feb. 1920): 329–345; Paul F. Brissenden, "Occupational Incidence of Labor Mobility," *Journal of the American Statistical Association* 18 (December 1923): 978–992; David Montgomery, *Workers' Control in America: Studies in the History of Work, Technology, and Labor Struggles* (Cambridge: Cambridge University Press, 1979), 35; David Brody, *Workers in Industrial America: Essays on the Twentieth Century Struggle* (New York: Oxford University Press, 1993), 12–13.
5. Lizebeth Cohen, *Making a New Deal: Industrial Workers in Chicago, 1919–1939* (Cambridge: Cambridge University Press, 1990), 50; Oscar Handlin, *The Uprooted* (Boston: Little, Brown, 1973); Gerald Rosenblum, *Immigrant Workers: Their Impact on American Labor Radicalism* (New York: Basic Books, 1973); Mark Wyman, *Round-Trip to America: The Immigrants Return to Europe, 1880–1930* (Ithaca, NY: Cornell University Press, 1993).
6. James R. Barrett, "Americanization from the Bottom Up: Immigration and the Remaking of the Working Class in the United States, 1880–1930," *The Journal of American History* 79, no. 3 (1992): 996–1020; John J. Kulczycki, *The Polish Coal Miner's Union and the German Labor Movement in the Ruhr, 1902–1934: National and Social Solidarity* (Oxford: Berg, 1997).
7. Herbert Gutman, "The Negro and the United Mine Workers of America: The Career and Letters of Richard L. Davis and Something of Their Meaning, 1890–1900," in *The Negro and the American Labor Movement,* ed. Julius Jacobson (New York: Doubleday, 1968).
8. On the use of race and "national origin" in the formation of the Immigration Act of 1924, see Mae Ngai, *The Architecture of Race in American Immigration Law: A Reexamination of the Immigration Act of 1924,* Vol. 86, No. 1 (June 1999): 67–92.
9. E.D. McCallum, *The Iron and Steel Industry in the United States* (London: P.S. King and Son, 1931), 25–26.

10. Gunther Peck, *Reinventing Free Labor: Padrones and Immigrant Workers in the North American West, 1880–1930* (Cambridge: Cambridge University Press, 2000).
11. McCallum, *The Iron and Steel Industry*, 59–63; D.G. Sofchalk, "Organized Labor and the Iron Ore Miners of Northern Minnesota, 1907–1936," *Labor History* 12, no. 2 (1971): 214–242; John Sirjamaki, "Development of Mesabi Communities" (Ph.D. diss., Yale, 1940); Paul Henry Landis, *Three Iron Mining Towns, a Study in Cultural Change* (Ann Arbor: Edwards Brothers, 1938); Joseph C. Mullin and Wallace P. Mullin, "United States Steel's Acquisition of the Great Northern Ore Properties: Vertical Foreclosure or Efficient Contractual Governance?" *Journal of Law, Economics, & Organization* 13, no. 1 (April 1997): 74–100.
12. John R. Commons, "The Delivered Price Practice in the Steel Market," *The American Economic Review* 14, no. 3 (September 1924): 505–519; William Cronon, *Nature's Metropolis: Chicago and the Great West*, 1st ed. (New York: W.W. Norton, 1991).
13. J. McCallum, *The Iron and Steel Industry*, 51, 65; David Brody, *In Labor's Cause: Main Themes on the History of the American Worker* (New York: Oxford University Press, 1993), 131.
14. Sydney A. Hale, "Marketing of Bituminous Coal," in Records of the U.S. Coal Commission, Commission Reports and Related Correspondence, December 1922 to July 1923 (Entry 3, Box 2, Record Group 68), National Archives.
15. McCallum, 119–122; Alfred Dupont Chandler, *The Visible Hand: The Managerial Revolution in American Business* (Cambridge, MA: Belknap Press of Harvard University Press, 1977), 105–311; Gabriel Kolko, *Main Currents in Modern American History* (New York: Pantheon Books, 1984), 105–311; Vladimir Ilyich Lenin, *Imperialism, the Highest Stage of Capitalism: A Popular Outline* (Moscow, Russia: Progress Publishers, 1975).
16. Hideki Yamawaki, "Dominant Firm Pricing and Fringe Expansion: The Case of the U.S. Iron and Steel Industry, 1907–1930," *The Review of Economics and Statistics* 67, no. 3 (August 1985): 429–437; James P. Johnson, *The Politics of Soft Coal: The Bituminous Industry from World War I Through the New Deal* (Urbana: University of Illinois Press, 1979).
17. Johnson, *Politics of Soft Coal*, 21.
18. Ibid., 13–15, 27.

Chapter 1

1. For a contemporary description of the segregation of mill towns and mill neighborhoods, see Margaret F. Byington, "Homestead: The Households of a Mill Town," in *The Pittsburgh Survey: Findings in Six Volumes*, ed. Paul Underwood Kellogg (New York: Charities Publication, 1910) and Breckinridge and Abbott, "Chicago Housing Conditions." The best work on space and social relations in coal mining towns is the Ph.D. dissertation by Caroline Merithew (née Waldron), "The Great Spirit of Solidarity: The Illinois Valley Mining Communities and the Formation of Interethnic Consciousness, 1889–1917" (Ph.D. diss., University of Illinois, Urbana-Champaign, 2000).
2. See for example, E.A. Ross, *The Old World in the New: The Significance of Past and Present Immigration to the American People* (New York: The Century Company, 1914); Madison Grant, *The Passing of the Great Race: Or, the Racial Basis of European History* (New York: Scribner's Sons, 1916); Jerome Davis, *The Russians and Ruthenians in America*, 104.
3. On the Progressive preoccupation with new immigrants, see for example James R. Barrett, *Work and Community in the Jungle: Chicago's Packinghouse Workers, 1894–1922* (Urbana: University of Illinois Press, 1990), 64–67; Jane Addams, *Twenty Years at Hull-House: With Autobiographical Notes*, ed. Victoria Bissell Brown (Boston: Bedford/St. Martin's, 1999); Hutchins Hapgood, *The Spirit of the Ghetto*, ed. James R. Barrett (Cambridge: Belknap Press, 1967). For organized labor's attitude toward new immigrants, see Gwendolyn Mink, *Old Labor and New Immigrants in American Political Development: Union, Party, and State, 1875–1920* (Ithaca: Cornell University Press, 1986). For the relationship between new immigrants and American radicalism, consult the Paul Buhle and Dan Georgekas edited volume, *The Immigrant Left in the United States* (Albany: State University of New York Press, 1996).
4. On the international and cosmopolitan character of the new immigration, see for examples Donna Gabaccia and Franca Iacovetta (eds.), *Women, Gender and Transnational Lives: Italian Workers of the World* (Toronto: University of Toronto Press, 2002); and Donna Gabaccia and Fraser Ottanelli (eds.), *Italian Workers of the World: Labor Migration and the Formation of Multiethnic States* (Urbana: University of Illinois Press, 2001).
5. All three terms are problematic. As applied to European nationalities, "ethnic"—today's preferred term—did not exist at the time. "National" was also infrequently used, and

is doubly problematic in since that which constituted a "nation" or "national group" in Eastern Europe at the time was quite fluid and in many cases was at an incipient state. Both terms, furthermore, are pregnant with present-day-ist political and racial assumptions. Though it is itself impossible to define in any meaningful way, I will use the term "race" since that was the most frequently used term of the period, and it reflects, moreover, a closer connotation for today's readers' eyes to the marginalized position that new immigrants actually confronted, as opposed to the more neutral or positive "ethnic" and "national."

6. John Fitch, "The Steel Workers," *Pittsburgh Survey*, ed. Paul Kellogg (Pittsburgh: Russell Sage Foundation, 1910), 142–149.

7. Bruno Ramirez, *When Workers Fight: The Politics of Industrial Relations in the Progressive Era, 1898–1916* (Westport, CT: Greenwood, 1978), 133; David Montgomery, *The Fall of the House of Labor: The Workplace, the State, and American Labor Activism, 1865–1925* (Cambridge: Cambridge University Press, 1987); Adam Walaszek, "Was the Polish Worker Asleep? Immigrants, Unions, and Workers' Control in America, 1900–1922," *Polish American Studies* 78 (Spring 1989).

8. Ivan Cizmic, "The Involvement of Yugoslav Socialists in the Socialist Party of America and the Socialist Labor Party of America, 1903–1924," *Labor Newspaper Preservation Project*, eds. Christine Harzig and Dirk Hoerder (Bremen: Universitat Bremen, 1985), 463; Frances Krljic, "Round Trip Croatia," in *Labor Migration in the Atlantic Economies: The European and North American Working Classes During the Period of Industrialization*, ed. Dirk Hoerder (Westport, CT: Greenwood, 1985), 407.

9. Julianna Puskas, *Ties That Bind, Ties That Divide: 100 Years of Hungarian Experience in the United States*. Ellis Island Series (New York: Holmes & Meier, 2000), 115; For a discussion of leadership among new immigrant groups see Victor R. Greene, *American Immigrant Leaders, 1800–1910: Marginality and Identity* (Baltimore: Johns Hopkins University Press, 1987) and David Montgomery, "Nationalism, American Patriotism, and Class Consciousness Among Immigrant Workers in the United States in the Epoch of World War I," 327–351, in *Struggle a Hard Battle*, ed. Dirk Hoerder (DeKalb, IL: Northern Illinois University Press, 1986) and Elisabetta Vezzosi, "Radical Ethnic Brokers: Immigrant Socialist Leaders in the United States between Ethnic Community and the Larger Society," 134. The work of Hoerder has been foundational in the continuing defense of understanding the new immigration, and immigration more generally as a labor migration. See for example his edited volume *American Labor and Immigration History, 1877–1920s: Recent European Research* (Urbana: University of Illinois Press, 1983). For a description of Czech and Finnish farming, see *They Chose Minnesota: A Survey of the State's Ethnic Groups* (St. Paul: Minnesota Historical Society Press, 1981); Puskas, *Ties That Bind*, 119 and *From Hungary to the United States* (1880–1914), Studia historica Academiae Scientiarum Hungaricae (Budapest: Akademiai Kiad, 1982), 148–153.

10. Michael La Sorte, *La Merica: Images of the Italian Greenhorn Experience* (Philadelphia: Temple University Press, Philadelphia, 1985); Walaszek, "Polish Worker," 47–49; Mark Wyman, *Round-Trip to America: The Immigrants Return to Europe, 1880–1930* (Cornell: Cornell University Press, 1993); Jerome Davis, *The Russian Immigrant* (New York: Macmillan, 1922), 16–17; Carl Ross, *The Finn Factor in American Labor, Culture, and Society* (New York Mills, MN: Parta Printers, 1977), 100–101; Jett Lauck and Edgar Sydenstricker, *Conditions of Labor in American Industries: A Summarization of the Results of Recent Investigations* (New York: Funk & Wagnalls, 1917); Barrett, *Work and Community in the Jungle*, 36–47; Puskas, *From Hungary to the United States*, 127–148; Timothy L. Smith, "Religious Denominations as Ethnic Communities: A Regional Case Study," *Church History* 35, no. 2 (1966): 207–226.

11. U.S. Senate, *Reports of the Immigration Commission, Immigrants in Industries*, Volume 16, Part 18, "Iron Ore Mining," 339–34; Senate Documents, 61st Congress, 2nd Session 1909–1910, volume 78 (Washington, D.C.: Government Printing Office, 1911).

12. The term "Austrian" referred to any emigrant from the Austrian portion of the Austro-Hungarian Empire. In census and industrial investigations, however, the term very rarely referred to German-speaking Austrians, but commonly referred to Poles, Czechs, and Yugoslavs—Slovenians, Croatians, Serbs, Bosnians, and Montenegrins. The category "Russian" likewise seems to have usually referred to non–Russian nationalities under the Tsar's empire, Lithuanians, for example. "Hungarian" perhaps in most cases referred to Magyars, but could also have subsumed Slovaks, Croatians, and Ruthenians, and perhaps occasionally Slovenians and Romanians as well.

13. Ross, *Finn Factor*, 107; Department of the Interior, Census Office, Report of the Population of the United States, Thirteenth Census, Part I, 1910 (Washington D.C.: Government Printing Office, 1912–1914), Volume II, St. Louis County, Minnesota, T624-722-725.

14. McCallum, *The Iron and Steel Industry in the U.S.*, 213–214; David Brody, *Labor in Crisis: The Steel Strike of 1919* (Philadelphia: Lippincott, 1965), 39.
15. U.S. Senate, *Reports of the Immigration Commission*, Volume 1, Part 2, "Iron and Steel Manufacturing" (Washington, D.C.: 1911), 32.
16. J.M. Gilette, "The Culture Agencies of a Typical Manufacturing Group: South Chicago," *The American Journal of Sociology* 7, no. 1 (July 1901); U.S. Senate, *Reports of the Immigration Commission*, Volume 1, Part 2, "Iron and Steel Manufacturing" (Washington, D.C.: 1911), 32.
17. Department of the Interior, Census Office, *Report of the Population of the United States*, Thirteenth Census, Part I, 1910 (Washington, D.C.: Government Printing Office, 1912–1914), Volume II, Cook County, Illinois, and Lake County, Indiana, T624-279, T624, 237, 238 and T624-361 T624-362.
18. Montgomery, *Fall of the House of Labor*, 335.
19. Victor Hicken, "Mine Union Radicalism in Macoupin and Montgomery Counties," *Western Illinois Regional Studies* 3, no. 2 (1980): 173–191; Immanuel Wallerstein, *World-Systems Analysis: An Introduction* (Durham: Duke University Press, 2004); Montgomery, *The Fall of the House of Labor*, 335; Waldron, "The Great Spirit of Solidarity," 57–58 and 79–137; Stephanie Booth, "The Relationship Between Radicalism and Ethnicity in Southern Illinois Coal Fields, 1870–1940" (Ph.D. diss., Illinois State University, 1983), 104–105.
20. U.S. Commission on Industrial Relations, "The Trade Agreement in the Bituminous Field from the Standpoint of Men and Union Officials," J.H. Bradford, January 1914; Joe William Trotter, *Coal, Class, and Color: Blacks in Southern West Virginia, 1915–32* (Urbana: University of Illinois Press, 1990).
21. U.S. Senate, *Reports of the Immigration Commission*, Volume 2, Part 1, "Bituminous Coal Mining" (Washington, D.C.: 1911), 581–585, 586; John H.M. Laslett, *Colliers Across the Sea: A Comparative Study of Class Formation in Scotland and the American Midwest, 1830–1924* (Urbana: University of Illinois Press, 2000); Waldron, "The Great Spirit of Solidarity," 54–69 and 79–137.
22. U.S. Senate, *Reports of the Immigration Commission*, Volume 2, Part 1, "Bituminous Coal Mining" (Washington, D.C.: 1911).
23. On the relationship between skill and nationality or "race," see for example Barrett and Roediger, "Inbetween Peoples," 3–44; Brody, *Steelworkers in America: The Nonunion Era* (New York: Russell, 1970); Isaac Hourwich, *Immigration and Labor* (New York: G.P. Putnam's Sons, 1912); Barrett, *Work and Community in the Jungle*, 54–58.
24. Ross, *Finn Factor*, 108; U.S. Senate, *Reports of the Immigration Commission*, Volume 16, Part 18, "Iron Ore Mining," 314, 340.
25. Cliff Brown, "Racial Conflict and Split Labor Markets: The A.F.L. Campaign to Organize Steel Workers, 1918–1919," *Social Science History* 22, no. 3, Special Issue: Migration and the Labor Markets (Autumn 1998): 319–347; Barrett and Roediger, "Inbetween Peoples"; Brody, *Steelworkers in America*; William Z. Foster, *The Great Steel Strike and Its Lessons* (New York: B.W. Huebsch, 1920); Charles Adams Gulick, *Labor Policy of the United States Steel Corporation* (New York: Columbia University, 1924), 107–133; Interchurch World Movement of North America, and Bureau of Industrial Research, *Report on the Steel Strike of 1919* (New York: Harcourt, Brace and Howe, 1920); Hourwich, *Immigration and Labor*, 148–176 and 394–413.
26. U.S. Senate, *Reports of the Immigration Commission*, Volume 2, Part 1, "Bituminous Coal Mining" (Washington, D.C.: 1911), 615; Hourwich, *Immigration and Labor*, 414–457.
27. U.S. Senate, *Reports of the Immigration Commission*, Volume 2, Part 1, "Bituminous Coal Mining" (Washington, D.C.: 1911), 656.
28. Booth, "The Regulation of the Coal Mining Industry in Illinois," 220–222.
29. See for example Roger Waldinger, "Another Look at the International Ladies' Garment Workers' Union: Women, Industry Structure and Collective Action," in *Women, Work, and Protest: A Century of U.S. Women's Labor History*, ed. Ruth Milkman (Boston: Routledge & Kegan Paul, 1985); Patricia Cooper, *Once a Cigar Maker: Men, Women, and Work Culture in American Cigar Factories, 1900–1919* (Urbana: University of Illinois Press, 1987); Carolyn Daniel McCreesh, *Women in the Campaign to Organize Garment Workers, 1880–1917* (New York: Garland, 1985); Leslie Woodcock Tentler, *Wage-Earning Women: Industrial Work and Family Live in the United States, 1900–1930* (Oxford: Oxford University Press, 1979); Barrett, *Work and Community*, 154–187.
30. Carter Goodrich, *The Miner's Freedom*, 113–114.
31. Ramirez, *When Workers Fight*; Andrea Graziosi, "Common Laborers, Unskilled

Workers, 1880–1915," *Labor History* 22 (Fall 1981): 512–544; Montgomery, *Workers Control*, 34.

32. Gordon, et.al., *Segmented Work, Divided Workers*, 146–149; Barrett, *Work and Community in the Jungle*, 240–241.

33. Sumner H. Slichter, "The Scope and Nature of the Labor Turnover Problem," *The Quarterly Journal of Economics* 34, no. 2 (February 1920): 329–345.

34. U.S. Senate, *Reports of the Immigration Commission*, Volume 1, Part 2, "Iron and Steel Manufacturing" (Washington, D.C.: 1911), 331, 381; Carl Weinberg, "The Tug of War: Labor, Loyalty and Rebellion in the Southwestern Illinois Coalfields, 1914–1920" (Ph.D. diss., Yale, 1995), 105–106.

35. Correspondence from Slovenian miners reproduced in *Glas Svobode*, 8 June 1906 and *Proletarec*, 23 May 1911, 7 May 1912 and 18 February 1913. Reproduced in Neil Betten, "The Origins of Ethnic Radicalism in Northern Minnesota, 1900–1920," *International Migration Review* 4, no. 2 (1970): 44–56.

36. David Montgomery, *Workers' Control in America: Studies in the History of Work, Technology, and Labor Struggles* (Cambridge: Cambridge University Press, 1979); Martha Ellen Shiells, "Collective Choice of Working Conditions: Hours in British and U.S. Iron and Steel, 1890–1923," *Journal of Economic History* 50, no. 2 (1990): 379–392; McCalhun, 242–245; Graziosi, "Common Laborers, Unskilled Workers, 1880–1915," 512–544; Fitch, "The Steel Workers," *Pittsburgh Survey*, 166–191.

37. *Proletarec*, 7 April 1914, reproduced in Neil Betten, "The Origins of Ethnic Radicalism."

38. U.S. Senate, *Reports of the Immigration Commission*, Volume 16, Part 18, "Iron Ore Mining," 332; Betten, "The Origins of Ethnic Radicalism," 48.

39. Michael Nash, *Conflict and Accommodation: Coal Miners, Steel Workers, and Socialism, 1890–1920*, Contributions in Labor History (Westport, CT: Greenwood, 1982), 19; U.S. Senate, *Reports of the Immigration Commission*, Volume 16, Part 18, "Iron Ore Mining," 332; Montgomery, *The Fall of the House of Labor*; "Making Steel and Killing Men," *Everybody's Magazine*, Vol. 17, No. 5 (November 1907): 579. Dorothy Schweider includes a lengthy and telling description of the actual labor of coal mining and the various dangers and injuries that resulted in her *Black Diamonds: Life and Work in Iowa's Coal Mining Communities, 1895–1925* (Ames: Iowa State University Press, 1983), 27–58; Fitch, "The Steel Workers," 57–71.

40. "Relief Plan of the United States Steel Corporation," in John Fitch, "The Steel Workers" *Pittsburgh Survey*; U.S. Senate, *Reports of the Immigration Commission*, Volume 16, Part 18, "Iron Ore Mining," 335.

41. Paul F. McGouldrick and Michael B. Tannen, "Did American Manufacturers Discriminate Against Immigrants Before 1914?" *The Journal of Economic History* 37, no. 3 (September 1977): 723–746.

42. U.S. Senate, *Reports of the Immigration Commission*, Volume 16, Part 18, "Iron Ore Mining," 315–31; U.S. Senate, *Reports of the Immigration Commission*, Volume I, Part 2, "Iron and steel Manufacturing," 20–24; Fitch, "The Steel Workers," *Pittsburgh Survey*, 207–220; Edwards, *Contested Terrain*, 94–97.

43. U.S. Senate, *Reports of the Immigration Commission*, Volume 2, Part 1, "Bituminous Coal Mining," 635–640; Price Van Meter Fishback, *Soft Coal, Hard Choices: The Economic Welfare of Bituminous Coal Miners, 1890–1930* (New York: Oxford University Press, 1992), 102–126. For more on wages in the steel industry, see John Fitch, "The Steel Workers," 150–165.

44. Edwards, *Contested Terrain*, 62–65.

45. Gordon, *Segmented Work, Divided Workers*; Andrew Sturdy, David Knights, and Hugh Willmott, eds., *Skill and Consent: Contemporary Studies in the Labour Process* (London: Routledge, 1992). Within the field of labor history, David Montgomery and his students have produced the most important studies relating to control and the work process. The classic is Montgomery's *Workers' Control*.

46. For an enlightening discussion of the relationship between the development of U.S. industry and the growth of labor migration, see Ramirez, *When Workers Fight*, 131–133.

47. On the characteristics of new immigrant communities see as examples: David Brody's chapter on mill towns in *Steelworkers in America*; John E. Bodnar, *Steelton: Immigration and Industrialization, 1870–1940* (Pittsburgh: University of Pittsburgh Press, 1990); Byington, "Homestead: The Households of a Mill Town"; R. Harris, "Chicago's Other Suburbs," *The Geographical Review* 84, no. 4 (1994).

48. Mary Heaton Vorse, *Men and Steel* (New York: Boni and Liveright, 1920), 14.

49. Breckinridge and Abbott, "Chicago Housing Conditions," 145–176.

50. U.S. Public Health Service Sanitary Survey of Coal Commission, April-June 1923, "Summarized Report on the Sanitation of 123 Communities in the Bituminous Coal Districts of 9 States," Records of the U.S. Coal Commission, Record Group 68, Entry 13, National Archives and Records Administration.

51. Vorse, *Men and Steel.*

52. Bituminous Operators' Special Committee, 17 September 1923, Records of the U.S. Coal Commission, Record Group 68, Entry 13, National Archives and Records Administration.

53. Mildred A. Beik, *The Miners of Windber: The Struggles of New Immigrants for Unionization, 1890s–1930s* (University Park: Pennsylvania State University Press, 1996), 82–106; U.S. Senate, *Reports of the Immigration Commission,* Volume 2, Part 1, "Bituminous Coal Mining" (Washington, D.C.: 1911), 615; Waldron, "The Great Spirit of Solidarity," 142–148; Dorothy Schwieder, *Black Diamonds: Life and Work in Iowa's Coal Mining Communities, 1895–1925* (Ames: Iowa State University Press, 1983), 99, 109; Montgomery, *The Fall of the House of Labor,* 337.

54. Tentler, *Wage-earning Women;* Alice Kessler-Harris, *Out to Work.*

55. Wyman, *Round-Trip to America,* 50; Jerome Davis, *The Russians and Ruthenians in America: Bolsheviks or Brothers* (New York: George H. Doran Company, 1922), 24–25.

56. Donna R. Gabaccia, *Italy's Many Diasporas* (Seattle: University of Washington Press, 2000); Ron Rothbart, "'Homes Are What Any Strike Is About': Immigrant Labor and the Family Wage," *Journal of Social History* 23, no. 2 (1989): 267–284; Frances Krljic, "Round Trip Croatia," 412–413; Schweider, *Black Diamonds,* 69.

57. S.J. Kleinberg, *The Shadow of the Mills: Working-Class Families in Pittsburgh, 1870–1907* (Pittsburgh: University of Pittsburgh Press, 1989); Davis, *The Russians and Ruthenians in America,* 24, 36; Schwieder, *Black Diamonds,* 95–97; Puskas, *Ties That Bind,* 124–126.

58. U.S. Senate, *Reports of the Immigration Commission,* Volume 16, Part 18, "Iron Ore Mining," 321–325.

59. U.S. Senate, *Reports of the Immigration Commission,* Volume 2, Part 1, "Bituminous Coal Mining," 643–645; Breckinridge and Abbott, "Chicago Housing Conditions," 145–176; Weinberg, "Labor, Loyalty, and Rebellion," 185; Raymond A. Mohl and Neil Betten, *Steel City: Urban and Ethnic Patterns in Gary, Indiana, 1906–1950* (New York: Holmes and Meier, 1986), 18–19; Beik, *Miners of Windber,* 90–96.

60. Andrew Vazsonyi, "The Cicisbeo and the Magnificent Cuckold: Boardinghouse Life and Lore in Immigrant Communities," *The Journal of American Folklore* 91, no. 360 (June 1978): 641–656.

61. Joseph Mavetz, interview by Mary Joy Lenont, *Ely Oral History Project:* A-95-3583, Ely, Minnesota, July 6, 1975.

62. U.S. Senate, *Reports of the Immigration Commission,* Volume 16, Part 18, "Iron Ore Mining," 321–325, 365–369, 371; U.S. Senate, *Reports of the Immigration Commission,* Volume 2, Part 1, "Bituminous Coal Mining," 687–692, 696; Carl Weinberg, "The Tug of War: Labor, Loyalty and Rebellion in the Southwestern Illinois Coalfields, 1914–1920" (Ph.D. diss, Yale, 1995), 181–188.

63. "Newsy Items of the Coal Mines," *Divernon News,* 29 October 1915.

64. These two features have been noted by scholars for nearly every individual new immigrant group. See for example, Antanas Kučas, *Lithuanians in America,* trans. Joseph Boley (Boston: Encyclopedia Lituanica, 1975), 42–43; Davis, *The Russian Immigrant,* 18.

65. Betten, "The Origins of Ethnic Radicalism in Northern Minnesota, 1900–1920," *International Migration Review* 4, no. 2 (1970): 51; U.S. Senate, *Reports of the Immigration Commission,* Volume 16, Part 18, "Iron Ore Mining," 339–341.

66. U.S. Senate, *Reports of the Immigration Commission,* Volume 16, Part 18, "Iron Ore Mining," 339–341.

67. *Ibid.*

68. U.S. Senate, *Reports of the Immigration Commission,* Volume 2, Part 1, "Bituminous Coal Mining"; U.S. Claude Rice to John R. Commons, "Suggestions Regarding Mining Conditions and Points to be Brought out by Federal Investigation," September 3, 1914, Commission on Industrial Relations, Papers.

69. Davis, *The Russian Immigrant,* 30–36; Santina Gambucci and Celeseste Gambucci, interview by Mary Ellen Batinich, Eveleth, August 4, 1981, and Salvatore (Sam) Aluni, interview by Batinich, Nov. 2, 1981, Batinich Oral History Collection, Immigration History Research Center, Minneapolis, Minnesota; Schwieder, *Black Diamonds,* 104–105.

70. Saposs, "Interview with Five Lithuanians and One Italian Young Fellows, All Born in E. Vandergrift and Educated through Grade School. 10/30/19," in *Saposs Papers* (1919).

71. Celeste Gambucci and Santina Gambucci, interview by Mary Ellen Batinich, Aug. 4, 1981.
72. Weinberg, "The Tug of War," 253.
73. Salvatore Aluni, interview by Mary Ellen Batinich, Nov. 2, 1981.
74. Paul Henry Landia, *Three Iron Mining Towns, a Study in Cultural Change* (Ann Arbor, MI: Edwards Brothers, 1938); Mohl and Betten, *Urban and Ethnic Patterns in Gary*, 18–19.
75. Weinberg, "The Tug of War," 146; James R. Barrett and David Roediger, "The Irish and the 'Americanization' of the 'New Immigrants' in the Streets and in the Churches of the Urban United States, 1900–1930," *The Journal of American Ethnic History* (Summer 2005), and "Inbetween Peoples"; Avinere Toigo, interview by Cullom Davis, 1972–73, interview T573, transcript, Illinois State Oral History Collection, Springfield, Illinois; John Bodnar's research on Steelton, Pennsylvania, turns up similar findings: *Immigration and Industrialization: Ethnicity in an American Mill Town, 1870–1940* (Pittsburgh: University of Pittsburgh Press, 1977), 21 and 51–75.
76. Mink, *Old Labor and New Immigrants*; David R. Roediger, *Working Toward Whiteness: How America's Immigrants Became White: The Strange Journey from Ellis Island to the Suburbs* (New York: Basic Books, 2005); Davis, *The Russian Immigrant*, 40–42; see also David Emmons' analysis of ethnicity and the Butte Miners Union, "The Aristocracy Besieged," in *The Butte Irish: Class and Ethnicity in an American Mining Town, 1875–1925* (Urbana: University of Illinois Press, 1990), 255–291.
77. Montgomery, *The Fall of the House of Labor*; Brody, *Steelworkers in America*; Ramirez, *When Workers Strike*; Fitch, "The Steel Workers" *Pittsburgh Survey*, 140–142. The most thorough treatment of the elimination of the craft unions from the steel industry, even after more than forty years, remains David Brody's *Steelworkers in America: The Non-union Era*. A similar process took place in Chicago's meatpacking industry. See James R. Barrett's chapter, "Work Rationalization and the Struggle for Control, 1900–1904," in *Work and Community in the Jungle*.
78. On the U.M.W.'s role in the rationalization of the coal industry in the C.C.F., see Craig Phelan, "John Mitchell and the Politics of the Trade Agreement," in *The United Mine Workers of America: A Model of Industrial Solidarity?* ed. John H.M. Laslett (University Park: Pennsylvania State University Press, 1996), 72–103; David Brody, *In Labor's Cause: Main Themes on the History of the American Worker* (New York: Oxford University Press, 1993), 139–142; Montgomery, *The Fall of the House of Labor*, 341–344; Ramirez, *When Workers Fight*, 104–125; Michael Nash, *Conflict and Accommodation: Coal Miners, Steel Workers, and Socialism, 1890–1920* (Westport, CT: Greenwood, 1982), 90–92; on low capitalization of some coal mines and the lack of rationalization of the coal industry, see Goodrich, *The Miner's Freedom*; Gottlieb, "The Regulation of the Coal Mining Industry in Illinois," 105–106; Weinberg, "The Tug of War"; For the garment industry, see Steven Fraser, *Labor Will Rule: Sidney Hillman and the Rise of American Labor* (New York: Free Press, 1991); Waldinger, "Another Look at the International Ladies' Garment Workers' Union: Women, Immigrant Structure and Collective Action," in *Women, Work and Protest: A Century of U.S. Women's History*, ed. Ruth Milkman (Boston: Routledge and Kegan Paul, 1986); on monopolization and rationalization of steel, see David Brody, *Steelworkers in America: The Nonunion Era*.
79. U.S. Senate, *Reports of the Immigration Commission*, Volume 2, Part 1, "Bituminous Coal Mining," 654; John H.M. Laslett, "British Immigrant Colliers, and the Origins and Early Development of the U.M.W., 1870–1912," in *The United Mine Workers of America*, ed. John H.M. Laslett, 38–41; J.H. Bradford, "The Trade Agreement in the Bituminous Field from the Standpoint of Men and Union Officials," 14 January 1914, U.S. Commission on Industrial Relations, Papers; Barrett, "Americanization from the Bottom Up," 996–1020.
80. Grace Abbott, *The Immigrant and Coal Mining Communities of Illinois* (Springfield, IL: Illinois Immigrants Commission, 1920), 36.
81. *Ibid.*; Laslett, "British Immigrant Colliers," 44–50.
82. U.S. Senate, *Reports of the Immigration Commission*, Volume 2, Part 1, "Bituminous Coal Mining"; Weinberg, "Tug of War," 145–146.
83. J.H. Bradford, "The Trade Agreement in the Bituminous Field from the Standpoint of Men and Union Officials," 14 January 1914, U.S. Commission on Industrial Relations, Papers.
84. *Ibid.*; Vecoli, "The Italian Immigrants in the United States Labor Movement from 1880 to 1929," 284–285; U.S. Senate, *Reports of the Immigration Commission*, Volume 2, Part 1, "Bituminous Coal Mining," 651–656; Jerome Davis testified to both the inclusiveness of Russian immigrants in the U.M.W. and the de facto segregation that existed nonetheless: *The Russian Immigrant*, 40–42; Nash, *Conflict and Accommodation*, 95–97.

85. U.S. Senate, *Reports of the Immigration Commission*, Volume 2, Part 1, "Bituminous Coal Mining," 651–656.
86. Brody, "Steelworkers in America," 73, 75.
87. Donald Sofchalk, "Organized Labor and the Iron Ore Miners of Northern Minnesota, 1907–1936," *Labor History*, 215–217.

Chapter 2

1. "The present war, indeed, has been referred to by various writers as 'a war of coal and iron,' or 'a war of metals,' and the like." Joseph E. Pogue, "Mineral Resources in War and Their Bearing on Preparedness," *The Scientific Monthly* 5, no. 2 (August 1917): 120–134.
2. Edwards, *Contested Terrain*, 65–71.
3. Quoted in David Montgomery, "Immigrants, Industrial Unions, and Social Reconstruction in the United States, 1916–1923," *Laboour/Le Travail*, Volume 13 (1984): 104.
4. Montgomery, *The Fall of the House of Labor* (Cambridge: Cambridge University Press: 1987), 6, 369; Barrett, *Work and Community*, 188–190.
5. Historical Statistics of the United States (Washington, D.C.: 1975), 119.
6. Gary Marks and Matthew Burbank, "Immigrant Support for the American Socialist Party, 1912 and 1920," *Social Science History* 14, no. 2 (Summer 1990): 175–202.
7. Vecoli, "The Making and Un-Making of the Italian American Working Class," in *The Lost World of Italian-American Radicalism*, eds. Philip Cannistraro and Gerald Meyer (Westport, CT: Praeger, 2003), 52; Puskas, *Ties That Bind, Ties That Divide*, 179–186; Mildred A. Beik, *The Miners of Windber: The Struggles of New Immigrants for Unionization, 1890s–1930s* (University Park: Pennsylvania State University Press, 1996), 231–239; Elizabeth McKillen, *Chicago Labor and the Quest for a Democratic Diplomacy, 1914–1924* (Ithaca, NY: Cornell University Press, 1995); Montgomery, "Immigrants, Industrial Unions, and Social Reconstruction," 111.
8. "Socialism Wins in Debate," 12 January 1915, *Naujienos*, Chicago Foreign Language Press Survey, Reel 42.
9. Ivan Cizmic, "The Involvement of Yugoslav Socialists in the Socialist Party of America and the Socialist Labor Party of America, 1903–1924," *Labor Migration Project Labor Newspaper Preservation Project*, Christaine Harzig and Dirk Horeder, eds. (Universitat Bremen, 1985): 459–473; Julianna Puskas, *From Hungary to the United States (1880–1914)* (Budapest: Studia historica Academiae Scientiarum Hungaricae, Budapest Akadthniai Kiado, 1982), 157–169.
10. Zefffiro Ciuffoletti, "Il Movimento Sindicale Italiano e L'emigrazione dalle Origini al Fascismo," in B. Bezza ed., *Gli Italiani Fuori D Italia: Gli Emigrati Italian mi Movimenti Operai dei Paesi d'Adozione, 1880–1940* (Milan: Franco Angeli, 1983), 203, 220; Nick Salvatore, *Eugene V. Debs, Citizen and Socialist*, 183–184; John I. Kolehmainen, *A History of the Finns in Ohio, Western Pennsylvania, and West Virginia: From Lake Erie's Shores to the Mahoning and Monongahela Valleys* (New York Mills, MN: Parta Printers, Inc., 1977).
11. Peter Kivisto, *Immigrant Socialists in the United States: The Case of Finns and the Left* (Rutherford, NJ: Associated University Press, 1984), 121.
12. Ibid.; "From Socialism to Industrial Unionism (I.W.W.): Social Factors in the Emergence of Left-Labor Radicalism Among Finnish Workers on the Mesabi, 1911–19," in Kami et al., eds., *The Finnish Experience*; Kohlemainen, *A History of the Finns in Ohio, Western Pennsylvania, and West Virginia*, 208; E.V. Cleef, "The Finn in America," *Geographical Review* 6, no. 3 (1918): 185–214; Neal Betten, "The Origins of Ethnic Radicalism in Northern Minnesota, 1900–1920," *International Migration Review* 4, no. 2 (1970): 44–56; Kathleen Blee and Al Gedicks, "The Emergence of Socialist Political Culture Among Finnish Immigrants in Minnesota Mining Communities," 172–192; Sally M. Miller, "The Ethnic Press and its Labor Component: Patterns of Selected Ethnic Groups," in *Labor Newspaper Preservation Project*; Hilja J. Karvonen, "Three Proponents of Women's Rights in the Finnish-American Labor Movement from 1910–1930: Selma Jokela Mcone, Maiju Nurmi, and Helmi Mattson," *For the Common Good*, Kami, ed.: 202–204.
13. Arthur Liebman, *The Jews and the Left* (New York: John Wiley, 1979); Paul Buhle, "Themes in American Jewish Radicalism," *In The Immigrant Left in the United States*, Buhle and Georgakas, eds.: 77–118; Salvatore, *Eugene V. Debs*, 284–285; Buhle, "Jews and American Communism: The Cultural Question," Radical History Review 23 (Spring): 9–33; Moses Rischin, *The Promised City: New York's Jews, 1870–1914* (Cambridge: Harvard University

Press, 1962); Irving Howe, *World of Our Fathers*, 1st ed. (New York: Harcourt Brace Jovanovich, 1976), 97–118.

14. "Naujienos Observes Second Anniversary," 20 Oct. 1916, *Naujienos*, Chicago Foreign Language Press Survey, Reel 42; Miller, "The Ethnic Press and its Labor Component," 412–414; Antanas Kučas, *Lithuanians in America*, Trans. by Joseph Boley (Boston: Encyclopedia Lituanica, 1975), 94–100; Jaan Pennar, *The Estonians in America, 1627–1975: A Chronology and Fact Book* (Dobbs Ferry, NY: Oceana Publications, 1975): viii.

15. Mary Cygan, "The Polish-American Left," in *The Immigrant Left in the United States*, SUNY Series in American Labor History (Albany: State University of New York Press, 1996), 148–184; Miroslav Boruta and Andrzej Porobski, "The Polish Labor Press and Workers' Acculturation in the United States, 1918–1929," *Labor Migration Project Labor Newspaper Preservation Project*, 487–503; Ewa Morawska, "From Myth to Reality: America in the Eyes of East European Peasant Migrant Laborers," *Distant Magnets: Expectations and Realities in the Immigrant Experience, 1840–1930*, Ellis Island series (New York: Holmes & Meier, 1993): 241–263.

16. Timothy L. Smith, "Religious Denominations as Ethnic Communities: A Regional Case Study," *Church History* 35, no. 2 (1966): 207–226; Matjai Klemenčič, "Proletarec and the Acculturation of Slovene Workers in the United States," *Labor Migration Project*, 479.

17. Davis, *The Russian Immigrant*, 114–126; Miller, "The Ethnic Press," *Labor Newspaper Preservation Project*, 411–412; "Russian Workingmen's Association," April 14, 1917, Prepared by the Army War College U.S. Military Intelligence Files, Surveillance of Radicals, Reel 1.

18. Waldron, "The Great Spirit of Solidarity," 285–293.

19. Bruno Cartosio, "Gli Emigrati Italiani e l'Industrial Workers of the World," in B. Bezza ed., *Gli Italiani Fuori D 'Italia: Gli Emigrati Italian nei Movimenti Operai dei Paesi d'Adozione, 1880–1940* (Milan: Franco Angeli, 1983), 380.

20. The literature on Italian immigrant radicalism has become extensive. See for example, Rudolph Vecoli, "The Making and Un-Making of the Italian American Working Class," in *The Lost World of Italian-American Radicalism*, Philip Cannistraro and Gerald Meyer, eds. (Westport, CT: Praeger, 2003); Michael Miller Topp, *Those Without a Country: The Political Culture of Italian American Syndicalists* (Minneapolis: University of Minnesota Press, 2001); Bruno Cartosio, "Italian Workers and Their Press in the United States, 1900–1920," 443–457, in Sally M. Miller, ed., *The Ethnic Press and its Labor Component: Patterns of Selected Ethnic Groups*, Labor Newspaper Preservation Project, and Labor Migration Project, The Press of Labor Migrants in Europe and North America 1880s to 1930s (Bremen: Universitat Bremen, 1985). Dubofsky discusses Ettor and Giovanitti in *We Shall Be All*, in 236–237; Caroline Merithew, "Anarchist Motherhood in Illinois Coal Towns," in Donna Gabaccia and Franca Iacovetta, eds., *Women, Gender and Transnational Lives: Italian Workers of the World* (Toronto: University of Toronto Press, 2002), 217–246; Donna Gabaccia, *Militants and Migrants: Rural Sicilians Become American Workers* (New Brunswick, NJ: Rutgers University Press, 1988), 117–118; Vecoli offers the most succinct coverage of the development of Italian American radicalism. "The Italian Immigrants in the United States Labor Movement from 1880 to 1929," in B. Bezza ed., *Gli Italiani Fuori D 'Italia: Gli Emigrati Italian nei Movimenti Operai dei Paesi d'Adozione, 1880–1940* (Milan: Franco Angeli, 1983), 270–282; See also Michael Miller Topp, "The Italian-American Left: Transnationalism and the Quest for Unity," *The Immigrant Left in the United States*, SUNY Series in American Labor History (Albany: State University of New York Press, 1996), 119–147.

21. Kivisto, *Immigrant Socialists in the United States*, 139–142.

22. "The Differentiation of the Hungarian Newspapers, Reflecting Some Aspects of Acculturation, 1853–1914," *Labor Newspaper Preservation Project*: 396–397; Puskas, *From Hungary to the U.S.*, 165–166.

23. Elisabetta Vezzosi, "Class, Ethnicity, and Acculturation in Il Proletario: The World War One Years," *Labor Newspaper Preservation Project*: 444–445; Puskas, *From Hungary to the U.S.*, 165–166.

24. Michael Nash, *Conflict and Accommodation: Coal Miners, Steel Workers, and Socialism, 1890–1920* (Westport, CT: Greenwood, 1982); John H.M. Laslett, *Colliers Across the Sea: A Comparative Study of Class Formation in Scotland and the American Midwest, 1830–1924* (Urbana: University of Illinois Press, 2000).

25. Laslett, *Colliers Across the Sea*, 186–189; Nash, *Conflict and Accommodation*, 86–99; Stephane Elise Booth, "The Relationship Between Radicalism and Ethnicity in Southern Illinois Coal Fields, 1870–1940," (Ph.D. Diss., Illinois State University, 1983), 148; Salvatore, *Eugene V. Debs*, 284–285; See also Vecoli, "The Italian Immigrants in the United States Labor

Movement," 283–285; Waldron, "The Great Spirit of Solidarity"; Cygan, "The Polish-American Left," 148–149.

26. Hyman Berman, "Education for Work and Labor Solidarity," unpublished manuscript in the possession of author.

27. Louis L. Gerson, *Woodrow Wilson and the Rebirth of Poland, 1914–1920: A Study in the Influence on American Policy of Minority Groups of Foreign Origin* (New Haven: Yale University Press, 1953), 46.

28. "War Notices Posted About Town," *Chisholm Herald Tribune*, 17 July 1914; "Great Interest Here in War Situation: Countries Involved Have Many Citizens in Eveleth; Few Leaving to Take up Arms," *The Eveleth News*, 6 Aug. 1914; Waldron, "The Great Spirit of Solidarity," 319; on the patriotic response among Italians, see Vecoli, "The Italian Immigrants in the United States Labor Movement from 1880 to 1929," 299–301; Bodnar includes a very interesting discussion of the impact of the war on Steelton's sizable population of Slovenians, Croatians, Serbs, Bulgarians, and Italians: *Immigration and Industrialization*, 118–126, as does Mildred Beik for Winber, Pennsylvania: *The Miners of Windber: The Struggles of New Immigrants for Unionization, 1890s–1930s* (University Park: Pennsylvania State University Press, 1996), 234–237; Puskas, *Ties That Bind, Ties That Divide*, 179–181. According to Puskas, most Hungarians in the U.S. opposed the war, not supporting either Austria-Hungary or the Allies after the U.S. entered.

29. Puskas, *Ties That Bind, Ties That Divide*, 170.

30. Montgomery, "Nationalism, American Patriotism, and Class Consciousness Among Immigrant Workers in the United States in the Epoch of World War One."

31. Puskas, *From Hungary to the U.S.*, 89–90.

32. Gerson, *Woodrow Wilson and the Rebirth of Poland*, 46–54.

33. Vecoli, "The Italian Immigrants in the United States Labor Movement from 1880 to 1929," 301.

34. Vezzosi, "Class, Ethnicity, and Acculturation in Il Proletario," *Naujienos*, 12 January 1915, Chicago Foreign Language Press Survey, Reel 42; Topp, "The Italian-American Left," 134–135.

35. Cygan, "The Polish-American Left," 166–167.

36. "Russian Workingmen's Association," April 14, 1917, Prepared by the Army War College, U.S. Military Intelligence Files, Surveillance of Radicals, Reel 1.

37. "Debs Gives Most Interesting Talk," *Chisholm Herald Tribune*, 4 May 1915; "Election," *Divernon News*, 23 April 1915; "Political Meetings," *Divernon News*, 16 October 1914.

38. "Barclay Mining Company Organized," *American Coal Journal*, 3 Oct. 1914; "Against Co-operative Mines:. Illinois Union Miners Go on Record Against Mines Run on Co-operative Basis. Farrington Issues Letter," *American Coal Journal*, 10 July 1915; Schwieder, *Black Diamonds*, 142–143.

39. "Peabody Interest at Springfield," *American Coal Journal*, 6 November 1915: 6; "Company Accepts Peabody Terms," *American Coal Journal*, 13 November 1915: 6; "Peabody Helps Springfield Trade," *American Coal Journal*, 13 November 1915: 2.

40. "Bituminous Coal Affected by War: Discontinuance of Export Trade Has Caused Bituminous Market to Suffer," *American Coal Journal*, 22 Aug. 1915; "Illinois Figures Show Big Decrease," *American Coal Journal*, 9 Oct. 1915; "Iron Ore Output Shows Decrease," *Chisholm Herald Tribune*, 22 January 1914; "Pawnee Mine Closed," *Divernon News*, 5 March 1915; Gertrude Schroeder, *The Growth of Major Steel Companies, 1900–1950* (Baltimore: Johns Hopkins University Press, 1952), 216; "Finding Work for the Unemployed Is a Big Task Fellows Are Facing," *Chicago Tribune*, 9 Oct. 1914: 5; Weinberg, 110–117; "Cheer Up," *Chisholm Herald Tribune*, 28 June 1914; "No Employment Commits Suicide," *Chisholm Herald Tribune*, July 5, 1914; "Report Peabody Buys More Mines," *American Coal Journal*, 24 April 1915; "Peabody Interests at Springfield," *American Coal Journal*, 1 June 1915; "Peabody Helps Springfield Trade," *American Coal Journal*, 19 June 1915.

41. "Effect of European War on Coal Trade: Opinions and Suggestions from Some of our Leading Coal Men," *American Coal Journal*, 15 Aug. 1914; "The Export Situation" and "No Coal From England," *American Coal Journal*, 21 Aug. 1915; "England Fears American Competition," *American Coal Journal*, 11 March 1916; James P. Johnson, *The Politics of Soft Coal: The Bituminous Industry from World War I Through the New Deal* (Urbana: University of Illinois Press, 1979), 31; Mildred A. Beik, *The Miners of Windber: The Struggles of New Immigrants for Unionization, 1890s–1930s* (University Park: Pennsylvania State University Press, 1996), 53–54.

42. Robert C. Allen, "International Competition in Iron and Steel, 1850–1913," *The Journal*

of Economic History 39, no. 4 (December 1979): 911–937; Montgomery, *The Fall of the House of Labor*, 331, 352.

43. "Steel Trade Shows Big Improvement," *Chisholm Herald Tribune*, 15 Jan. 1915; "Mining Outlook Much Brighter," "Steel Orders Growing Fast" *Chisholm Herald Tribune*, 2 July 1915; "Steel Industry Shows Capacity: Mills at Pittsburgh Are Getting Behind on Orders; Mines to Work at Full Capacity," *Chisholm Herald Tribune*, 9 July 1915; "Mine Not to Close Down on April First," *Divernon News*, 24 March 1916; "The Divernon Mine Is Working," *Divernon News*, 16 June 1916; "Mines Opening at Springfield," *The American Coal Journal*, 28 Aug. 1915; "Big Improvement at Springfield," *The American Coal Journal*, 4 Sept. 1915; "Business Brisk at Springfield," *The American Coal Journal*, 11 Sept. 1915; Edwards, *Contested Terrain*, 69.

44. "Miners Leaving Illinois Field," *American Coal Journal*, 22 Oct. 1914; "Opinions of Others," *Chisholm Herald Tribune*, 8 Jan. 1915; *Divernon News*, 8 Oct. 1916.

45. Puskas, *From Hungary to the U.S.*, 148–149; Davis, *The Russian Immigrant*, 13–15; Brody, *Steelworkers in America*, 96–111.

46. Kathleen Blee, "Family Ties and Class Conflict: The Politics of Immigrant Communities in the Great Lakes Region, 1890–1920," *Social Problems* 31, no. 3 (1984): 311–321.

47. James R. Grossman, *Land of Hope: Chicago, Black Southerners, and the Great Migration* (Chicago: University of Chicago Press, 1989); Thomas Lee Philpott, *The Slum and the Ghetto: Immigrants, Blacks, and Reformers in Chicago, 1880–1930* (Belmont, CA: Wadsworth Pub. Co., 1991), 117.

48. Victor R. Greene, *The Slavic Community on Strike: Immigrant Labor in Pennsylvania Anthracite*. (Notre Dame: University of Notre Dame Press, 1968), xv, 79–110.

49. On Jewish and Italian women's garment workers, see Susan Anita Glenn, *Daughters of the Shtetl: Life and Labor in the Immigrant Generation* (Ithaca: Cornell University Press, 1990) and Jennifer Guglielmo, "Negotiating Gender, Race, and the Coalition: Italian Women and Working-Class Politics in New York City, 1880–1945," Ph.D. dissertation, University of Minnesota, 2003. On the I.W.W. involvement in Lawrence and McKee's Rock, see 199, and 227–262 in Melvyn Dubofsky's *We Shall Be All: A History of the Industrial Workers of the World*, 2nd edition (Urbana: University of Illinois Press, 1988) and "Lawrence, Massachusetts, Textile Strike," Case file 16–26, in The Strike Files of the U.S. Department of Justice, Part I, 1894–1920; on the Copper Country strike, see Arthur Puotinen's "Copper Country Finns and the Strike of 1913," in *The Finnish Experience in the Western Great Lakes Region*, 143–155; Adam Walaszek, "Was the Polish Worker Asleep? Immigrants, Unions, and Workers' Control in America, 1900–1922," 74–96.

50. "Tabulation of Work Suspensions at Mines of Members of Illinois Coal Operators Association, Luke Grant, March 31–Aprill, 1915," U.S. Commission on Industrial Relations. Reel 7, 0429; Jon Amsden and Stephen Brier, "Coal Miners on Strike: The Transformation of Strike Demands and the Formation of a National Union," *Journal of Interdisciplinary History* 7, no. 4 (Spring 1977): 583–616.

51. Leopold Haimson, "The Problem of Social Stability in Urban Russia, 1905–1917 (Part One)," *Slavic Review* 23, no. 4 (December 1964): 619–642; Diane Koenker and William G. Rosenberg, *Strikes and Revolution in Russia, 1917* (Princeton, NJ: Princeton University Press, 1989); Spencer Di Scala, "'RedWeek' 1914: Prelude to War and Revolution," in *Studies in Modern Italian History: From the Risorgimento to the Republic*, ed. Frank Coppa (New York: Peter Lang, 1986), 123–33; James E. Cronin, "The Peculiar Pattern of British Strikes Since 1888," *The Journal of British Studies* 18, no. 2 (Spring 1979): 118–141. One author usefully charts a number of countries, see Douglas A. Hibbs, "On the Political Economy of Long-Run Trends in Strike Activity," *British Journal of Political Science* 8, no. 2 (April 1978): 153–175. On international working class sentiment, see the final chapter of Waldron's dissertation, "The Great Spirit of Solidarity."

52. "Labor Troubles Cut Down New Consumption of Steel," *Chicago Daily Tribune*, 4 May 1916.

53. The Interchurch World Movement Commission of Inquiry, *Report on the Steel Strike of 1919* (New York: Harcourt, Brace, and Howe, 1920), 30–31.

54. Booth, "The Relationship Between Radicalism and Ethnicity in Southern Illinois Coal Fields," 118–148; "1 Dead, Five Shot in Strike Riot at War Plant," *Chicago Tribune*, 20 Jan. 1916; "Labor Blames U.S. Steel for Riots in Youngstown," *Chicago Tribune*, 17 Jan. 1916; "Strikers Force Entrance into Four Big Mills," *Chicago Tribune*, 2 May 1916; Barrett, *Work and Community in the Jungle*, 193.

55. Dubovsky, *We Shall Be All*, 20–21.

56. Frank Tobias Higbie, *Indispensable Outcasts: Hobo Workers and Community in the American Midwest, 1880-1930* (Urbana: University of Illinois Press, 2003).
57. Melanina (Amato) Degubellis, *Italians on the Iron Range*, interviewed August 1, 1985, by Mary Battanich in Chisholm, MN.
58. Salvatore (Sam) Aluni, *Italians on the Iron Range*, interviewed Nov. 2, 1981, by Mary Battanich in Virginia, MN.
59. *Ibid.*; Topp, "Those Without a Country," 177-218.
60. Andy Johnson, *Iron Range Oral History Collections*, Interviewed August 25, 1983, by Tom Rukavina, in Babbitt. MN.
61. Quinto Aluni, *Italians on the Iron Range*, interviewed by Mary Batinich, September 18, 1990, Virginia, MN.
62. David Sofchalk, "Organized Labor and the Iron Ore Miners of Northern Minnesota, 1907-1936," *Labor History*, 226-240.
63. Quinto Aluni interview; "Tolerance Will Win," "I.W.W. Open Agitation Here," *Chisholm Herald Tribune*, 23 June 1916; "IWW Strike About at an End," "Two Actions Needed for Village Good," *Chisholm Herald Tribune*, 30 June 1916; "Near Riot When Striker Is Arrested by Oliver Deputy," *The Eveleth News*, 29 June 1916; "Two Killed at Biwabik," *The Eveleth News*, 6 July 1916; "IWW Dynamite House of Miner at Virginia" *The Eveleth News*, 13 July 1916; "Eveleth Miners Hear Mrs. Flynn," *The Eveleth News*, 3 Aug. 1916; "Open Meeting Held by IWW" *The Eveleth News*, 10 Aug. 1916; Kivisto, *Immigrant Socialists in America*, 141-146.
64. Salvatore Aluni interview.
65. Melanina Degubellis interview.
66. "Sindicato Giallo," *Il Proletario*, 14 August 1916.
67. P. Vipartas, "An Appeal to Stockyard Workers," *Naujienos*, 11 May 1916: 135.

Chapter 3

1. Salvatore, *Eugene V. Debs*, 283-285; Gary Gerstle, *American Crucible: Race and Nation in the Twentieth Century* (Princeton, NJ: Princeton University Press, 2001), 65-90; Preston, *Aliens and Dissenters*, 1-35; Higham, *Strangers in the Land*, 195-204.
2. Gerstle, *American Crucible*; Montgomery, *The Fall of the House of Labor*, 370-410; Joseph McCartin, *Labor's Great War: The Struggle for Industrial Democracy and the Origins of Modern American Labor Relations, 1912-1921* (Chapel Hill: University of North Carolina Press, 1997); Frank L. Grubbs, *The Struggle for Labor Loyalty: Gompers, the A.F. of L., and the Pacifists, 1917-1920* (Durham, NC: Duke University Press, 1968).
3. Barrett, "Americanization from the Bottom Up," 996-1020; Gary Gerstle, *Working Class Americanism: The Politics of Labor in a Textile City, 1914-1960* (Cambridge: Cambridge University Press, 1989).
4. Russell A. Kazal, "Revisting Assimilation: The Rise, Fall, and Reappraisal of a Concept in American Ethnic History," *American Historical Review* 100, no. 2 (April 1995): 437-471; Richard Alba and Victor Nee, "Rethinking Assimilation Theory for a New Era of Immigration," *International Migration Review* 31, no. 4, Special Issue: Immigrant Adaptation and Native-Born Responses in the Making of Americans (Winter 1997): 826-874.
5. Murray, *Red Scare: A Study in National Hysteria, 1919-1920*; Higham, *Strangers in the Land: Patterns of American Nativism, 1860-1925*. More recent accounts that, at least implicitly, support this view, are the prominent works of Gerstle, *Working Class Americanism*, McCartin, *Labor's Great War*, and Cohen, *Making a New Deal*.
6. According to Gabaccia, the diasporic nature of Italian immigration lent itself to various forms of worker internationalism, or conversely to nationalism. Donna Gabaccia and Fraser Ottanelli, "Diaspora or International Proletariat? Italian Labor, Labor Migration, and the Making of Multiethnic States, 1815-1939," 116-128. See also McKillen, *Chicago Labor*, 344; Topp, *Those Without a Country*.
7. Gordon S. Watkins, "Labor Problems and Labor Administration in the United States During the War," Outgoing Letters of J.W. Sullivan, July-December 1917, Committee on Labor, Council of National Defense, National Archives, RG 101, A6; Johnson, *Politics of Soft Coal*, 88-92.
8. Paul H. Douglas, "The Problem of Labor Turnover," *The American Economic Review* 8, no. 2 (June 1918): 306-316; Sumner Slichter, *The Turnover of Factory Labor* (New York: D. Appelton, 1919), and "The Scope and Nature of the Labor Turnover Problem," *Quarterly Journal of Economics* 34 (Feb. 1920): 329-345; Paul F. Brissenden, "Occupational Incidence of

Labor Mobility," *Journal of the American Statistical Association* 18 (Dec. 1923): 978–992; Montgomery, *Workers Control*, 35; Barrett, *Work and Community*, 193; Brody, *Workers in Industrial America*, 12–13; Fishback, *Soft Coal, Hard Choices*, 28–31.

9. "Labor Turnover: Facts and Causes" Section on Industrial Service C.N.D., Committee on Labor, Chairman's Office, January 1918, Committee of National Defense, Box 360, 10A–C2.

10. Frank Julian Warne, *The Workers at War* (New York: The Century Co., 1920), 116; Betten and Mohl, *Steel City*, 30; Johnson, *Politics of Soft Coal*, 81; Brody, *In Labor's Cause*, 146–147.

11. Laslett, *Colliers Across the Sea*, 197.

12. Johnson, *The Politics of Soft Coal*, 31–51.

13. Letters to Francis S. Peabody from businessmen angry about their energy costs indicate some of this rivalry. "Correspondence of Francis S. Peabody," May 1917–April 1918, Committee on Coal Production, C.N.D., 9A–1C; Johnson, *The Politics of Soft Coal*, 32 and 31–51, 93–94.

14. Quote from Johnson, *Politics of Soft Coal*, 40–41. Johnson includes a lengthy discussion of the various phases of operator and governmental cooperation and lack thereof, 31–81.

15. Montgomery, *The Fall of the House of Labor*, 6.

16. McCallum, *The Iron and Steel Industry in the United States*, 124–125.

17. Edwards, *Contested Terrain*, 66–71; Montgomery, *Workers' Control*, 101–113; Alan Dawley, *Changing the World: American Progressives in War and Revolution* (Princeton, NJ: Princeton University Press, 2003), 143–180; McCartin, *Labor's Great War*, 1–11, 63–93.

18. Edwards, *Contested Terrain*, 125.

19. Weinstein, in his *The Decline of Socialism in America, 1912–1925*, includes a telling discussion of the large anti-war feeling across the nation (New Brunswick, NJ: Rutgers University Press, 1984), 134–142. See also McKillen, *Chicago Labor and the Quest for a Democratic Diplomacy*; David W. Detjen, *The Germans in Missouri, 1900–1918: Prohibition, Neutrality, and Assimilation* (Columbia: University of Missouri Press, 1985); Charles T. Johnson, *Culture at Twilight: The National German-American Alliance, 1901–1918* (New York: Peter Lang, 1999); Malcolm Campbell, "Emigrant Responses to War and Revolution, 1914–1921: Irish Opinion in the United States and Australia," *Irish Historical Studies* 32, no. 125 (2000): 75–92; Thomas J. Rowland, "Strained Neutrality: Irish-American Catholics, Woodrow Wilson, and the 'Lusitania,'" *Éire-Ireland* 30, no. 4 (1996): 58–75; Theodore Kornweibel, *Investigate Everything: Federal Efforts to Compel Black Loyalty During World War I* (Bloomington: Indiana University Press, 2002), 1–75; Christopher Sterba, *Good Americans: Italian and Jewish Immigrants During the First World War* (Oxford: Oxford University Press, 2003); Preston, *Aliens and Dissenters*, 88–117; Jim Bissett, *Agrarian Socialism in America: Marx, Jefferson, and Jesus in the Oklahoma Countryside, 1904–1920* (Norman: University of Oklahoma Press, 1999), 142–173.

20. "Americanization," *Chicago Daily Tribune*, 23 February 1916: 6.

21. Joan M. Jensen, *The Price of Vigilance* (Chicago: Rand McNally, 1969); George Creel, *How We Advertised America: The First Telling of the Amazing Story of the Committee on Public Information That Carried the Gospel of Americanism to Every Corner of the Globe* (New York: Harper and Brothers, 1920); Preston, *Aliens and Dissenters*; Dawley, *Changing the World*, 111, 115–123, 153, 170–176, 375; Weinstein, *The Decline of Socialism in America*, 159–162, 182–183.

22. Letter from Solon J. Buck of the Minnesota Historical Society in Saint Paul, MN, May 31, 1917, to Prof. G.S. Ford, Director's Office of the Foreign Section, General Correspondence, Jan–March 1919, 17–1, Box 2, Entry 105, Records of the Committee on Public Information, National Archives RG 63; see also, "Correspondence of G.S. Ford During the Conclusion of His Work with the Committee," Nov.–Dec. 1918, 3-A5. Entry 31, Box 1, Records of the Committee on Public Information, National Archives RG 63.

23. P. George Hummasti, "'The Workingman's Daily Bread,' Finnish-American Working Class Newspapers, 1900–1921," in Karni, ed., *For the Common Good: Finnish Immigrants and the Radical Response to Industrial America* (Superior, WI: Tyomies Society, 1977), 167–194; Dubofsky, *We Shall Be All*, 382–383, 405; Montgomery, *Fall of the House of Labor*, 376; Weinstein, *The Decline of Socialism in America*, 90–93.

24. Simeon Larson, *Labor and Foreign Policy: Gompers, the A.F.L., and the First World War, 1914–1918* (Cranbury, NJ: Associated University Presses, 1975), 47–64; Ronald Radosh, *American Labor and United States: Foreign Policy* (New York: Random House, 1969); Weinstein, *The Decline of Socialism in America, 1912–1925*, 46–47; Edwards, *Contested Terrain*, 69.

25. Montgomery, *The Fall of the House of Labor*, 357, 358.

26. James P. Cannon, *The First Ten Years of American Communism: Report of a Participant* (New York: Lyle Stuart, 1962), 266.
27. Montgomery, *The Fall of the House of Labor*, 357, 358.
28. Weinstein, *The Decline of Socialism*, 125–132, 146–159, 173–176; Michael K. Rosenow, "Divided They Fell: The Cook County S.P. and the Decline of Socialism in America, 1917–1921," unpublished undergraduate thesis, in possession of author; McKillen, *Chicago Labor and the Quest for a Democratic Diplomacy*, 12–13; Errol Wayne Stevens, "The Socialist Party of America in Municipal Politics: Canton, Illinois, 1911–1920," *Journal of the Illinois State Historical Society* 72, no. 4 (1979): 257–272; Gary Marks and Matthew Burbank, "Immigrant Support for the American Socialist Party, 1912 and 1920," *Social Science History* 14, no. 2 (Summer 1990): 175–202.
29. Gary Marks and Matthew Burbank, "Immigrant Support for the American Socialist Party, 1912 and 1920," *Social Science History* 14, no. 2 (Summer 1990): 175–202; Letter from Arvid Nelson to Emil Seidel, in Milwaukee, Wisconsin, Secretary of the Socialist Party of Wisconsin, 29 April 1920, Arvid Nelson Papers, FF8, Box 2, Immigration History Research Center; Mark Pittenger, *American Socialist and Evolutionary Thought, 1870–1920* (Madison: University of Wisconsin Press, 1985), 167–172; Sally M. Miller, *Victor Berger and the Promise of Constructive Socialism* (Westport, CT: Greenwood, 1973), 51; Sally M. Miller, *The Radical Immigrant* (New York: Twayne Publishers, 1974), 120; Mink, *Old Labor and New Immigrants* (Ithaca: Cornell University Press, 1986), 41; Eugene Debs, "A Letter from Debs on Immigration," *International Socialist Review*, July 11, 1920, cited in Sally M. Miller ed., *Race, Ethnicity, and Gender in Early Twentieth-Century American Socialism* (New York: Garland Publishing, 1996), 232; Salvatore, *Eugene V. Debs*, 285.
30. Booth, "The Relationship Between Radicalism and Ethnicity in Southern Illinois Coal Fields, 1870–1940," 175–176, 186; Laslett, *Colliers Across the Sea*, 186–189; Nash, *Conflict and Accommodation*, 86–99, 210; Philip S. Foner, *The Bolshevik Revolution: Its Impact on American Radicals, Liberals, and Labor: A Documentary Study* (New York: International Publishers, 1967), 20–45; Michael Karni, "The Forging of Finnish-American Communism, 1917–1924: A Study in Ethnic Radicalism," in Auvo Kostiainen, ed., *Migration Studies*, C 4 (Turku, Finland: The Migration Institute, 1978), 69. On growth of the I.W.W., see Dubofsky, *We Shall Be All*; on growth of A.F.L., see Montgomery, *The Fall of the House of Labor*, 332, 370–372; Salvatore, *Eugene V. Debs*, 290; Rosenow, "Divided They Fell," 85–87; Mary Senior interview with an American skilled worker, July 30th, Saposs Papers, B26, F9.
31. Letter to the Wisconsin Central Committee of the S.P., sent from Superior Wisconsin, 24 April 1916, Arvid Nelson Papers, Immigration History Research Center; Ross, *The Finn Factor*, 145.
32. Letter from Kalle Tahtela, 11 February 1917, Secretary of the Central Committee of the S.P. of Douglas County, Arvid Nelson Papers.
33. Weinstein, *The Decline of Socialism in America*, 162, 179–181.
34. Letter from Arvid Nelson to George W. Lippert, District Attorney, Marathon County, Wausau, Wisconsin, 10 June 1918, Arvid Nelson Papers. On the popularity of the Russian Revolution with Finns, see Kostiainen, "The Forging of Finnish-American Communism," 46–47.
35. Letter from John Wiita to Mike Karni, 15 October 1976, John Wiita Papers, Folder 1, Immigration History Research Center; Kostiainen, "The Forging of Finnish-American Communism," 46–48, 63–64; Foner, *The Bolshevik Revolution*, 20–45.
36. "Are Lithuanians Undesirable?" *Lietuva*, 26 April 1918, Chicago Foreign Language Press Survey.
37. Mirosław Boruta and Andrzej Porębski, "The Polish Labor Press and Workers' Acculturation in the United States, 1918–1929," *The Press of Labor Migrants in Europe and North America, 1880s to 1930s*, 487–503, 489; Joseph John Parot, *Polish Catholics in Chicago: 1850–1920* (DeKalb, IL: Northern Illinois University Press, 1981); Kučas, *Lithuanians in America*, 100–102; Maria Woroby, "The Ukrainian Immigrant Left in the United States, 1890–1950," in *The Immigrant Left in the United States*, 194–202; Foner, *The Bolshevik Revolution*, 21–22; Vecoli, "The Making and Un-Making of the Italian American Working Class," 51–76; Report from John R. Dillon, 25 May 1917, Surveillance of Radicals, U.S. Military Intelligence Files, Reel 8; Davis, *The Russians and Ruthenians*, 38; Weinstein, *The Decline of Socialism in America*, 184.
38. Gerson, *Woodrow Wilson and the Rebirth of Poland*, 26; Cygan, "The Polish-American Left."
39. Ivan Čizmić, "The Involvement of Yugoslav Socialists in the SP of America and the

Socialist Labor Party of America, 1903–1924," *The Press of Labor Migrants in Europe and North America 1880s to 1930s,* 465–469.

40. Of the 12,000 workers at Overland, only 2,500 remained at work. "When I asked him which of the people had remained at work and did not go out he answered, 'I am sorry to say it was the so-called Americans.'" Letter from W.M. Leiserson "Re: glass workers' strike in Toledo, Ford Plate Glass Works at Rossford, Overland Strike," 3 July 1919, Saposs Papers, Box 1, F9; "Soldiers, Sailors, and Marines Soviet," 6 May 1919, from "Intelligence Officer, Pittsburgh, PA," U.S. Military Intelligence Files, Surveillance of Radicals, Reel 8.

41. Letter from Toledo, Ohio, to Attorney General A. Mitchell Palmer, Washington, D.C., 10 June 1919, Strike Files, U.S. Department of Justice; Letter from Toledo, Ohio. On the subject of workers' control, see Montgomery, *Workers Control in America,* and for a local example, see Adam Jonathan Hodges, "World War I and Local Change in America: Federal War Production and Class Relations in Portland, Oregon," (PhD. Diss., University of Illinois at Urbana-Champaign, 2002), 167–178.

42. "Conditions at Sault St. Marie, Detroit, and Duluth; Neutrality Matter," Agent Kenny, June 18, 1917, U.S. Military Intelligence Files, Surveillance of Radicals, Reel 1; "Duluth Neutrality Matter," Agent Kenny, June 18, 1917, U.S. Military Intelligence Files, Surveillance of Radicals, Reel 1; Weinberg, *Tug of War,* 320–326; Thomas Mackaman, "Life and Labor in Ely, Minnesota, 1886–1919: Community and Worker Identity on the American Industrial Frontier" (BA Thesis, University of Minnesota, 1998), in possession of author.

43. Gerald Ronning, "Jackpine Savages: Discourses of Conquest in the 1916 Mesabi Iron Range Strike," *Labor History* 44, no. 3 (2003): 359–382; "Statement of John S. Pardee Secretary of the Minnesota Commission of Public Safety in Regard to the I.W.W.," C.N.D. Papers, State Council Sections, 14-A1, General Correspondence April–December 1917, Minnesota State Council of National Defense, September, Record Group 62; Report from James Daly, Biwabik, MN, 31 May 1917, U.S. Military Intelligence Files, Surveillance of Radicals; Report from James H. Daly, Duluth, Minnesota, 21 May 1917, U.S. Military Intelligence Files, Surveillance of Radicals; Report from John T. Kenney, 18 June 1917, U.S. Military Intelligence Files, Surveillance of Radicals; Report from Troyer, 17 July 1917, U.S. Military Intelligence Files, Surveillance of Radicals; Ross, *The Finn Factor,* 146; Gary London, "The Finnish-American Anti-Socialist Movement, 1908–1918," in Michael G. Karni, Olavi Koivukangas, and Edward W. Laine, eds., *Finns in North America: Proceedings of Finn Forum III* (Turku, Finland: Institute of Migration, 1988), 211–226; Kivisto, *Immigrant Socialists in the United States,* 156–158; Dubofsky, *We Shall Be All,* 407–408.

44. Weinberg, "The Tug of War," 343–346; Betten and Mohl, *Steel City,* 33–34.

45. "Are Lithuanians Undesirable?" 26 April 1918, *Lietuva,* Chicago Foreign Language Press Survey.

46. Letter from E.H. Hatch, mayor of Eveleth, MN, to George Creel, 19 February 1918, Papers of the Committee on Public Information, "Executive Division: Answers by Mayors to Americanization Survey Letters, Feb–April 1918, Box 1, Entry No. 2, National Archives; Ross, *The Finn Factor,* 145–157, quote from Creel on page 151; London, "The Finnish-American Anti-Socialist Movement, 1908–1918," 211–226; Montgomery, *Fall of the House of Labor,* 376; Mackaman, "Life and Labor in Ely, Minnesota"; "Italian Societies March for Liberty," *Chicago Daily Tribune,* 22 April 1918: 5; Montgomery, "Nationalism, American Patriotism, and Class Consciousness," 327–351.

47. Jack Battuello, interviews conducted by Nick Cherniavsky and Bobbie Herndon, April 1973, Sangamon State Oral History Collection, Transcript: Part 6., no. 4: 36; Carl Weinberg's dissertation includes a very good account of developments in the Illinois U.M.W. and among coal miners: "Tug of War," 266–285.

48. Weinberg, "Tug of War," 453–522; "Tar and Feather Chicago Lawyer as an I.W.W. Aid," *Chicago Daily Tribune,* 13 February 1918: 1.

49. Waldron, "The Great Spirit of Solidarity," 320–322; David Dechenne, "Recipe for Violence: War Attitudes, the Black Hundred Riot, and Superpatriotism in an Illinois Coalfield, 1917–1918," *Illinois Historical Journal,* 80(4) 1987: 221–238; Booth, "The Relationship Between Radicalism and Ethnicity," 118–120, 149; Weinberg, "The Tug of War," 118–119; Laslett, *Colliers Across the Sea,* 198, 210.

50. Alan Singer, "'Something of a Man': John L. Lewis, the U.M.W., and the CIO, 1919–1943," Laslett, ed., *The U.M.W. of America,* 104–106; Laslett, *Colliers Across the Sea,* 208–209.

51. Salvatore, *Eugene V. Debs,* 286–288.

52. Letter from Frank Farrington to Peter Grubich, "Sec. L.U. 620, La Salle, Illinois," 14,

February, 1917, Duncan McDonald Collection, Box 1 Folder 3, Abraham Lincoln Library, Springfield, Illinois.

53. Letter from Farrington to "The Officers and Members, District 12, U.M.W. of America" 11 October 1917, and to "The Officers and Members, District 12, U.M.W. of America," 20 July 1917, Folder 4, Abraham Lincoln Library, Springfield, Illinois; Laslett, *Colliers Across the Sea*, 198.

54. Barrett, *Work and Community*, 192–195.

55. Letter from Farrington to "The Officers and Members, District 12, U.M.W. of America," 20, July, 1917, MacDonald Papers; Foner, *History of the Labor Movement in the United States*, 141.

56. Weinberg, "Tug of War," 348, 368, 372–373, 438–441.

57. "Engine Car Men out on a Strike at Springfield," and "Man Is Shot above Eye in Outbreak at State Capital," *Chicago Daily Tribune*, 26 July 1917: 1; "Policeman Shot During Car Riot at Springfield," *Chicago Daily Tribune*, 8 August 1917: 1.

58. "Strike Beyond Union Control; Asks State Aid; Miners' Head Wants the Council of Defense to Check Spread," *Chicago Daily Tribune*, 14 August 1917: 13; "Rebel Miners Imperil Illinois Coal Price Plan," *Chicago Daily Tribune*, 15 August 1917: 17; "Strikers: More Men Will Walk Out at Mines, Is Fear Now," *Chicago Daily Tribune*, 15 August 1917: 17.

59. "Springfield, Illinois," Papers of the National War Labor Board, Microfilm reels 2 and 22; Kenton Gatyas, "Springfield's General Strike of 1917," *Journal of Illinois History*, Vol. 1, No. 1 (1998): 43–56; "Bayonets End Riot of 2,000 in Springfield," *Chicago Daily Tribune*, 4 September 1917: 1; "State Capital in Strike Grip; More Quit Work," *Chicago Daily Tribune*, 12 September 1917: 5; "10,000 Join Big Strike at Springfield," *Chicago Daily Tribune*, 14 September 1917: 1; "Strikers March, Berate Judges, Vote for Peace," *Chicago Daily Tribune*, 17 September 1917: 1.

Chapter 4

1. Johnson, *The Politics of Soft Coal*, 101. Inflation of major food products had increased by 85 percent between 1914 and 1919, while real wages had declined. Beik, *The Miners of Windber*, 257.

2. "Interview with Peter Furrara, Ex. Ed. Member, Dist. No. 2, United Mine Workers," Interviewed by David Saposs, 1919, Saposs Papers.

3. "The Revolt of the Rank and File," *The Nation*, 25 October, 1919.

4. David Saposs, "Problems Encountered in Organizing Immigrant Workers, Cohesiveness and Uniformity of Purpose, Discipline and Control." From Saposs, *The Immigrant and the Labor Movement*, Saposs Papers, 1920; "Interview with Carl Andelin, Local Organizer, Boot and Shoe Workers Union, Chicago, Ill, January 2nd, 1919," Interviewed by Saposs, Saposs Papers.

5. Foster, *The Great Steel Strike and Its Lessons*, 16–27; Brody, *Labor in Crisis*, 45–77 and *Steelworkers in America*, 214–230.

6. Mackaman, "Life and Labor in Ely, Minnesota, 1886–1919."

7. Brody, *Labor in Crisis*; David Montgomery, "The 'New Unionism' and the Transformation of Workers' Consciousness in America, 1909–1922," *Journal of Social History* 7 (1974): 509–29; Barrett, *William Z. Foster* and *Work and Community in the Jungle*; Brody, *Labor in Crisis*.

8. "Standard Steel Car Company Hammond, Ind.," Letter to Hugh Kerwin from Edward J. Evans, Secretary Treasurer, Chicago District National Committee for Organizing Iron and Steel Workers, 20 March 1919, and telegram from John J. Walsh to Kerwin, Received 15 April 1919, Federation Mediation and Reconciliation Service, Box 102, 170–262, National Archives, RG 280.

9. James R. Barrett, *William Z. Foster and the Tragedy of American Radicalism* (Urbana: University of Illinois Press, 1999), 84–90.

10. Barrett, "Americanization from the Bottom Up," 1009; Foster, *The Great Steel Strike*, 52, 51–67, 110–139; Brody, *Labor in Crisis*, 87–89.

11. Betten and Mohl, *Steel City*, 41.

12. Foster, *The Great Steel Strike*, 194–211; Brody, *Labor in Crisis*, 132–136, 149–151, 156–159.

13. Brody, *Labor in Crisis*, 205–210; Betten and Mohl, *Steel City*, 28; James R. Barrett, *William Z. Foster*, 95–96.

14. Chicago Commission on Race Relations, *The Negro in Chicago: A Study of Race Relations and a Race Riot* (Chicago: University of Chicago Press, 1923), 11–17; William M. Tuttle, *Race Riot: Chicago in the Red Summer of 1919* (New York: Atheneum, 1970), 103–104; Lee E. Williams and Lee E. Williams II, *Anatomy of Four Race Riots: Racial Conflict in Knoxville, Elaine (Arkansas), Tulsa, and Chicago, 1919–1921* (Jackson: University and College Press of Mississippi, 1972), 87; "How the Lawrence Ku Klux Gang Taught Me American Democracy," letter to "Look, Dr. Percey J., Andover, Mass," Anthony Capraro papers, Immigration History Research Center; Horace R. Cayton, George S. Mitchell, "Blacks and Organized Labor in the Iron and Steel Industry, 1880–1939," in John H. Bracey, *Black Workers and Organized Labor* (Belmont, CA: Wadsworth, 1971), 132–154; Bernard Mandel, "Samuel Gompers and the Negro Workers, 1886–1914," in John H. Bracey, *Black Workers and Organized Labor* (Belmont, CA: Wadsworth, 1971), 26–43.

15. "Notes on Conference of District Secretaries in Charge During Steel Strike, 20 January 1920," Saposs Papers.

16. Carol Marks, *Farewell—We're Good and Gone: The Great Black Migration* (Bloomington: Indiana University Press, 1989), 3; Cannon, *The First Ten Years of American Communism*, 233.

17. James R. Bartett, *The Irish Way: Becoming American in the Multiethnic City* (New York: Penguin, 2012); James Barrett and David Roediger, "The Irish and the 'Americanization' of the 'New Immigrants' in the Streets and in the Churches of the Urban United States, 1900–1930," *Journal of American Ethnic History* 24, no. 4 (2005): 4–33; Chicago Commission on Race Relations, *The Negro in Chicago*, 11–17.

18. Betten and Mohl, *Steel City*, 52.

19. "Letter from W.M. Leiserson, Chief of Division, Industrial and Economics Amalgamated," 26 February, 1919," Saposs Papers.

20. Brody, *Steelworkers in America*, 80–95; Barrett and Roediger. "Inbetween Peoples," 3–44; "Interview with James Bissell," 2 August 1920, Saposs Papers; "Interview with Robert Allan, New Kensington," 1920, Saposs Papers; "Interview with Frank Kasten, United Brick and Clay Workers of Am., Chicago., 20 Dec. 1918," Saposs Papers; "Geo. Bechtold, General Secretary-Treasurer, International Foundry Employees, St. Louis. Mo." 21 Dec. 1918, Saposs Papers; "Letter from W.A. Logan, General President for the United Automobile, Aircraft and Vehicle Workers of America, Located in Dearborn, Michigan," 1919, Saposs Papers; "Interview with Edward J. Evans, Secretary-Treasurer. Chicago District Organization Committee of the National Committee for Organizing Iron and Steel Workers, Chicago, 27 December 1918," Saposs Papers; "Interview with Dalton C. Clarke, Pres., the National Co-Operative Association, Pittsburgh," 14 April 1919, Saposs Papers.

21. "Interview with Tom Manseel, 11th Ave., Homestead," 18 July 1920, Saposs Papers.

22. "Interview with Mr. Lane, 2431 Arlington Ave, South Side," 5 August 1920, Saposs Papers; and "Interview with an American worker," 1920, Saposs Papers.

23. "Engineers' Head Says His Union Will Not Strike: Comerford Blames Steel Trouble on Radicals and Foreigners," *Chicago Daily Tribune*, 23 September 1919; Foster, *The Great Steel Strike*, 194.

24. "Foreigners Feel Slur of Corrupt Editors," *The New Majority*, 1 Nov. 1919: 1.

25. Barrett, *William Z. Foster*, 94.

26. Foster, *The Great Steel Strike and Its Lessons*, 200.

27. Mary Heaton Vorse, *Men and Steel* (New York: Boni and Liveright, 1920), 163–177.

28. "Interview with Five Lithuanians and One Italian Young Fellows, All Born in E. Vandergrift and Educated through Grade School," 30 October 1919, Saposs Papers.

29. Commission of Inquiry, *Report on the Steel Strike of 1919*, 162.

30. Vorse, *Men and Steel*, 112.

31. "Letter from Jere L. Sullivan, Secretary-Treasurer of Hotel and Restaurant Employees' International Alliance and Bartenders' International League of America," 1919, Saposs Papers.

32. "Interview with J.E. Roach, in Charge of New York Office American Federation of Labor," 1919, Saposs Papers.

33. Montgomery, "Immigrants, Industrial Unions, and Social Reconstruction in the United States, 1916–1923," 112. See also Barrett, *Work and Community in the Jungle*, 224–231.

34. "An Interview with David Saposs," interview by Alice M. Hoffman, 1967, Saposs Papers, Box 26, F5; "Interview with Joe Dick, 2306 Patterson St., South Side," 7 August 1920, Saposs Papers B26, F9; Kessler-Harris, *Out to Work*, 138; Weiler, "The Uprising in Chicago," 117–118; Maurine Weiner Greenwald, "Women and Class in Pittsburgh, 1850–1920," Samuel

P. Hays, ed., *City at the Point: Essays on the Social History of Pittsburgh* (Pittsburgh: University of Pittsburgh Press, 1989), 40–41, 47.
35. Foster, *The Great Steel Strike*, 17–27.
36. Barrett, *Work and Community in the Jungle*, 242.
37. "Impromptu Remarks by Elbert H. Gary, Chairman at the Annual Meeting of the Stockholders of the United States Steel Corporation, April 21, 1919."
38. Leonardo Minelli, Interview by Mary Ellen Batinich, 28 October 1987, Batinich Collection.
39. McKillen, *Chicago Labor*, 3.
40. Johnson, *The Politics of Soft Coal*, 100–104; Brody, *In Labor's Cause*, 147.
41. Laslett, *Colliers Across the Sea*, 202–203; Montgomery, *The Fall of the House of Labor*, 391; Booth, "The Relationship Between Radicalism and Ethnicity in Southern Illinois Coal Fields," 120–126; Weinberg, "The Tug of War," 558–570, 579–594.
42. Singer, "'Something of a Man': John L. Lewis, the U.M.W.A, and the CIO," 107–110; Mildred Beik, *The Miners of Windber*, 260.
43. Barrett, *William Z. Foster*, 84–85, 89–90; Foster, *The Great Steel Strike and Its Lessons*, 26.
44. Brecher, *Strike!*, 115; "Radical Organizations in Gary, Ind.," Report of Agent. J. Spolansky, 8 January 1919, U.S. Military Intelligence Files, Surveillance of Radicals, Reel 13; Commission of Inquiry, *Report on the Steel Strike of 1919*, 15, 39–40; "Interview with Edward J. Evans," 27 December 1918, Saposs Papers.
45. Montgomery, "Immigrants, Industrial Unions, and Social Reconstruction in the United States, 1916–1923", 113.
46. Commission of Inquiry, *Report on the Steel Strike of 1919*, 20.
47. Saposs, "The Problem of Making Permanent Trade Unionists out of the Large Number of Recently Organized Immigrant Workers," 1919, Saposs Papers.
48. "Interview with Edward J. Evans," Saposs Papers.
49. Saposs Papers, Folder 26, File 6.
50. "Digest of Interviews with Trade Union Officials, by DJ Saposs, 1919," Saposs Papers.
51. "Letter from W.M. Leiserson," 3 July 1919, "Re: Glass Workers' Strike in Toledo, Ford Plate Glass Works at Rossford, Overland Strike," Saposs Papers.
52. "Interview with Graff," 19 July 1920, Box 26, Folder 8, Saposs Papers.
53. "Geo. Bechtold," 1919, Saposs Papers.
54. "Interview with Edward J. Evans," Saposs Papers.
55. "Interview with John Howard, Secretary Local Amalgamated Iron, Sheet and Steel Workers, Indiana Harbor, Indiana," 1919, Saposs Papers.
56. "Letter from W.M. Leiserson," Saposs.
57. "Standard Steel Car Company Hammond, Ind.," Letter to Hugh Kerwin from Edward J. Evans, Secretary Treasurer, Chicago District National Committee for Organizing Iron and Steel Workers, 20 March 1919, and telegram from John J. Walsh to Kerwin, Received 15 April 1919, Federation Mediation and Reconciliation Service, Box 102, 170–262, National Archives, RG 280.
58. "Interview with John Corpi, Organizer for Metal Mine Workers' Industrial Union, I.W.W., Duluth, Minn.," 9 July 1919, Saposs Papers; Brecher, *Strike!*, 115.
59. Preston, *Aliens and Dissenters*, 88–151, 181–237; Murray, *Red Scare*, 135–153.
60. "Interview with Edward J. Evans," 27 December 1918, Saposs Papers.
61. McKillen, "Chicago Labor and the Quest for a Democratic Diplomacy," 17; Wyman, *Round-Trip to America*, 63, 65.
62. Montgomery, "Nationalism, American Patriotism, and Class Consciousness," 330–331.
63. "The Barbers' Strike," *La Fiaccola*, 1918, in *Chicago Foreign Language Press Survey*.
64. "The Strike of the Macaroni Workers," *L'Italia*, 1919, in *Chicago Foreign Language Press Survey*.
65. Pacyga, *Polish Immigrants and Industrial Chicago: Workers on the South Side, 1880–1922*, 233–234.
66. John J. Bukowzyk, "The Transformation of Working-Class Ethnicity: Corporate Control, Americanization, and the Polish Immigrant Middle Class in Bayonne, New Jersey, 1915–1925," in Robert and Charles Stephenson Asher, eds., *Labor Divided: Race and Ethnicity in United States Labor Struggles, 1835–1960* (New York: State University of New York Press, 1990); N. Costanzo, "Auburn N.Y.," *Il Proletario*, 21 May 1921.
67. "Interview with Mr. Tarkangi, Editor of Hungarian Herald, Pittsburgh," 1920, Saposs Papers.

68. "Interview with Budimer Grahavoc, Editor, the *American Srbobran*, Official Organ of the Servian O.S. Srbron and Serbian National Defense League of America," 1920, Saposs Papers.
69. "Interview with Albert Mamatey, President, National Slovak Society," 1920, in Saposs Papers.
70. "Interview with Ivan Bielek, Editor and O.D. Koreff, Assistant Editor, Narodne Noving (National News)," 1920, Saposs Papers.
71. "Interview with G. Guntkiewicz, Treasurer, Polish Falcons Alliance of America, Pittsburgh," 1920, Saposs Papers.
72. Saposs, "Interview with Edward J. Evans, Secretary-Treasurer. Chicago District Organization Committee of the National Committee for Organizing Iron and Steel Workers, Chicago, December 27th, 1918."
73. "Interview with G. Guntkiewicz," Saposs Papers.
74. Hummasti, "The Workingman's Daily Bread," 167–194; Karni, *The Forging of Finnish-American Communism, 1917–1924*, 69–96.
75. Rosenow, "Divided They Fell," 94–95; Letter from Arvid Nelson to Emil Seidel, 29 April 1920; Nelson to Seidel, 26 July 1920.Correspondence between Arvid Nelson and Emile Seidel from Arvid Nelson Papers, FF8, Box 2: Letter to Nelson from Seidel; Letter from Nelson to Seidel, 8 July 1920; "Finnish Convention in Chicago," 17 Dec. 1918, U.S. Military Intelligence Files, Surveillance of Radicals; Maria Woroby, "The Ukrainian Immigrant Left in the United States," 196–202.
76. Weinstein, *The Decline of Socialism*, 192, 199–200, 210–211, 222–230, 237; Mirosłav Boruta and Andrzej Porębski, "The Polish Labor Press and Workers' Acculturation in the United States, 1918–1929," *The Press of Labor Migrants in Europe and North America 1880s to 1930s*, 489.
77. Draper, *Roots of American Communism*, 148–175; Bryan D. Palmer, *James P. Cannon and the Origins of the American Revolutionary Left, 1890–1928* (Urbana: University of Illinois Press, 2007), 87–128; John Howard Keiser, "John Fitzpatrick and Progressive Unionism, 1915–1925," (PhD. Diss., Northwestern University, Illinois), 106–154.
78. "I.W.W. Meeting, June 7, 1919, Chicago," "Chicago, April 14, 1919," Meeting of Czech and Slovak socialists, "Russian Mass Meeting Held at Walsh's Hall, May 31st, 1919," U.S. Military Intelligence Files, Reel 10; "Radical Situation in Gary," correspondence from "Department of Intelligence Officer, Chicago." May 1, 2, 5, October 9, 28, November 11, 12, 18, 1919, U.S. Military Intelligence Files, Reel 13; Weinberg, "Tug of War," 556–557.
79. Michael M. Passi, "Finnish Immigrants and the Radical Response to Industrial America" in Michael Karni, ed., *For the Common Good: Finnish Immigrants and the Radical Response to Industrial America* (Superior, WI: Tyomies Society, 1977), 12–19; Hummasti, "'The Workingman's Daily Bread,' Finnish-American Working Class Newspapers, 1900–1921," in *For the Common Good*, 189–190; Karni, *The Forging of Finnish-American Communism*, 92–97.
80. Vecoli, *The Italian Immigrants in the United States Labor Movement*, 303.
81. "Communism vs. Socialism," Anthony Capraro Papers, Box 2, Folder, "Communist Party of Italy"; Anthony Capraro Papers, Box 3, Folder, "Untitled"; Box 4, Folder "Unidentified" Letter from *Partito Communista D'Italia*, sent from *il Comitato Esecutivo*, December 1, 1923; and letter from Capraro to "Sig. Egidio Gennari *Casa del Popolo*," Via Capo d'Africa, Roma, Italy, 12 October 1922.
82. Dubofsky, *We Shall Be All*, 445–468.

Chapter 5

1. Frank L. Palmer, *Spies in Steel: An Expose of Industrial War* (Denver, CO: Labor Press, 1928).
2. Sofchalk, "Organized Labor and the Iron Ore Miners of Northern Minnesota," 214–242; David Brody, "The Origins of Modern Steel Unionism: The SWOC Era," in Paul F. Clark, Peter Gottlieb, and Donald Kennedy, eds., *Forging a Union of Steel: Philip Murray, SWOC, and the United Steelworkers* (Ithaca: ILR Press of Cornell University, 1987), 13–29.
3. McCallum, *The Iron and Steel Industry in the United States*, 300–304; Edwards, *Contested Terrain*, 70; For the counteroffensive in meatpacking, see Barrett, *Work and Community in the Jungle*, 255–263; Dawley, *Changing the World*, 259–296.
4. Cohen, *Making a New Deal*. For the strategies of the early communist movement in the face of the postwar reaction, see Palmer, *James P. Cannon*, and Barrett, *William Z. Foster*.

5. This outlook is the dominant position of the great majority of labor and immigration histories of the period—it is more of an implicit viewpoint than a theoretical enunciation. See for examples, Brody, *Steelworkers in America*, Dubovsky, *We Shall Be All*.
6. Murray, *Red Scare*; Preston, *Aliens and Dissenters*; Higham, *Strangers in the Land*.
7. Theodore Draper, *The Roots of American Communism*, 345–346. This is the perspective of most of the analyses of the various immigrant groups, see for example Gerald Meyer, "Italian Americans and the American Communist Party," in *The Lost World of Italian American Radicalism*, and P. Kivisto. "The Decline of the Finnish American Left, 1925–1945," *International Migration Review* 17, no. 1 (1983): 65–94.
8. T. Iván Berend, *Decades of Crisis: Central and Eastern Europe Before World War II* (Berkeley: University of California Press, 1998); Robert Lee Wolff, *The Balkans in Our Time* (New York: W.W. Norton, 1967), 101–190; Lewin Moshe, *Lenin's Last Struggle* (New York: Monthly Review Press, 1978); R.J.B. Bosworth, *Mussolini's Italy: Life Under the Dictatorship, 1915–1945* (New York: Penguin, 2006).
9. Arno Mayer, *Politics and Diplomacy of Peacemaking Containment and Counterrevolution at Versailles, 1918–1919* (New York: Knopf, 1967); Thomas J. McCormick, *America's Half-Century*, 17–28.
10. McCallum, *The Iron and Steel Industry in the United States*, 125–126.
11. David Montgomery, "New Tendencies in Union Struggles and Strategies in Europe and the United States, 1916–1922," in *Work, Community, and Power: The Experience of Labor in Europe and America, 1900–1925* (Philadelphia: Temple University Press, 1983); Irving Bernstein, *The Lean Years: A History of the American Worker, 1920–1933* (Baltimore, MD: Penguin, 1966).
12. Keith Dix, "Mechanization, Workplace Control, and the End of the Hand-Loading Era," in John H.M. Laslett, ed., *The United Mine Workers of America*, 190–197; John H.M. Laslett, *Colliers Across the Sea*, 203.
13. David Corbin, *Life, Work, and Rebellion in the Coal Fields: The Southern West Virginia Miners, 1880–1922* (Urbana: University of Illinois Press, 1981).
14. Singer, "'Something of a Man': John L. Lewis, the U.M.W.A, and the CIO," 190–195; Laslett, *Colliers Across the Sea*, 200–201.
15. "Price of Bituminous Coal in 1921 Lowest Since 1916," *Coal Age*, Vol. 21, No. 3 (19 January 1922): 81.
16. "Telegram" from John L. Lewis to Woodrow Wilson, 19 August 1920, Federal Mediation and Reconciliation Service, Case Files, Dispute Case Files, "Bituminous Coal Miners Illinois (Springfield), 1913–1948," Box 126, 170–1215, National Archives, Record Group 280.
17. "To the Members of the United Mine Workers of America," 20 July 1920, Woodrow Wilson, Federal Mediation and Reconciliation Service, Case Files, Dispute Case Files, "Bituminous Coal Miners Illinois (Springfield), 1913–1948," Box 126, 170–1215, National Archives, Record Group 280.
18. "Memorandum for the President," 29 July 1920, Secretary Wilson, Federal Mediation and Reconciliation Service, Case Files, Dispute Case Files, "Bituminous Coal Miners Illinois (Springfield), 1913–1948," Box 126, 170–1215, National Archives, Record Group 280.
19. "Department of Labor Telegram," 31 July 1920, Frank Farrington to Sec. Wilson, Federal Mediation and Reconciliation Service, Case Files, Dispute Case Files, "Bituminous Coal Miners Illinois (Springfield), 1913–1948," Box 126, 170–1215, National Archives, Record Group 280.
20. Letter from Sec. Wilson to Kerwin, Dept. of Labor, 3 August 1920 and Letter from Hugh Kerwin to Deward Kenny, 9 February 1921, Federal Mediation and Reconciliation Service, Case Files, Dispute Case Files, "Bituminous Coal Miners Illinois (Springfield), 1913–1948," Box 126, 170–1215, National Archives, Record Group 280; "The Report of the Sub-Scale Committee," 26 August 1920, Federal Mediation and Reconciliation Service, Case Files, Dispute Case Files, "Bituminous Coal Miners Illinois (Springfield), 1913–1948," Box 126, 170–1215, National Archives, Record Group 280; "Mines Closed by Second Outbreak of Daymen's Strike in Indiana," prepared by F.G. Tryon, United States Geological Survey, 15 August 1920, Federal Mediation and Reconciliation Service, Case Files, Dispute Case Files, "Bituminous Coal Miners Illinois (Springfield), 1913–1948," Box 126, 170–1215, National Archives, Record Group 280; Telegram, 19 August 1920, From John L. Lewis via Philip Murray to Sec. Wilson, Federal Mediation and Reconciliation Service, Case Files, Dispute Case Files, "Bituminous Coal Miners Illinois (Springfield), 1913–1948," Box 126, 170–1215, National Archives, Record Group 280; "Confidential Memorandum on Effects of Illinois-Indiana Miners' Strike on Production of Soft Coal," 26 August 1920, F.G. Tryon, U.S. Geological Survey, Federal Mediation and Reconciliation Service, Case Files, Dispute Case Files, "Bituminous Coal Miners Illinois (Springfield),

1913–1948," Box 126, 170–1215, National Archives, Record Group 280; "Telegram to President Wilson," 29 July 1920, from Wyllys W. Baird, President of the Chicago Association of Commerce, Federal Mediation and Reconciliation Service, Case Files, Dispute Case Files, "Bituminous Coal Miners Illinois (Springfield), 1913–1948," Box 126, 170–1215, National Archives, Record Group 280; "Department of Labor Telegram," 26 July 1920, from Rogers, Lennon, Walsh (labor conciliators) to Kerwin, Federal Mediation and Reconciliation Service, Case Files, Dispute Case Files, "Bituminous Coal Miners Illinois (Springfield), 1913–1948," Box 126, 170–1215, National Archives, Record Group 280; "Statement of John L. Lewis, President United Mine Workers of America," 24 July 1920, Federal Mediation and Reconciliation Service, Case Files, Dispute Case Files, "Bituminous Coal Miners Illinois (Springfield), 1913–1948," Box 126, 170–1215, National Archives, Record Group 280.

21. "Department of Labor Telegram from Walsh," 7 August 1920, Federal Mediation and Reconciliation Service, Case Files, Dispute Case Files, "Bituminous Coal Miners Illinois (Springfield), 1913–1948," Box 126, 170–1215, National Archives, Record Group 280; "Assures Protection to Aliens: Riots Are Renewed at West Frankfort," *New York Times*, 15 August 1920: 26; "The Harvest," *The Chicago Defender*, 14 August 1920: 12; "Race Riots and War," *Chicago Daily Tribune*, 9 August 1920: 8; "Italian Consul Asks Reparation for Mob's Prey: Troops Capture Pair in Downstate Murder," *Chicago Daily Tribune*, 8 August 1920: 3; "The Mob Reveals Our Needs," *Chicago Daily Tribune*, 7 August 1920: 4.

22. "Miners' Convention Adopts 'Suicidal' List of Demands," *Coal Age*, Vol. 21, 8 (23 February 1922): 337; Johnson, *Politics of Soft Coal*, 95–123.

23. Paul M. Angle's coverage of the massacre and the events leading up to it remain the most descriptive coverage of the event: *Bloody Williamson: A Chapter in American Lawlessness* (Urbana: University of Illinois Press, 1992), 3–71; Johnson, *The Politics of Soft Coal*, 114.

24. Brody, *In Labor's Cause*, 131, 144, 149–150.

25. "Underground Management in Bituminous Coal Mines," Sanford E. Thomas, August 1923, Drafts of Commission Reports, 1922–23, Entry 4, Records of the U.S. Coal Commission Reports, 1922–23, Records of the U.S. Coal Commission, National Archives, RG 68; "April 1, 1922," *Coal Age*, Vol. 21, 13 (March 30, 1922): 521; "The Principle at Stake," *Coal Age*, Vol. 2, 15 (13 April 1922): 1; "Can One Coal Company Cover United States?," *Coal Age*, Vol. 21, 16.

26. "Working Papers and Copies of Reports Relating to the Coal Industry, January 1923–May 1924," Records of the U.S. Coal Commission, National Archives, RG 68, Entry 6; Brody, *In Labor's Cause*, 142, 152.

27. L.F. "Fra I Minatori," *Il Proletario*, 8 January 1921; Carl D. Oblinger, *Divided Kingdom: Work, Community, and the Mining Wars in the Central Illinois Coal Fields During the Great Depression* (Springfield: Illinois State Historical Society, 1991); John M. Laslett, "Swan Song or New Social Movement? Socialism and District 12, United Mine Workers of America, 1919–1926," in *Socialism in the Heartland: The Midwestern Experience*, Donald T. Critchlow ed. (South Bend, IN: University of Notre Dame Press, 1986).

28. Higham, *Strangers in the Land*; Mae Ngai, "The Architecture of Race in American Immigration Law: A Reexamination of the Immigration Act of 1924," *The Journal of American History* 86, no. 1 (June 1999): 67–92.

29. Dawley, *Changing the World*, 259–296; Ronald E. Powaski, *Toward an Entangling Alliance: American Isolationism, Internationalism, and Europe, 1901–1950* (Westport, CT: Greenwood, 1991); Stanley Coben, *Rebellion Against Victorianism: The Impetus for Cultural Change in 1920s America* (New York: Oxford University Press, 1991).

30. McCartin, *Labor's Great War*; Gerstle, *Working Class Americanism*.

31. Leonard Joseph Moore, *Citizen Klansmen: The Ku Klux Klan in Indiana, 1921–1928* (Chapel Hill: University of North Carolina Press, 1991); Leonard Joseph Moore, "Review: Historical Interpretations of the 1920's Klan: The Traditional View and the Populist Revision," *Journal of Social History* 24, no. 2 (Winter 1990): 341–357.

32. William Pencak, *For God and Country: The American Legion, 1919–1941* (Boston: Northeastern University Press, 1989); David Mark Chalmers, *Hooded Americanism: The History of the Ku Klux Klan* (Chicago: Quadrangle Books, 1968); Shawn Lay, *Hooded Knights on the Niagara: The Ku Klux Klan in Buffalo, New York* (New York: New York University Press, 1995); William D. Jenkins, *Steel Valley Klan: The Ku Klux Klan in Ohio's Mahoning Valley* (Kent, OH: Kent State University Press, 1990); Kenneth T. Jackson, *The Ku Klux Klan in the City, 1915–1930* (New York: Oxford University Press, 1967); Robert Alan Goldberg, *Hooded Empire: The Ku Klux Klan in Colorado* (Urbana: University of Illinois Press, 1981); "The A.F.L. and the Ku Klux Klan," 18 June 1921, *New York Call*, clipping in Anthony Capraro Papers, Box 2, Folder "The Ku Klux Klan."

33. Letter from Arvid Nelson to Enoch Nelson, 21 January 1920, Arvid Nelson Paper, FF5, Box 5.
34. "Raid Finn Reds and Force 150 to Kiss the Flag," *New York Times*, 8 October 1919: 1.
35. Betten and Mohl, *Steel City*, 28.
36. "Injustice to Foreign Workmen," *Znanje*, 24 November 1919, Chicago Foreign Language Press Survey.
37. Dominick DeJohn, "Italians in Illinois: A Memoir of an Ethnic Mining Community," *Italian Americana*. Vol. 7, 2 (1983): 30.
38. Ron and Molly Morcum, interview by Tom Rukavina, Soudan, MN, 1 September 1983, Iron Range Oral History Project.
39. Nick Camp, interview by Bobbie Herndon, Spring 1974, Sangamon State Oral History Project; Larry Mantowich, interview by Bobbie Herndon, Spring 1974, Sangamon State Oral History Project. Mildred Beik has found similar tendencies at play in the coal fields of Pennsylvania. There the Klan also burnt crosses across from mines. Immigrant workers fought back. See *The Miners of Windber*, 310–316; Letter from Arvid Nelson to Enoch Nelson, 1 January 1919, Arvid Nelson Papers, Box 5, F4; Dennis C. Dickerson, *Out of This Crucible: Black Steelworkers in Western Pennsylvania, 1875–1980* (Albany: State University of New York Press, 1986), 64; Jenkins, *Steel Valley Klan*, 120–140.
40. William Fitzhugh Brundage, *Lynching in the New South: Georgia and Virginia, 1880–1930* (Urbana: University of Illinois Press, 1993), 58–63.
41. Letter from Arvid Nelson to Enoch Nelson, 21 January 1920, Arvid Nelson Papers, Box 5, F5; Letter from Arvid Nelson to Enoch Nelson, 18 June 1920, Arvid Nelson Papers, Box 5, F5.
42. Jackson, *The Ku Klux Klan in the City, 1915–1930*, 93–126; Philpott, *The Slum and the Ghetto*, 188–190.
43. Jackson, *The Ku Klux Klan in the City, 1915–1930*, 108.
44. Betten and Mohl, *Steel City*, 33–34.
45. Angle, *Bloody Williamson*, 134–205; "Disputes Herrin Picture," *New York Times*, 26 August 1924, clipping in Anthony Capraro Papers, Box 3, Folder "The Mining Industry in U.S."; Henry Pappone, Interviewed by Mary Ellen Batinich, 4 September 1984, Virginia, MN.
46. "Italophobia," *Bulletin* of the Italian American National Union, April 1925, Chicago Foreign Language Press Survey.
47. "Gompers Points out Seven Dominant Issues for Labor," *New York World*, 26 June 1924, clipping in Anthony Capraro Papers, B3, Folder, "American Federation of Labor."
48. Santina Gambucci and Celeste Gambucci, interview by Mary Ellen Batinich, Eveleth, August 4, 1981.
49. Giovanni Arrighi and Beverly J. Silver, "Labor Movements and Capital Migration: The United States and Western Europe in World-Historical Perspective," in C. Bergquist, ed., *Labor in the Capitalist World-Economy* (Beverly Hills, CA: Sage, 1984), 183–216.
50. The collected volume *Native Fascism in the Successor States, 1918–1945*, edited by Peter F. Sugar, contains suggestive case studies of Austrian, Czechoslovakian, Hungarian, Polish, Romanian, and Yugoslavian forms of fascism and fascistic movements, as well as insightful commentary on the social and political situations in these countries; Berend, *Decades of Crisis*; Wolfe, *The Balkans in Our Time*, 101–190; Bosworth, *Mussolini's Italy*, 93–150.
51. Paolo Spriano, *The Occupation of the Factories: Italy 1920* (London: Pluto Press, 1975); Oreste Scalzone, *Biennio Rosso, '68–'69: Figure E Passaggi Di Una Stagione Rivoluzionaria* (Milano, Italia: SugarCo, 1988).
52. Giuseppe Berta, "The Interregnum: Turin, Fiat and Industrial Conflict Between War and Fascism," Chris Wrigley, ed., *Challenges of Labour: Central and Western Europe, 1917–1920* (London: Routledge, 1993), 105–124.
53. Fraser Ottanelli, "'If Fascism Comes to America We Will Push It Back into the Ocean': Italian American Anti-Fascism in the 1920s and 1930s," in Luciano Tosi, ed., *Europe, Its Borders, and the Others* (Napoli: Edizioni scientifiche italiane, 2000), 361–381; J.P. Diggins, "The Italo-American Anti-Fascist Opposition," *The Journal of American History* (1967): 579–598; Letter from Capraro to Gennari, Roma," and "To and From Giovanitti," 9 April 1923, Anthony Capraro Papers, Box 3, Folder "Communist Party of Italy"; Domenico Fabiano, "I Fasci Italiani all'Estero," in B. Bezza ed., *Gli Italiani Fuori D'Italia*, 221–236; Vecoli, *The Making and Un-Making of the Italian American Working Class*, 51–56.
54. Auvo Kostiainen, "The Tragic Crisis: Finnish-American Workers and the Civil War in Finland," in Michael Karni, ed., *For the Common Good* (Superior, WI: Tyomies, 1977), 217–235; Kivisto, *Immigrant Socialists in the United States*, 158–162.

55. Kostiainen, "The Tragic Crisis."
56. Kostiainen, "The Tragic Crisis"; "Synopsis of the Case of Santeri Nuorteva," compiled by First Lieutenant Horgan, Reel 9, U.S. Military Intelligence Files; Karni, *The Forging of Finnish-American Communism*, 109, 162.
57. Karni, *The Forging of Finnish-American Communism*, 123–128; Weinstein, *The Decline of Socialism in America*, 254–255; John Earl Haynes and Harvey Klehr, *In Denial: Historians, Communism and Espionage* (San Francisco, CA: Encounter Books, 2005), 115–119, 132.
58. Wyman, *Round-Trip to America*, 113–118; Mackaman, "Life and Labor in Ely, Minnesota," 42.
59. "Injustice to Foreign Workmen," *Znanje*, 24 November 1919, Chicago Foreign Language Press Survey.
60. "They Are Going," *Magyar Tribune*, 16 January 1920, Chicago Foreign Language Press Survey; Frances Krljic, "Round Trip Croatia," in Dirk Hoerder, ed., *Labor Migration in the Atlantic Economies: The European and North American Working Classes During the Period of Industrialization* (Westport, CT: Greenwood, 1985), 418; Adam Walaszek, "Return Migration from the USA to Poland," in *The Politics of Return: International Return Migration in Europe Proceedings of the First European Conference on International Return Migration* (Rome: Centro studi emigrazione, 1984), 213–220; see also Juliana Puskás, "Some Results of My Research on the Transatlantic Emigration from Hungary on the Basis of Macro- and Micro-Analysis," in Julianna Puskás, ed., *Overseas Migration from East-Central and South Eastern Europe, 1880–1940* (Budapest: Akadémiai Kiadó, 1990), 43–58; Davis, *The Russians and Ruthenians in America*, 25; Puskás, *Ties That Bind*, 193; Joseph John Parot, "Review: [untitled]," *International Migration Review* 19, no. 1 (Spring 1985): 167–168.
61. Vesna Mikačić, "Overseas Migration of the Yugoslav Population in the Period Between the Two World Wars," in Puskás, *Overseas Migration from East-Central and South Eastern Europe, 1880–1940* (Budapest: Akadémiai Kiadó, 1990), 168–190; Ngai, *The Architecture of Race in American Immigration Law*.
62. Wyman, *Round-Trip to America*.
63. Maier, *Recasting Bourgeois Europe*, 3–18.

Epilogue

1. "Gompers Points out Seven Dominant Issues for Labor," *New York World*, 26 June 1924, Anthony Capraro Papers, B3, Folder "American Federation of Labor."
2. Kivisto, *Immigrant Socialists*, 168.
3. William M. Leiserson, *Adjusting Immigrant and Industry* (New York: Harper, 1924), 105, quoted in Montgomery, *Workers' Control*, 32.
4. Stephen Meyer, "Adapting the Immigrant to the Line: Americanization in the Ford Factory, 1914–1921," *Journal of Social History* 14, no. 1 (Autumn 1980): 67–82; Barrett, "Americanization from the Bottom Up," 996–997.
5. Antonio Gramsci, *Selections from the Prison Notebooks of Antonio Gramsci* (New York: International Publishers, 1971), 280–28; Edwards, *Contested Terrain*, 121.
6. Montgomery, *Workers' Control*, 44, 32–47.
7. Gordon, et al., *Segmented Work, Divided Workers*, 146–149; Edwards calls these "experiments," *Contested Terrain*, 20, 95–97, 100–104; Brody, *Workers in Industrial America*, 12–13; Barrett, *Work and Community in the Jungle*, 240–255; Montgomery, *Workers' Control*, 32–39.

Bibliography

Manuscript Collections

Batinich Oral History Collection, Immigration History Research Center, Minneapolis.
Anthony Capraro Papers, Immigration History Research Center, Minneapolis.
Council of National Defense, Records, National Archives and Records Administration.
Duncan McDonald Collection, Abraham Lincoln Library, Springfield Illinois.
Federal Mediation and Reconciliation Service, Papers, National Archives and Records Administration.
Iron Range Oral History Projects, Iron Range Research Center, Chisholm, Minnesota.
Italians in Chicago Project, University of Illinois Historical Survey, Urbana, Illinois.
National War Labor Board, Papers, University of Illinois Library, Urbana, Illinois.
Arvid Nelson Papers, Immigration History Research Center, Minneapolis.
Oliver Iron Mining Company Papers, Minnesota State Historical Society, St. Paul, Minnesota.
Records of the Committee on Public Information, National Archives and Records Administration.
Records of the U.S. Coal Commission, National Archives and Records Administration.
Sangamon State University Oral History Collection, Illinois Historical Survey, Urbana, Illinois.
David Saposs Papers, State Historical Society, Madison, Wisconsin.
James Steele Papers, Minnesota State Historical Society, St. Paul, Minnesota.
Strike Files of the United States Department of Justice, University of Illinois Library, Urbana, Illinois.
U.S. Commission on Industrial Relations (CIR), University of Illinois Library, Urbana, Illinois.
U.S. Military Intelligence Files, Surveillance of Radicals, University of Illinois Library, Urbana, Illinois.
University of Chicago Foreign Language Press Survey, Microfilm, University of Illinois Library, Urbana, Illinois.
John Wiita Papers, Immigration History Research Center, University of Minnesota, Minneapolis.

Government Publications

Department of the Interior, Census Office. *Report of the Population of the United States, Thirteenth Census.* Part I, 1910. Washington, D.C. Government Printing Office, 1912–1914.
Historical Statistics of the United States. Washington, D.C.: Government Printing Office, 1975.
U.S. Senate. *Reports of the Immigration Commission, Immigrants in Industries.* Washington, D.C.: Government Printing Office, 1911.

Newspapers and Periodicals

American Coal Journal
Chicago Tribune
Chisholm Herald Tribune

Divernon News, Divernon, Illinois
Eveleth News, Eveleth, Minnesota
Everybody's Magazine
Il Martello
The New Majority
New York Times
Il Proletario
Työmies

Books and Articles

Abbott, Edith. "Federal Immigration Policies, 1864–1924." *The University Journal of Business* 2, no. 2 (March 1924): 133–156.
Abbott, Grace. *The Immigrant and Coal Mining Communities of Illinois*. Springfield, IL: Illinois Immigration Commission, 1920.
Addams, Jane. *Twenty Years at Hull-House: With Autobiographical Notes*. Edited by Victoria Bissell Brown. Boston: Bedford/St. Martens, 1999.
Allen, Robert C. "International Competition in Iron and Steel, 1850–1913." *The Journal of Economic History* 39, no. 4 (December 1979): 911–937.
Amsden, Jon, and Stephen Brier. "Coal Miners on Strike: The Transformation of Strike Demands and the Formation of a National Union." *Journal of Interdisciplinary History* 7, no. 4 (Spring 1977): 583–616.
Angle, Paul M. *Bloody Williamson: A Chapter in American Lawlessness*. Urbana: University of Illinois Press, 1992.
Arrighi, Giovanni, and Beverly J. Silver. "Labor Movements and Capital Migration: The United States and Western Europe in World-Historical Perspective." In C. B Bergquist, ed., *Labor in the Capitalist World-Economy*: 183–216. Beverly Hills, CA: Sage.
Barkan, Elliott Robert, and Michael Robert Lemay, eds. *Immigration and Naturalization Laws and Issues: A Documentary History*. Westbrook, CT: Greenwood Press, 1999.
Barrett, James R. "Americanization from the Bottom Up: Immigration and the Remaking of the Working Class in the United States, 1880–1930." *The Journal of American History* 79, no. 3 (1992): 996–1020.
_____. *The Irish Way: Becoming American in the Multiethnic City*. New York: Penguin, 2012.
_____. *William Z. Foster and the Tragedy of American Radicalism*. Urbana: University of Illinois Press, 1999.
_____. "Women's Work, Family Economy, and Labor Militancy: The Case of Chicago's Immigrant Packinghouse Workers, 1900–1922." In *Labor Divided: Race and Ethnicity in United States Labor Struggles, 1835–1960*, eds. Robert Asher and Charles Stephenson. Albany: State University of New York, 1990.
_____. *Work and Community in the Jungle: Chicago's Packinghouse Workers, 1894–1922*. Urbana: University of Illinois Press, 1990.
Barrett, James R., and David Roediger. "Inbetween Peoples: Race, Nationality and the 'New Immigrant' Working Class." *Journal of American Ethnic History* 16, no. 3 (1997): 3–44.
_____. "The Irish and the 'Americanization' of the 'New Immigrants' in the Streets and in the Churches of the Urban United States, 1900–1930." *Journal of American Ethnic History* 24, no. 4 (2005): 4–33.
Beik, Mildred A. *The Miners of Windber: The Struggles of New Immigrants for Unionization, 1890s–1930s*. University Park: Pennsylvania State University Press, 1996.
Berend, T. Iván. *Decades of Crisis: Central and Eastern Europe Before World War II*. Berkeley: University of California Press, 1998.
Bernstein, Irving. *The Lean Years: A History of the American Worker, 1920–1933*. Baltimore: Penguin, 1966.
Betten, Neil. "The Origins of Ethnic Radicalism in Northern Minnesota, 1900–1920." *International Migration Review* 4, no. 2 (1970): 44–56.
Betten, Neil, and Raymond A. Mohl. *Steel City: Urban and Ethnic Patterns in Gary, Indiana, 1906–1950*. New York: Holmes and Meier, 1986.
Bezza, B., ed. *Gli Italiani Fuori D'Italia: Gli Emigrati Italian nei Movimenti Operai dei Paesi d'Adozione, 1880–1940*. Milan: Franco Angeli, 1983.
Blee, Kathleen. "Family Ties and Class Conflict: The Politics of Immigrant Communities in the Great Lakes Region, 1890–1920." *Social Problems* 31, no. 3 (1984): 311–321.

Bodnar, John. *Steelton: Immigration and Industrialization, 1870–1940*. Pittsburgh: University of Pittsburgh Press, 1990.
———. *The Transplanted: A History of Immigrants in Urban America*. Bloomington: Indiana University Press, 1987.
———. *Workers' World: Kinship, Community, and Protest in an Industrial Society, 1900–1940*. Baltimore: Johns Hopkins University Press, 1982.
Bonacich, Edna. "Advanced Capitalism and Black/White Race Relations in the United States: A Split Labor Market Interpretation." *American Sociological Review* 41, no. 1 (1976): 34–51.
Booth, Stephanie. "The Relationship Between Radicalism and Ethnicity in Southern Illinois Coal Fields, 1870–1940." Ph.D. diss., Illinois State University, 1983.
Bosworth, R.J.B. *Mussolini's Italy: Life Under the Dictatorship, 1915–1945*. New York: Penguin, 2006.
Bracey, John H., ed. *Black Workers and Organized Labor*. Belmont, CA: Wadsworth, 1971.
Brecher, Jeremy. *Strike!* Boston, MA: South End Press, 1997.
Breckinridge, S.P., and E. Abbott. "Chicago Housing Conditions, V: South Chicago at the Gates of the Steel Mills." *The American Journal of Sociology* 17, no. 2 (1911): 145–176.
Brissenden, Paul F. "Occupational Incidence of Labor Mobility." *Journal of the American Statistical Association* 18 (December 1923).
Brody, David. *In Labor's Cause: Main Themes on the History of the American Worker*. New York: Oxford University Press, 1993.
———. *Labor in Crisis: The Steel Strike of 1919*. Philadelphia: Lippincott, 1965.
———. *Steelworkers in America: The Nonunion Era*. New York: Russell, 1970.
———. *Workers in Industrial America: Essays on the Twentieth Century Struggle*. New York: Oxford University Press, 1993.
Brown, Cliff. "Racial Conflict and Split Labor Markets: The AFL Campaign to Organize Steel Workers, 1918–1919." *Social Science History* 22, no. 3, Special Issue: Migration and the Labor Markets (Autumn 1998): 319–347.
Brundage, William Fitzhugh. *Lynching in the New South: Georgia and Virginia, 1880–1930*. Urbana: University of Illinois Press, 1993.
Buhle, Paul. "Jews and American Communism: The Cultural Question," *Radical History Review* 23 (Spring): 9–33.
Buhle, Paul, and Dan Georgekas, eds. *The Immigrant Left in the United States*. Albany: State University of New York Press, 1996.
Bukowzyk, John J. "The Transformation of Working-Class Ethnicity: Corporate Control, Americanization, and the Polish Immigrant Middle Class in Bayonne, New Jersey, 1915–1925." In *Labor Divided: Race and Ethnicity in United States Labor Struggles, 1835–1960*, edited by Robert Asher and Charles Stephenson. New York: State University of New York Press, 1990.
Byington, Margaret F. "Homestead: The Households of a Mill Town." *The Pittsburgh Survey: Findings in Six Volumes*, ed. Paul Underwood Kellogg. New York: Charities Publication, 1910.
Cannon, James P. *The First Ten Years of American Communism: Report of a Participant*. New York: L. Stuart, 1962.
Chalmers, David Mark. *Hooded Americanism: The History of the Ku Klux Klan*. Chicago: Quadrangle Books, 1968.
Chandler, Alfred Dupont. *The Visible Hand: The Managerial Revolution in American Business*. Cambridge, MA: Belknap Press of Harvard University Press, 1977.
Chency, O.H. "America in the World Steel Markets." *Proceedings of the Academy of Political Science in the City of New York* 12, no. 4, America as a Creditor Nation (January 1928): 128–132.
Cleef, E.V. "The Finn in America." *Geographical Review* 6, no. 3 (1918): 185–214
Coben, Stanley. *Rebellion Against Victorianism: The Impetus for Cultural Change in 1920s America*. New York: Oxford University Press, 1991.
Cohen, Lizabeth. *Making a New Deal: Industrial Workers in Chicago, 1919–1939*. Cambridge: Cambridge University Press, 1990.
Collomp, Catherine. "Immigrants, Labor Markets, and the State, a Comparative Approach: France and the United States, 1880–1930." *The Journal of American History* 86, no. 1 (June 1999): 41–66.
Commission of Inquiry, Interchurch World Movement. *Public Opinion and the Steel Strike*. New York: Harcourt, Brace, and Company, 1921.
———. *Report on the Steel Strike of 1919*. New York: Harcourt, Brace, and Howe, 1920.

Commons, John R. "The Delivered Price Practice in the Steel Market." *The American Economic Review* 14, no. 3 (September 1924): 505–519.
Cooper, Patricia. *Once a Cigar Maker: Men, Women, and Work Culture in American Cigar Factories, 1900–1919.* Urbana: University of Illinois Press, 1987.
Corbin, David. *Life, Work, and Rebellion in the Coal Fields: The Southern West Virginia Miners, 1880–1922.* Urbana: University of Illinois Press, 1981.
Cronin, James E. "The Peculiar Pattern of British Strikes since 1888." *The Journal of British Studies* 18, no. 2 (Spring 1979): 118–141.
Cronon, William. *Nature's Metropolis: Chicago and the Great West.* New York: W.W. Norton, 1991.
Davis, Jerome. *The Russian Immigrant.* New York: Macmillan, 1922.
———. *The Russians and Ruthenians in America: Bolsheviks or Brothers.* New York: George H. Doran Company, 1922.
Dawley, Alan. *Changing the World: American Progressives in War and Revolution.* Princeton: Princeton University Press, 2003.
DeJohn, Dominick. "Italians in Illinois: A Memoir of an Ethnic Mining Community," *Italian Americana.* Vol. 7, no. 2 (1983).
Dickerson, Dennis C. *Out of This Crucible: Black Steelworkers in Western Pennsylvania, 1875–1980.* Albany: State University of New York Press, 1986.
Diggins, J.P. "The Italo-American Anti-Fascist Opposition." *The Journal of American History* (1967): 579–598.
Di Scala, Spencer. "'Red Week' 1914: Prelude to War and Revolution." In *Studies in Modern Italian History: From the Risorgimento to the Republic,* ed. Frank Coppa: 123–33. New York: Peter Lang, 1986.
Draper, Theodore. *Roots of American Communism.* New York: Viking Press, 1957.
Dubofsky, Melvyn. *We Shall Be All: A History of the Industrial Workers of the World.* Urbana: University of Illinois Press, 1988.
Edwards, Richard. *Contested Terrain: The Transformation of the Workplace in the Twentieth Century.* New York: Basic Books, 1979.
Edwards, Richard, David M. Gordon, and Michael Reich, eds. *Segmented Work, Divided Workers: The Historical Transformations of Labor in the United States.* New York: Cambridge University Press, 1982.
Emmons, David. *The Butte Irish: Class and Ethnicity in an American Mining Town, 1875–1925.* Urbana: University of Illinois Press, 1990.
Fishback, Price Van Meter. *Soft Coal, Hard Choices: The Economic Welfare of Bituminous Coal Miners, 1890–1930.* New York: Oxford University Press, 1992.
Fitch, J. "The Steel Workers." In *Pittsburgh Survey,* ed. Paul Kellogg. Pittsburgh: Russell Sage Foundation, 1910.
Foley, Barbara. *Spectres of 1919: Class and Nation in the Making of the New Negro.* Urbana: University of Illinois Press, 2003.
Foster, William Z. *The Great Steel Strike and Its Lessons.* New York: B.W. Huebsch, 1920.
Fraser, Steven. *Labor Will Rule: Sidney Hillman and the Rise of American Labor.* New York: Free Press, 1991.
Gabaccia, Donna. *Italy's Many Diasporas.* Seattle: University of Washington Press, 2000.
———. *Militants and Migrants: Rural Sicilians Become American Workers.* New Brunswick: Rutgers University Press, 1988.
Gabaccia, Donna, and Franca Iacovetta, eds. *Women, Gender and Transnational Lives: Italian Workers of the World.* Toronto: University of Toronto Press, 2002.
Gabaccia, Donna, and Fraser Ottanelli, eds. *Italian Workers of the World: Labor Migration and the Formation of Multiethnic States.* Urbana: University of Illinois Press, 2001.
Garrett, Paul Willard. "American Control Over War Prices." *Annals of the American Academy of Political and Social Science* 89: Prices (May 1920): 22–43.
Gerson, Louis. *Woodrow Wilson and the Rebirth of Poland, 1914–1920: A Study in the Influence on American Policy of Minority Groups of Foreign Origin.* New Haven: Yale University Press, 1953.
Gerstle, Gary. *Working Class Americanism: The Politics of Labor in a Textile City, 1914–1960.* Cambridge: Cambridge University Press, 1989.
Gerstle, Gary, and John Mollenkopf. *E Pluribus Unum? Contemporary and Historical Perspectives on Immigrant Political Incorporation.* New York: Russell Sage Foundation, 2001.
Gilette, J.M. "The Culture Agencies of a Typical Manufacturing Group: South Chicago." *The American Journal of Sociology* 7, no. 1 (July 1901).

Glenn, Anita. *Daughters of the Shtetl: Life and Labor in the Immigrant Generation*. Ithaca: Cornell University Press, 1990.
Goldberg, Robert Alan. *Hooded Empire: The Ku Klux Klan in Colorado*. Urbana: University of Illinois Press, 1981.
Goodrich, Carter. *The Miner's Freedom*. New York: Arno Press, 1977.
Grant, Madison, *The Passing of the Great Race: Or, the Racial Basis of European History*. New York: Scribner's Sons, 1916.
Graziosi, Andrea. "Common Laborers, Unskilled Workers: 1880–1915." *Labor History* 22, no. 4 (1981): 512–544.
Greene, Victor R. *American Immigrant Leaders, 1800–1910: Marginality and Identity*. Baltimore, MD: Johns Hopkins University Press, 1987.
_____. *The Slavic Community on Strike: Immigrant Labor in Pennsylvania Anthracite*. Notre Dame: University of Notre Dame Press, 1968.
Greenwald, Maurine Weiner. "Women and Class in Pittsburgh, 1850–1920." In *City at the Point: Essays on the Social History of Pittsburgh*, ed. Samuel P. Hays, ed. Pittsburgh: University of Pittsburgh Press, 1989.
Grossman, James R. *Land of Hope: Chicago, Black Southerners, and the Great Migration*. Chicago: University of Chicago Press, 1989.
Guglielmo, Jennifer. "Negotiating Gender, Race, and the Coalition: Italian Women and Working-Class Politics in New York City, 1880–1945." Ph.D. diss., University of Minnesota, 2003.
Guglielmo, Jennifer, and Salvatore Salerno, eds. *Are Italians White? How Race Is Made in America*. New York: Routledge, 2003.
Guglielmo, Thomas A. *White on Arrival: Italians, Race, Color, and Power in Chicago, 1890–1945*. Oxford: Oxford University Press, 2003.
Gulick, Charles Adams. *Labor Policy of the United States Steel Corporation*. New York: Columbia University, 1924.
Gutman, Herbert. "The Negro and the United Mine Workers of America: The Career and Letters of Richard L. Davis and Something of Their Meaning, 1890–1900." In *The Negro and the American Labor Movement*, ed. Julius Jacobson. New York: Doubleday, 1968.
Gutman, Herbert G. *Work, Culture, and Society in Industrializing America: Essays in American Working-Class and Social History*. New York: Vintage Books, 1977.
Haimson, Leopold. "The Problem of Social Stability in Urban Russia, 1905–1917 (Part One)." *Slavic Review* 23, no. 4 (December 1964): 619–642.
Handlin, Oscar. *The Uprooted*. Boston: Little, Brown, 1973.
Hapgood, Hutchins. *The Spirit of the Ghetto*, edited by James R. Barrett. Cambridge: Belknap Press, 1967.
Harris, Richard. "Chicago's Other Suburbs." *The Geographical Review* 84, no. 4 (1994).
Hibbs, Douglas A. "On the Political Economy of Long-Run Trends in Strike Activity." *British Journal of Political Science* 8, no. 2 (April 1978): 153–175.
Hicken, Victor. "Mine Union Radicalism in Macoupin and Montgomery Counties." *Western Illinois Regional Studies* 3, no. 2 (1980): 173–191.
Higbie, Frank Tobias. *Indispensable Outcasts: Hobo Workers and Community in the American Midwest, 1880–1930*. Urbana: University of Illinois Press, 2003.
Higham, John. *Strangers in the Land: Patterns of American Nativism, 1860–1925*. New Brunswick, NJ: Rutgers University Press, 1988.
Hing, Bill Ong. "Beyond the Rhetoric of Assimilation and Cultural Pluralism: Addressing the Tension of Separatism and Conflict in an Immigration-Driven Multiracial Society." *California Law Review* 81, no. 4 (July 1993): 863–925.
Hoerder, Dirk. *American Labor and Immigration History, 1877–1920s: Recent European Research*. Urbana: University of Illinois Press, 1983.
_____. *Cultures in Contact: World Migrations in the Second Millennium. Comparative and International Working-Class History*. Durham: Duke University Press, 2002.
_____. *The Immigrant Labor Press in North America, 1840s–1970s: An Annotated Bibliography*. New York: Greenwood Press, 1987.
_____, ed. *Labor Migration in the Atlantic Economies: The European and North American Working Classes During the Period of Industrialization*. Westport, CT: Greenwood Press, 1985.
_____, ed. *Struggle a Hard Battle: Essays on Working Class Immigrants*. DeKalb, IL: Northern Illinois University Press, 1986.
Hoerder, Dirk, and Christiane Harzig, eds. *The Press of Labor Migrants in Europe and North America, 1880s to 1930s*. Bremen: Universität Bremen, 1985.

Hoerder, Dirk, and Diethelm Knauf, eds. *Fame, Fortune and Sweet Liberty: The Great European Emigration.* Bremen: Edition Temmen, 1992.
Hoerder, Dirk, and Leslie Page Moch. *European Migrants: Global and Local Perspectives.* Boston: Northeastern University Press, 1996.
Hoerder Dirk, and Horst Rössler. *Distant Magnets: Expectations and Realities in the Immigrant Experience, 1840–1930.* New York: Holmes and Meier, 1993.
Holmquist, June Drenning, ed. *They Chose Minnesota: A Survey of the State's Ethnic Groups.* St. Paul: Minnesota Historical Society Press, 1981.
Hourwich, Isaac. *Immigration and Labor.* New York: G.P. Putnam's Sons, 1912.
Howe, Irving. *World of Our Fathers.* New York: Harcourt Brace Jovanovich, 1976.
Jackson, Kenneth T. *The Ku Klux Klan in the City, 1915–1930* New York: Oxford University Press, 1967.
Jenkins, William D. *Steel Valley Klan: The Ku Klux Klan in Ohio's Mahoning Valley.* Kent, OH: Kent State University Press, 1990.
Jensen, Joan M. *The Price of Vigilance.* Chicago: Rand McNally, 1969.
Johnson, James P. *The Politics of Soft Coal: The Bituminous Industry from World War I Through the New Deal.* Urbana: University of Illinois Press, 1979.
Karni, Michael G., Matti E. Kaups, and Douglas J. Ollila, eds. *The Finnish Experience in the Western Great Lakes Region: New Perspectives.* Turku, Finland: Institute for Migration, 1975.
Karni, Michael G., Olavi Koivukangas, and Edward W. Laine, eds. *Finns in North America: Proceedings of Finn Forum III.* Turku, Finland: Institute of Migration, 1988.
Karni, Michael G., and Douglas J. Ollila, eds. *For the Common Good: Finnish Immigrants and the Radical Response to Industrial America.* Superior, WI: Työmies Society, 1977.
Keiser, John Howard. "John Fitzpatrick and Progressive Unionism, 1915–1925." Ph.D. diss., Northwestern University, 1965.
Kessler-Harris, Alice. *Out to Work: A History of Wage-Earning Women in the United States.* New York: Oxford University Press, 1982.
Kivisto, Peter. *Immigrant Socialists in the United States: The Case of Finns and the Left.* Rutherford, NJ: Associated University Press, 1984.
Kleinberg, S.J. *The Shadow of the Mills: Working-class Families in Pittsburgh, 1870–1907.* Pittsburgh: University of Pittsburgh Press, 1989.
Koenker, Diane, and William G. Rosenberg. *Strikes and Revolution in Russia, 1917.* Princeton, NJ: Princeton University Press, 1989.
Kohlemainen, John I. *A History of the Finns in Ohio, Western Pennsylvania, and West Virginia: From Lake Erie's Shores to the Mahoning and Monongahela Valleys.* New York Mills, MN: Parta Printers, 1977.
Kolko, Gabriel. *Main Currents in Modern American History.* New York: Pantheon Books, 1984.
Krohe, James. *Midnight at Noon: A History of Coal Mining in Sangamon County.* Springfield, IL: Sangamon County Historical Society, 1975.
Kučas, Antanas. *Lithuanians in America.* Translated by Joseph Boley. Boston: Encyclopedia Lituanica, 1975.
Kulczycki, John J. *The Polish Coal Miner's Union and the German Labor Movement in the Ruhr, 1902–1934: National and Social Solidarity.* Oxford: Berg, 1997.
Landis, Paul Henry. *Three Iron Mining Towns: A Study in Cultural Change.* Ann Arbor, MI: Edwards Brothers, 1938.
Laslett, John H.M. *Colliers Across the Sea: A Comparative Study of Class Formation in Scotland and the American Midwest, 1830–1924.* Urbana: University of Illinois Press, 2000.
———. "Swan Song or New Social Movement? Socialism and District 12, United Mine Workers of America, 1919–1926." In *Socialism in the Heartland: The Midwestern Experience,* ed. Donald T. Critchlow. South Bend, IN: University of Notre Dame Press, 1986.
———, ed. *The United Mine Workers of America: A Model of Industrial Solidarity?* University Park: Pennsylvania State University Press, 1996.
La Sorte, Michael. *La Merica: Images of the Italian Greenhorn Experience.* Philadelphia: Temple University Press, 1985.
Lauck, W. Jett. *Conditions of Labor in American Industries: A Summarization of the Results of Recent Investigations.* New York: Funk and Wagnalls, 1917.
Lay, Shawn. *Hooded Knights on the Niagara: The Ku Klux Klan in Buffalo, New York.* New York: New York University Press, 1995.
LeMay, Michael Robert, and Elliott Robert Barkan, eds. *Immigration and Naturalization Laws and Issues: A Documentary History.* Westport, CT: Greenwood Press, 1999.

Lenin, Vladimir Illiich. *Imperialism, the Highest Stage of Capitalism: A Popular Outline*. Moscow: Progress Publishers, 1975.
Lewin, Moshe. *Lenin's Last Struggle*. New York: Monthly Review Press, 1978.
Liebman, Arthur. *The Jews and the Left*. New York: John Wiley, 1979.
Lubotina, Paul A. "Conflict and Community Building: The Dichotomy of Immigrant Life on Minnesota's Mesabi Iron Range, 1893–1930." Ph.D. diss., Saint Louis University, 2006.
Makalani, Minkah. "For the Liberation of Black People Everywhere: The African Blood Brotherhood, Black Radicalism, and Pan-African Liberation in the New Negro Movement, 1917–1936." Ph.D. diss., University of Illinois at Urbana–Champaign, 2004.
Marks, Carol. *Farewell—We're Good and Gone: The Great Black Migration*. Bloomington: Indiana University Press, 1989.
Marks, Gary, and Matthew Burbank. "Immigrant Support for the American Socialist Party, 1912 and 1920." *Social Science History* 14, no. 2 (Summer 1990): 175–202.
Mayer, Arno. *Politics and Diplomacy of Peacemaking Containment and Counterrevolution at Versailles, 1918–1919*. New York: Knopf, 1967.
McCallum, E.D. *The Iron and Steel Industry in the United States*. London: P.S. King and Son, 1931.
McCartin, Joseph. *Labor's Great War: The Struggle for Industrial Democracy and the Origins of Modern American Labor Relations, 1912–1921*. Chapel Hill: University of North Carolina Press, 1997.
McCormick, Thomas J. *America's Half-Century: United States Foreign Policy in the Cold War*. Baltimore: Johns Hopkins University Press, 1989.
McCreesh, Carolyn Daniel. *Women in the Campaign to Organize Garment Workers, 1880–1917*. New York: Garland, 1985.
McGouldrick, Paul F, and Michael B. Tannen. "Did American Manufacturers Discriminate Against Immigrants Before 1914?" *The Journal of Economic History* 37, no. 3 (September 1977): 723–746.
McKillen, Elizabeth. *Chicago Labor and the Quest for a Democratic Diplomacy, 1914–1924*. Ithaca, NY: Cornell University Press, 1995.
Merithew, Caroline (née Waldron). "The Great Spirit of Solidarity: The Illinois Valley Mining Communities and the Formation of Interethnic Consciousness, 1889–1917." Ph.D. diss., University of Illinois, Urbana-Champaign, 2000.
Miller, George J. "Some Geographic Influences of the Lake Superior Iron Ores." *Bulletin of the American Geographical Society* 46, no. 12 (1914): 881–916.
Miller, Sally M. *The Radical Immigrant*. New York: Twayne Publishers, 1974.
Miller, Sally M. *Victor Berger and the Promise of Constructive Socialism*. Westport, CT: Greenwood, 1973.
Mink, Gwendolyn. *Old Labor and New Immigrants in American Political Development: Union, Party, and State, 1875–1920*. Ithaca, NY: Cornell University Press, 1986.
Mohl, Raymond A., and Neil Betten. "Ethnic Adjustment in the Industrial City: The International Institute of Gary, 1919–1940." *International Migration Review* 6, no. 4 (Winter 1972): 361–376.
Montgomery, David. *The Fall of the House of Labor: The Workplace, the State, and American Labor Activism, 1865–1925*. Cambridge: Cambridge University Press, 1987.
_____. "Immigrants, Industrial Unions, and Social Reconstruction in the United States, 1916–1923." *Labour/Le Travail* 13 (1984): 101–13.
_____. "Nationalism, American Patriotism, and Class Consciousness among Immigrants Workers in the United States in the Epoch of World War I." In *Struggle a Hard Battle*, ed. Dirk Hoerden: 327–51. DeKalb, IL: Northern Illinois University Press, 1986.
_____. "New Tendencies in Union Struggles and Strategies in Europe and the United States, 1916–1922." In *Work, Community, and Power: The Experience of Labor in Europe and America, 1900–1925*. Philadelphia: Temple University Press, 1983.
_____. "The 'New Unionism' and the Transformation of Workers' Consciousness in America, 1909–1922." *Journal of Social History* 7 (1974): 509–29.
_____. *Workers' Control in America: Studies in the History of Work, Technology, and Labor Struggles*. Cambridge: Cambridge University Press, 1979.
Moore, Leonard Joseph. *Citizen Klansmen: The Ku Klux Klan in Indiana, 1921–1928*. Chapel Hill: University of North Carolina Press, 1991.
_____. "Review: Historical Interpretations of the 1920's Klan: The Traditional View and the Populist Revision." *Journal of Social History* 24, no. 2 (Winter 1990): 341–357.

Mullin, Joseph C., and Wallace P. Mullin. "United States Steel's Acquisition of the Great Northern Ore Properties: Vertical Foreclosure or Efficient Contractual Governance?" *Journal of Law, Economics, & Organization* 13, no. 1 (April 1997): 74–100.

Murray, Robert K. "Communism and the Great Steel Strike of 1919." *The Mississippi Valley Historical Review* 38, no. 3 (December 1951): 445–466.

———. *Red Scare: A Study in National Hysteria, 1919–1920*. Minneapolis: University of Minnesota Press, 1955.

Mussey, Henry Raymond. *Combination in the Mining Industry: A Study of Concentration in Lake Superior Iron Ore Production*. New York: Columbia University Press, 1905.

Nash, Michael. *Conflict and Accommodation: Coal Miners, Steel Workers, and Socialism, 1890–1920*. Westport, CT: Greenwood, 1982.

Ngai, Mae M. "The Architecture of Race in American Immigration Law: A Reexamination of the Immigration Act of 1924." *The Journal of American History* 86, no. 1 (June 1999): 67–92.

———. *Impossible Subjects: Illegal Aliens and the Making of Modern America*. Princeton: Princeton University Press, 2004.

Nuwer, Michael. "From Batch to Flow: Production Technology and Work-Force Skills in the Steel Industry, 1880–1920." *Technology and Culture* 29, no. 4, Special Issue: Labor History and the History of Technology (October 1988): 808–838.

Oblinger, Carl D. *Divided Kingdom: Work, Community, and the Mining Wars in the Central Illinois Coal Fields During the Great Depression*. Springfield: Illinois State Historical Society, 1991.

Ottanelli, Fraser. "All in the Family." *Reviews in American History* 22, no. 3 (1994): 468–473.

———. "'If Fascism Comes to America We Will Push It Back into the Ocean': Italian American Anti-Fascism in the 1920s and 1930s." In *Europe, Its Borders, and the Others*, ed. Luciano Tosi: 361–381. Napoli: Edizioni scientifiche italiane, 2000.

Pacyga, Dominic. *Polish Immigrants and Industrial Chicago: Workers on the South Side, 1880–1922*. Columbus: Ohio State University Press, 1991.

Palmer, Bryan D. *James P. Cannon and the Origins of the American Revolutionary Left, 1890–1928*. Urbana: University of Illinois Press, 2007.

Palmer, Frank L. *Spies in Steel: An Expose of Industrial War*. Denver, CO: Labor Press, 1928.

Peck, Gunther. *Reinventing Free Labor: Padrones and Immigrant Workers in the North American West, 1880–1930*. Cambridge: Cambridge University Press, 2000.

Pencak, William. *For God and Country: The American Legion, 1919–1941*. Boston: Northeastern University Press, 1989.

Pennar, Jaan. *The Estonians in America, 1627–1975: A Chronology and Fact Book*. Dobbs Ferry, NY: Oceana Publications, 1975.

Philpott, Thomas Lee. *The Slum and the Ghetto: Immigrants, Blacks, and Reformers in Chicago, 1880–1930*. Belmont, CA: Wadsworth, 1991.

Pogue, Joseph E. "Mineral Resources in War and Their Bearing on Preparedness." *The Scientific Monthly* 5, no. 2 (August 1917): 120–134.

Powaski, Ronald, E. *Toward an Entangling Alliance: American Isolationism, Internationalism, and Europe, 1901–1950*. Westport, CT: Greenwood Press, 1991.

Preston, William. *Aliens and Dissenters: Federal Suppression of Radicals, 1903–1933*. Urbana: University of Illinois Press, 1994.

Puskás, Julianna. *From Hungary to the United States (1880–1914)*. Budapest: Akadémiai Kiadó, 1982.

———. *Overseas Migration from East-Central and South Eastern Europe, 1880–1940*. Budapest: Akadémiai Kiadó, 1990.

———. *Ties That Bind, Ties That Divide: 100 Years of Hungarian Experience in the United States*. Ellis Island Series. New York: Holmes & Meier, 2000.

Ramirez, Bruno. *When Workers Fight: The Politics of Industrial Relations in the Progressive Era, 1898–1916*. Westport, CT: Greenwood Press, 1978.

Richards, David A.J. *Italian American: The Racializing of an Ethnic Identity*. New York: New York University Press, 1999.

Rischin, Moses. *The Promised City: New York's Jews, 1870–1914*. Cambridge: Harvard University Press, 1962.

Roediger, David R. *Working Toward Whiteness: How America's Immigrants Became White: The Strange Journey from Ellis Island to the Suburbs*. New York: Basic Books, 2005.

Rosales, F.A., and D.T. Simon. "Chicano Steel Workers and Unionism in the Midwest, 1919–1945." *Aztlán: A Journal of Chicano Studies* 6, no. 2 (1975): 266–275.

Rosenblum, Gerald. *Immigrant Workers: Their Impact on American Labor Radicalism.* New York: Basic Books, 1973.
Ross, Carl. *The Finn Factor in American Labor, Culture, and Society.* New York Mills, MN: Parta Printers, 1977.
Ross, E.A. *The Old World in the New: The Significance of Past and Present Immigration to the American People.* New York: The Century Company, 1914.
Rothbart, Ron. "'Homes Are What Any Strike Is About': Immigrant Labor and the Family Wage." *Journal of Social History* 23, no. 2 (1989): 267–284.
Salvatore, Nick. *Eugene V. Debs, Citizen and Socialist.* Urbana: University of Illinois Press, 1982.
Scalzone, Oreste. *Biennio Rosso, '68-'69: Figure E Passaggi Di Una Stagione Rivoluzionaria.* Milan: SugarCo, 1988.
Schroeder, Gertrude. *The Growth of Major Steel Companies, 1900–1950.* Baltimore: Johns Hopkins University Press, 1952.
Schwieder, Dorothy. *Black Diamonds: Life and Work in Iowa's Coal Mining Communities, 1895–1925.* Ames: Iowa State University Press, 1983.
Shields, Martha Ellen. "Collective Choice of Working Conditions: Hours in British and U.S. Iron and Steel, 1890–1923." *Journal of Economic History* 50, no. 2 (1990): 379–392.
Sirjamaki, John. "Development of Mesabi Communities." Ph.D. diss., Yale, 1940.
Slichter, Sumner H. "The Scope and Nature of the Labor Turnover Problem." *Quarterly Journal of Economics* 34 (February 1920): 329–345.
_____. *The Turnover of Factory Labor.* New York: D. Appleton, 1919.
Smith, Timothy L. "Religious Denominations as Ethnic Communities: A Regional Case Study." *Church History* 35, no. 2 (1966): 207–226.
Sofchalk, D.G. "Organized Labor and the Iron Ore Miners of Northern Minnesota, 1907–1936." *Labor History* 12, no. 2 (1971): 214–242.
Spriano, Paolo. *The Occupation of the Factories: Italy 1920.* London: Pluto Press, 1975.
Sugar, Peter F., ed. *Native Fascism in the Successor States, 1918–1945.* Santa Barbara, CA: ABC-Clio, 1971.
Tentler, Leslie Woodcock. *Wage-Earning Women: Industrial Work and Family Life in the United States, 1900–1930.* Oxford: Oxford University Press, 1979.
Topp, Michael Miller. *Those Without a Country: The Political Culture of Italian American Syndicalists.* Minneapolis: University of Minnesota Press, 2001.
Trotter, Joe William. *Coal, Class, and Color: Blacks in Southern West Virginia, 1915–32.* Urbana: University of Illinois Press, 1990.
Tuttle, William M. *Race Riot: Chicago in the Red Summer of 1919.* New York: Atheneum, 1970.
Vazsonyi, Andrew "The Cicisbeo and the Magnificent Cuckold Boardinghouse Life and Lore in Immigrant Communities." *The Journal of American Folklore* 91, no. 360 (June 1978): 641–656.
Vecoli, Rudolph. "Anthony Capraro and the Lawrence Strike of 1919." In *In Labor Divided: Race and Ethnicity in United States Labor Struggles, 1835–1960,* eds. Robert Asher and Charles Stephenson. New York: State University of New York Press, 1990.
_____. "Contadini in Chicago: A Critique of 'The Uprooted.'" *The Journal of American History* 51, no. 3 (1964): 404–417.
_____. "The Making and Un-Making of the Italian American Working Class." In *The Lost World of Italian-American Radicalism,* eds. Philip Cannistraro and Gerald Meyer. Westport, CT: Praeger, 2003.
Vorse, Mary Heaton. *Men and Steel.* New York: Boni and Liveright, 1920.
Walaszek, Adam. "Return Migration from the USA to Poland." In *The Politics of Return: International Return Migration in Europe Proceedings of the First European Conference on International Return Migration:* 213–220. Rome: Centro studi emigrazione, 1984.
_____. "Was the Polish Worker Asleep? Immigrants, Unions, and Workers' Control in America, 1900–1922." *Polish American Studies* 78 (Spring 1989).
Waldinger, Roger. "Another Look at the International Ladies' Garment Workers' Union: Women, Industry Structure and Collective Action." In *Women, Work, and Protest: A Century of U.S. Women's Labor History,* ed. Ruth Milkman. Boston: Routledge and Kegan Paul, 1985.
Wallerstein, Immanuel Maurice. *World-Systems Analysis: An Introduction.* Durham: Duke University Press, 2004.
Weinberg, Carl R. *Labor, Loyalty, and Rebellion: Southwestern Illinois Coal Miners and World War I.* Carbondale: Southern Illinois University Press, 2005.

———. "The Tug of War: Labor, Loyalty and Rebellion in the Southwestern Illinois Coalfields, 1914–1920." Ph.D. diss., Yale, 1995.
Weinstein, James. *The Decline of Socialism in America, 1912–1925*. New York: Vintage Books, 1969.
Whatley, W.C. "African-American Strikebreaking from the Civil War to the New Deal." *Social Science History* 17, no. 4 (1993): 525–558.
Williams, Lee E., and Lee E. Williams II. *Anatomy of Four Race Riots: Racial Conflict in Knoxville, Elaine (Arkansas), Tulsa, and Chicago, 1919–1921*. Jackson, MS: University and College Press of Mississippi, 1972.
Wolff, Robert Lee. *The Balkans in Our Time*. New York: W.W. Norton, 1967.
Wyman, Mark. *Round-Trip to America: The Immigrants Return to Europe, 1880–1930*. Ithaca: Cornell University Press, 1993.
Yamawaki, Hideki. "Dominant Firm Pricing and Fringe Expansion: The Case of the U.S. Iron and Steel Industry, 1907–1930." *The Review of Economics and Statistics* 67, no. 3 (August 1985): 429–437.
Zolberg, Aristide. *A Nation by Design: Immigration Policy in the Fashioning of America*. Cambridge: Harvard University Press, 2006.

Index

Abbott, Edith, and Sophia Sophonisba Breckinridge 37, 40, 43
African Americans 28, 29, 30, 32, 45, 73, 78, 96, 110, 156, 158, 171; coal industry and 30–32; Great Black Migration and 20, 78, 87; Great Steel Strike and 21, 120–126
Alien and Sedition Acts 98
Amalgamated Association of Iron and Steel Workers, "The Amalgamated" 57
American Alliance for Labor and Democracy, A.A.L.D. 99
American Federation of Labor, A.F.L. 9, 11, 21, 52–53, 57, 60, 62, 69, 82, 84, 88–89, 98–102, 109, 115–123, 126–128, 131–138, 141, 146, 151, 155, 159, 169
American Protective League, A.P.L. 9, 98, 107, 109, 159
American Srbobran 135
Americanization 9, 10, 13, 21, 31, 54, 86, 88, 96, 97, 119, 135, 165
"Anglo-Saxon" 155
Appeal to Reason 133
Austria-Hungary 70–71
"Austrian" 29, 51, 69, 71, 77, 107, 112, n. 177

Barrett, James R. 10, 88, 124
Belgian coal miners 19
Belleville, Illinois 130
Benld, Illinois 44
Berger, Victor 62, 68, 69, 101, 105, 110, 137
Black Belt, Chicago 30
Boarding houses 46–48
Bodnar, John 35
British Americans 31, 32, 35, 52, 109, 123
Brody, David 35
Bukharin, Nikolai 66, 104, 166
Bulgarian immigrants 46, 70, 117, 139, 166
Bulletin of the Italian American Union 159

The Call 133
Camera del lavoro, New York City 140
Cannon, James P. 121
Capraro, Anthony 66, 149, 162
Casa del popolo, Chicago 140

Cedar Point, Illinois 85
Central Competitive Field, C.C.F. 19, 41, 53–58, 73, 84, 92, 116, 129, 143–153
Chicago, Illinois 7, 10, 45, 78; and Great Steel Strike 119, 121, 133, 170; and immigrant workers 23, 30, 52, 79, 90, 116; and Ku Klux Klan 158; and radicals 65, 66, 68, 72, 74, 97, 100, 101, 103, 104, 107, 135, 137, 139, 140, 157, 160; and steel industry 13–16
Chicago Commission on Race Relations 122
Chicago Daily Tribune 97
Chicago Defender 78
Chicago Federation of Labor, C.F.L. 118, 131–132, 138
Chicago Heights, Illinois 29, 158
Chicago I.W.W. Trial 103, 107
Chicago Steamshovel Men's Union, C.S.M.U. 151
Chisholm, Minnesota 28, 73, 74, 82, 142
Cohen, Elizabeth 10–11, 144
Collinsville, Illinois 109
Committee for Industrial Organization, C.I.O. 143
Committee on Coal Production 93–94
Committee on Industrial Relations, C.I.R. 51, 55, 79, 85
Committee on Public Information, C.P.I. 97–98
Commons, John R. 51
Communist movement 138–141
Cook County Socialist Party (Chicago), C.C.S.P. 137
Cornish iron miners 19, 28, 34, 52, 62
Corpi, John 133
Corporate welfare 35, 39–40, 143, 171–173
Council of National Defense, C.N.D. 90–93, 101, 106
"Cousin Jack" 52
Craft Unions 11, 12, 20, 41, 53, 57–58, 86, 99, 118, 123, 181
Creel, George 98, 99, 107
Croatian immigrants 20, 29, 38, 39, 47, 48, 50, 65, 69, 70, 105, 157, 165

209

Cuyuna Iron Range 14
Czech immigrants 27, 29, 45, 70, 139
Czechoslovakia 160–161

Davis, Jerome 104
Debs, Eugene 62–63, 68, 72–73, 139
De Leon, Daniel 65, 68
Dillingham Commission, United States Immigration Commission 27–28, 31, 33–39, 46–51, 54, 56
Duluth, Minnesota 13, 14, 17, 83, 101, 102, 106, 138, 156, 158
"Dumbla Affair" 70

East Chicago, Indiana 29, 30, 47, 80
Edwards, Richard 96, 173
Edwards, Thyra J. 122
Ely, Minnesota 28, 41, 116
English Americans 29, 31, 33, 39, 40, 47, 48, 50, 41, 54, 55, 62, 67, 102
English language: barriers and immigrant acquisition 47, 51, 55–56, 67, 84–85, 98, 117, 124–126, 133, 135
Espionage Act 107, 109
Estonia 160
Estonian immigrant radicals 64
Ethnicity 10, 12, 20, 31, 70; see also Race
Ettor, Joseph 66
Evans, Edward J. 133
Eveleth, Minnesota 28, 69, 83, 157

Farrington, Frank 56, 68, 111, 129, 149–150
Fascism 22, 161–162
Federal Bureau of Investigation, F.B.I. 121
Federal Mediation and Reconciliation Service, F.M.R.S. 118
Federal Trade Commission, F.T.C. 94
Federazione Socialista Italiana (Italian Socialist Federation), F.S.I. 66, 68, 71, 84
Finland 28, 49, 103, 144, 161–164
Finnish immigrants 19, 27, 33, 39, 47, 50, 63–64, 67, 72–74, 79, 82, 84, 98, 101–103, 104, 106–108, 117, 134, 137, 139–140, 142, 156, 158, 163–167, 170
Finnish Seamen's Union 167
Finnish Socialist Federation, F.S.F. 63, 67, 72–73, 83, 84, 102–103, 140, 164
Fitch, John 35, 37
Fitzpatrick, John 117, 138
Flynn, Elizabeth Gurley 83
Ford Motor Company 172–173
Fordism 22, 90, 91, 141, 169–174
Foster, William Z. 119, 210, 224–128, 131
Fuel Administration 91–92, 111

Gabaccia, Donna 46
Garment industry 34, 45, 53, 54, 58, 59, 79, 116, 141
Gary, Indiana 52, 158
Germans 26, 27, 29, 31, 40, 46, 52, 61, 64, 70, 96, 109, 123, 151

Germany 71–72, 75–76, 80, 104, 129, 145, 160–164
Germer, Adolph 68–69, 73, 101, 110
Gerstle, Gary 88
Giovanitti, Arturo 66
Gompers, Samuel 9, 99, 115, 117–119, 127–128, 134, 136, 159, 169
Goodrich, Carter 34, 53
Gottlieb, Amy 34
Grahavoc 135
Gramsci, Antonio 172
Graziosi, Andrea 36
Great Britain 75
Great Depression 173
Great Lakes Region 1, 7, 13–18, 63, 76

Hammond, Indiana 118, 133
Harding, Warren G.: administration of 119, 152–153
Haywood, William "Big Bill" 61, 139
Herrin, Illinois 151, 159
Hibbing, Minnesota 28, 82, 142
Hillquit, Morris 62, 101, 105, 137
Hoover, Herbert 152–153
Hungarian immigrants 10, 19, 21, 27, 28, 29, 38, 47, 61, 68, 69, 70, 98, 135, 137, 165, 167, 171
Hungary, Austria-Hungary or Hapsburg Empire 70–71, 104, 161
"Hunky" 12, 25, 32–33, 49, 52, 117, 120, 124, 125, 170

Indiana: and coal industry 15–16, 19, 30–31, 54, 139, 148–150, 152; and steel industry 15–16, 28–29
Indianapolis, Indiana 139
Industrial Workers of the World, I.W.W. 8, 58, 61–62, 88–9, 100, 143, 164, 166, 167, 170; and coal mining 85, 108; and Great Steel Strike 131–139; Mesabi Range Strike 20, 82–86, 106; and Red Scare 88–89, 98, 106–107, 139, 142; and rift with Socialist Party 61–62; 66–68; 79, 81, 84; and Russian Revolution 102–103, 106, 140–141, 164; and Vermillion Range Strike 116–117
Irish immigrants and Irish Americans 26, 29, 31, 33, 39, 46, 50, 52, 54, 62, 96, 109, 122, 123, 126, 158
Italian immigrants 19, 29, 31, 33, 39, 40–41, 44–48, 50–55, 61, 66–70, 79, 82, 97, 101, 111, 117, 133, 150, 157, 162, 171
Italian Macaroni Manufacturers' Association 135
Italy 22, 66, 71, 80, 140, 144, 150, 160–163

Jewish immigrants 24, 31, 45, 64, 79, 97, 104, 138, 140, 158, 171
"Johnny Bull" 52
Johnson-Reed Act, National Origins Act of 1924 1, 7, 9, 13, 144, 154–155, 166–167

Kellor, Francis 97
Kentucky 12, 16, 19, 30, 151–153
Kollontai, Alexandra 166
Ku Klux Klan 9, 21, 154–159, 169
Kulczycki, John J. 10

Labor Party (U.S.) 138
Labor turnover 10, 90–96, 113, 170
Lake County, Indiana 29–30, 158
Lake Superior iron and steel region 13–18, 35, 63, 74, 140, 142
Larson, Simeon 99
Latvia 160
Latvian immigrant radicals 166
Leiserson, William 123
Lenin, Vladimir Ilyich 97
Lever Act 94–95, 131
Lewis, John. L. 12, 110, 116, 129–131, 147–149, 153
Lietuva 103
Lithuania 160
Lithuanian, immigrants 19, 31, 41, 44, 47, 54, 64, 72, 85–86, 101, 103, 107, 108, 137, 167, 171
Livingston, Illinois 44
Loyalty Leagues 106–108

MacDonald, Duncan 56, 68, 110
Magyar *see* Hungarian
Mamatey, Albert 136
Masters' Barber Association 135
McKee's Rocks, Pennsylvania: IWW strike 79
McKeesport, Pennsylvania 101
Mechanization 12, 32–35, 151
Mexican immigrants 20, 60, 87, 107, 122, 170, 173
Mexican Revolution 106
Michigan 14–16, 27, 64, 79
Mickevičius-Kapsukas, Vincas 167
Milwaukee, Wisconsin: socialism 101–103
Miners Examining Board 55
Minnesota Commission of Public Safety, C.P.S. 106
Montenegrin immigrants 19, 33, 48, 50, 82
Montgomery, David 35, 45, 60, 76, 100, 126, 173
Mooney, Tom: case of 139
Mount Olive, Illinois 109

Narodne Noving 136
The Nation 114
National Association of Manufacturers, N.A.M. 170
National Committee to Organize Iron and Steel Workers 12, 116–121, 124, 126–128, 132–136, 146
National Manufacturing and Trade Association, N.M.T.A. 76
National Mediation and Reconciliation Service, N.M.R.S. 148

National Origins Act of 1924 *see* Johnson-Reed Act
National Slovak Society 136
Native Americans 32
New Deal 10, 153
New Kennsington, Pennsylvania 52
The New Majority 124

"Old immigrants" 12, 20, 25, 27, 29–35, 38, 40, 48, 49, 52, 62, 68, 101, 102, 120, 122, 123
Oliver Iron Mining Company (U.S. Steel subsidiary) 27, 81, 84, 142
Open pit mining 34, 36, 41, 43–44

Pacyga, Dominic 135
Palmer, A. Mitchell: and the "Palmer Raids" 131, 134, 135, 137
Palmer, Frank 142
Panama, Illinois 110
Peabody, Francis 93
Peabody Coal 152
Peabody Commission *see* Committee on Coal Production
Pennsylvania 15–19, 30, 112, 119, 130, 148, 151
Pennsylvania Westinghouse Strike of 1916 80
Pittsburgh steel industry 13, 15, 16, 37, 104–105, 119, 133–135
Poland 29, 49, 70, 71, 104, 144, 161
Polish Falcons Alliance of America 136
Polish immigrants 11, 27, 29, 38, 47, 64, 65, 67, 70, 71, 72, 79, 104, 133, 135, 137, 139, 171
Polish Socialist Federation, P.S.F. 65, 72, 104
"Practical miner" 54–56
Prager, Robert: lynching of 109
President's Mediation Committee 91
Progressive Era, and progressivism 7, 42, 43, 50, 59, 88, 94–96, 98, 125, 154, 172
Progressive Miners of America 108
Prohibition of alcohol 143, 154, 159–160
Il Proletario 71, 85
Puskás, Julianna 70, 167

Race 10, 12, 20, 25, 31, 33, 49, 50, 51, 54, 56, 61, 106, 122, 128, 156, 169
Raivaaja 103
Ramirez, Bruno 26, 171
Red Scare 8, 21, 137, 154–155
Romanian immigrants 24, 46, 70
Rossoni, Edmondo 71
Rothbart, Ron 46
Russia 160–164, 166, 63–64, 70, 72, 80, 87, 103, 139; *see also* Soviet Union
Russian immigrants 24, 27, 28, 29, 38, 46, 47, 49, 51, 56, 65–66, 72, 77, 130, 139, 166, 171
Russian Revolution of 1905 64

Russian Revolution of 1917 5, 7, 21, 87, 89, 100–105, 113, 117, 137–141, 160, 163, 165
Russian Workmen's Association *see* Union of Russian Workers

Sacco and Vanzetti: case of 160, 162
Sangamon County, Illinois 36, 48, 55, 73, 74, 112
Saposs, David 51, 121, 123, 125–127, 132, 134, 136
Scandinavian Americans 26, 28, 29, 33, 49, 50, 123, 171
Scarlett, Sam 83
Scientific management 90, 95, 172–173
Scottish Americans 19, 31, 50, 51, 62, 85
Serbian immigrants 19, 46, 50, 65, 69, 105, 127, 135–136
Serbo-Croatians 65, 72, 84, 105, 123
Shaft mining 18, 34
Skill 20, 25, 27, 30–35, 50, 53–59, 90, 101, 103, 116, 118–131; 151, 155, 159, 171–172
Slovak immigrants 19, 29, 31, 36, 38, 55–56, 70, 136, 139
Slovene immigrants 19, 33, 36, 38, 39, 47–48, 65, 69, 72, 73, 79, 83, 94, 105, 108, 117, 157
Socialist Labor Party, S.L.P. 65, 67
Socialist Party, S.P. 8, 60, 63–72, 88–89, 98–108, 117, 137–138, 140–143; and rift with I.W.W. 61–62; 66–68; 79, 81, 84
South Chicago, Illinois 15, 28–29, 37–40, 43, 47, 48, 97
South Slavic immigrants *see* Yugoslavs
South Slavic Socialist Federation, S.S.S.F. 71–72, 104–105
Soviet Union 22, 103, 104, 137, 139, 142, 144–145, 163–166, 169
Soviets, in the U.S. 105
Spring Valley, Illinois 30–31, 108
Springfield, Illinois: and Amalgamated Association of Street and Electric Railway Employees of America 112–113; and coal mining 31, 42, 44, 77, 85, 148, 149, 157; and General Strike 21, 88, 108–114, 129; and Springfield Consolidated Railway Company 112
Steel Workers Organizing Committee, S.W.O.C. 143
Streator, Illinois 97
Strike wave of 1916–1922 5, 7, 9, 60, 80, 86, 89, 97, 115, 117, 131, 135–136, 146, 155, 162, 166
Superior, Wisconsin 101–103
Swedish Americans 19, 29, 39, 46, 49, 50, 52, 101, 102

"Taylorization" 12, 25, 35
Thayer, Illinois 44
The Toiler 133
Tokoi, Oskari 167
Toveri 103

Tresca, Carlo 67, 81, 83–84, 142
Trotsky, Leon 13, 104, 166
Trotskyism 122
Two Harbors, Minnesota 106
Työmies 103, 117

Ukrainian immigrants 103–104, 137
Union of Russian Workers, U.R.W. 65–66, 72
United Mine Workers of America: and Bituminous Strike of 1919, 116, 128–129; challenges to Lewis leadership 148–149, 153; and Cleveland Agreement 150–153; and cooperative movement 73, 109; decline of 141, 143, 146–148, 152–153; and eight-hour day 36; and Harding Administration 152–153; and immigrants 11, 30–32, 40–41, 51–53; International Executive Board (I.E.B.), of the 129–131; and non-union producers 12, 98, 121, 146–147; and radicalism 66, 68, 84–85, 95, 108, 110, 139, 170; rationalization of the coal industry 11–12, 40, 53–54; and Springfield General Strike 108, 112–113; and Washington Agreement 111, 129–130; wildcat strikes 79, 81, 84–85, 110–111, 129–130, 139, 149; and Wilson administration 92–94, 110–111, 131, 149

Vecoli, Rudolph 61, 67
Vermillion Iron Range 14, 117, 139, 157
Vermillion Strike 117, 139
Virginia Minnesota 28, 52, 64, 107, 134, 157
Vorst, Mary Heaton 43, 44, 125

Walker, John 68, 101
Walling, William English 59
Walsh, Frank 9
War Industries Board 91, 95
Weinberg, Carl 36, 55, 109
Welfare capitalism *see* corporate welfare
Welsh Americans 31, 62, 110
West Virginia 12, 16, 19, 30, 147, 153, 156
Western Federation of Miners, W.F.M. 79, 81
Whiting, Indiana 30
Williamson County, Illinois 151, 159
Wilson, Woodrow 145; and administration of 90–103; 116–121; 128–131; 138; 145–150
Wobblies *see* Industrial Workers of the World
Wood, Major General Leonard 119
Work People's College, Työvaen Opisto 67, 83, 107, 164
Workers Party of America, W.P.A. 140
World War I: and employment levels 77, 87, 90, 100, 113, 127; and inflation 9, 13, 42, 80, 87, 92–93, 99, 113, 115, 129, 131

Yugoslav immigrants 26, 29, 65, 69–71, 72, 82–84, 104, 166, 171
Yugoslavia 144, 161

www.ingramcontent.com/pod-product-compliance
Ingram Content Group UK Ltd.
Pitfield, Milton Keynes, MK11 3LW, UK
UKHW041959140426
5217IPUK00015B/890